BALANCE SHEET OF NARENDRA MODI GOVERNMENT

SHESHRAO CHAVAN

ATLANTIC
PUBLISHERS & DISTRIBUTORS (P) LTD

ATLANTIC
PUBLISHERS & DISTRIBUTORS (P) LTD

7/22, Ansari Road, Darya Ganj, New Delhi
Tel.: +91-11-4077 5252, 2327 3880
E-mail: orders@atlanticbooks.com
Web: www.atlanticbooks.com

Published by Atlantic Publishers & Distributors (P) Ltd 2024

Printed & bound in India by Atlantic Print Services

Contents

Preface

Narendra Modi is often seen as a political leader who exhibits qualities reminiscent of Mahatma Gandhi and Sardar Vallabhbhai Patel, while also displaying traits of both a democrat and a benevolent dictator.

Modi's dedication and commitment to Mahatma Gandhi, as he proclaimed in his speech on 15th August 2022 from the ramparts of the Red Fort, is evident through the various programs he has been implementing to fulfill Mahatma Gandhi's second dream, such as the Swachh Bharat Abhiyan (Clean India Campaign), Kaushalya Vikas (Skill Development), Har Ghar Jal (access to clean water in every household), Har Ghar Bijli (electricity for every household), boosting the Khadi industry, increasing farmers' income, combating corruption, empowering women, and ensuring that the poorest of the poor feel that their voices matter in the nation-building process.

Modi has shown unwavering admiration for Sardar Patel and his instrumental role in nation-building. Several key decisions and actions undertaken by Modi, such as the Abrogation of Article 370, the response to the Pulwama attack and the Balakot airstrike, demonetization, the National Monetization Pipeline, the Central Vista Project, the fight against corruption and black money, as well as the enforcement of law and order without bias, serve as notable examples. Additionally, one of his significant achievements is overseeing the completion of the Sardar Sarovar Project within a remarkable three-year period after assuming office as Prime Minister. On his 68th birthday, which falls on 17th September, 2017, Modi dedicated this project to the nation. It is worth noting that the foundation for the Sardar Sarovar

Dam was laid by Jawaharlal Nehru on 5th April, 1961, and the construction had been underway since then.

I have written a full-fledged book on Sardar Sarovar Project, tracing its origins from the visionary mind of Sardar Patel to the challenges faced during its implementation, including the withdrawal of funds by the World Bank and opposition from various national and international entities. It also explores a pivotal moment when Narendra Modi, the then Chief Minister of Gujarat, undertook a fast in support of the project's completion.

Narendra Modi carries a strong conviction that injustice had been done to Sardar Patel by Jawaharlal Nehru, and he is trying his utmost to do justice to him posthumously.

The combination of Modi as a democrat and a dictator is evident from the following.

Democrat: Modi enacted three Farm Laws, believing they were in the best interest of farmers. However, due to mounting opposition from farmers, he eventually decided to repeal them. A similar situation occurred with the Citizenship Amendment Act (CAA) and the National Register of Citizens (NRC). Recognizing the concerns and protests surrounding these issues, Modi decided to put both the CAA and NRC on hold.

The implementation of numerous welfare schemes under Modi's leadership can be seen as an indication of his commitment to the welfare of the masses. These schemes aim to address various social and economic challenges faced by different sections of society, such as access to healthcare, housing, sanitation, and financial inclusion. These initiatives demonstrate Modi's efforts to improve the overall well-being of the population and establish him as a true democrat.

Dictator: Today, while there is no formal declaration of Emergency, press censorship, or lawful suspension of the laws, the rise of Hindu nationalism has catapulted Narendra Modi into the kind of position that Indira Gandhi occupied only with the Emergency. When she could not get the constitutional democracy to bend to her will, she chose to suppress it with the arms of the State. Today, while the courts, the press, and political parties do not face overt repression, they seem to be either unwilling or incapable of effectively serving as the gatekeepers of democracy when confronted with the State power infused with populist sentiments. Similar to Indira Gandhi, Narendra Modi stands as the unquestioned leader of his party. The Bharatiya Janata Party, known for its roster of experienced politicians, now recognizes Modi as its supreme authority. He wields a significant influence in Indian politics, reminiscent of the stature once held by Indira Gandhi. His images, slogans, and initiatives are omnipresent, much like hers were in the past. Instead of engaging in press conferences and subjecting himself to questioning, Modi chooses to communicate directly with the people through his weekly radio address and, akin to Donald Trump, frequent tweets. Ironically, while Modi and BJP leaders criticize Indira Gandhi's concentration of executive powers during the Emergency, they themselves strive for a one-party state, exhibiting intolerance towards minorities and displaying contempt for dissent by branding it as 'anti-national'.

Smita Gupta, in her article in the book, *Reforming India: The Nation Today*, edited by Niraja Gopal Jayal and published by Penguin Viking at page 5 says: "For one, Modi runs, by far, the most opaque PMO to date. Communication under him has become a one-way street, with strictly regulated information being disseminated from his office, granting virtually no opportunity for journalists to seek clarification or a perspective on a government position or decision, leave alone ask actual questions of him or any of his associates. Two, Modi's dislike of being made accountable in Parliament too has ensured that even Opposition leaders rarely receive answers to their questions, and many feel this shows a lack of respect for any legislature. Three, Modi's desire for absolute control has reportedly meant that individual ministers have little authority; in most cases, not even the right to select their own officers, while civil servants are expected to be subservient. Four, Modi prefers to take major decisions with the minimum possible consultation, possibly emanating from his desire to shock and awe. Five, while Modi drives foreign policy, like many of his predecessors in office, extent to which he depends on personal diplomacy and informal summitry is unprecedented. It is also possibly, for the first time, a part of foreign policy has been 'outsourced' to bodies outside the government—the Vivekananda International Foundation (VIF) and the India Foundation—that have close connections with the RSS, the BJP's parent organization." She further says on page 11: "Modi has not just centralized all government policy making in the PMO but he also controls the selection of top officials in the GoI. The Appointments Committee of the Cabinet (ACC) that decides these appointments was earlier composed of the Prime Minister (chairman), the Home Minister and the Minister in-charge of the ministry concerned. An official notification issued on 18th June, 2014 announced that the ACC would henceforth have just two members, with the minister of the ministry concerned now excluded from the committee. According to one report, the bold print at the bottom of most proposals to the ACC reads: "Approval of the Home Minister will be obtained ex post facto in the ACC". In short, the Home Minister too, has no say, he just signs on the dotted line."

Justice Ajit Prasad Shah, former Chief Justice of Delhi and Madras High Court, says: "Parallels can be drawn with elected autocrats, where elected governments use the very institutions integrated to democracy to kill democracy itself and destroy civil liberties. We have heard nothing of the Lok Pal since. The National Human Rights commission has been made dormant. Investigation agencies are misused at the slightest opportunity, with action against activists, journalists, students, political opponents, or anyone who protests against the government. The Election Commission of India appears to have been clearly compromised. The Information Commission is almost non-functional. Others who can hold the executive accountable—academia, the press, and civil society—have also been systematically emasculated. Universities are under attack. An unbiased mainstream fourth estate in India no longer exists, and the media operates mostly as a propaganda machine. Civil society, too, is being slowly but surely strangled."

Press Conferences: Modi's relationship with the press betrays an intense distrust of journalists on the one hand and a desire to control them on the other. As the Prime Minister, he has seldom addressed press conferences, except on those occasions when he met heads of other foreign governments, when both heads are expected to brief the press on their deliberations. Such press conferences are controlled for the kind of questions that are permitted. His press interviews are particularly given to those journalists whose loyalty to him is beyond doubt.

Modi uses social media and those traditional media outlets controlled by the government to communicate directly with the masses. His monthly radio address is called *Mann Ki Baat*, for which questions from the people are sought online.

Dr. B.R. Ambedkar, speaking at the concluding session of the Constituent Assembly on 25th November, 1949, invoked John Stuart Mill to warn the citizens against placing their liberties at the feet of a great leader. He said: "All those interested in the maintenance of democracy, namely, not to lay their liberties at the feet of even a great man, or to trust him with powers which enable him to subvert their institutions. There is nothing wrong in being grateful to great men who have rendered lifelong services to the country. But there are limits to gratefulness. As has been well said by the Irish patriot Daniel O'Connel, no man can be grateful at the cost of his honour, no woman can be grateful at the cost of her chastity and no nation can be grateful at the cost of its liberty. This caution is far more necessary in the case of India than in the case of any other country. In India, *Bhakti* or what may be called a path of devotion or hero worship, plays a part in its politics unequalled in magnitude by the part it plays in the politics of any other country in the world. *Bhakti* in religion may be a road to the salvation of the soul. But, in politics, *Bhakti* or hero-worship is a sure road to degradation and eventual dictatorship."

Prophecy of a Sadhu: Around 1962-63, when Narendra Modi was hardly 12 years old, a Sadhu told his mother after seeing his horoscope that if he goes in politics, he would be as powerful as an emperor or else, he may become a sanyasi and eventually turned out to be like Shankaracharya. Modi wandered in Himalayas for three years with a view to become a sanyasi, but found that it was not his cup of tea and returned to Vadnagar to become as powerful as an emperor as Chief Minister and Prime Minister.

Interview with Mark Zuckerberg: On 27th September, 2015, a little over a year after Narendra Modi became the Prime Minister of India, he was interviewed by Mark Zuckerberg, the CEO of Facebook, at the Facebook Headquarters in San Jose, California. During the interview, Zuckerberg asked Modi a personal question about his childhood and teenage years. Here is how Modi described his early years:

> "I used to sell tea at the train station. My father is no more. My mother is still alive, over 90 years old. She is not educated. To make ends meet, she used to wash utensils in neighboring households, fill their water pots, and do a poor worker's manual work. You cannot imagine how much she suffered when she was raising me. Millions of mothers from *samanya parivar* (ordinary families) go through such sufferings." (*Reforming India: The Nation Today,* edited by Niraja Gopal Jayal, Penguin Viking, p. 336)

Modi was deeply attached and dedicated to his mother. She left for divine abode on 30th December, 2022, at the age of hundred years. Her last advice to him was *Kaam karo buddhi thi, jivan jivo suddhi thi* (work with wisdom and live a life of purity). Modi who performed her last rites along with his brothers said: "A glorious centenary rests at the feet of God. I have witnessed three qualities in mother—the journey of a *tapasvi* (saint), a selfless worker and a life dedicated to values". Hiraba reared Modi to rise to the position of the Prime Minister from a *chaiwala*. It is astounding.

Narendra Modi was sworn in as 15th Prime Minister of India on 26th May, 2014 in the Forecourt of Rashtrapati Bhavan, rather than in the magnificent hall inside, in the presence of heads of the SAARC countries and 8000 Indian and international invitees including politicians, diplomats, government officials, constitutional authorities and Chief Ministers of States.

Balance Sheet of Modi Government

I have dispassionately analyzed the issues addressed by Prime Minister Narendra Modi in his Independence Day address on 15th August, 2022, from the ramparts of the Red Fort in chapters 2 to 16. However, the following aspects have been highlighted.

Poverty: In May 2015, while launching social insurance schemes, the Prime Minister articulated his views on the poor and poverty as: "Poor people do not need help. We have to change our thinking, our outlook, our way of functioning. Poor people need to be empowered. If they are empowered then they would be all geared up to fight poverty on their own strength and free themselves of poverty."

Reiterating his views in his 2015 Independence Day speech, Modi said: "We have to strengthen the foundation of the bottom pyramid of development so as to ensure that these people are empowered. When purchasing power of the poorest of the poor in society increases, nobody can stop the economy to flourish. Therefore, it is our intention to give impetus to that. We have laid great stress upon social security and also the welfare of the poor."

In his 2016 Independence Day speech, the Prime Minister further emphasized this approach. "We stress upon integrated development rather than isolated development. We stress on empowerment and not entitlement," he said.

Every Prime Minister from Jawaharlal Nehru to Narendra Modi has been pledging to eradicate poverty, but none of them has been successful. The reason according to me is that the poverty has been made a lucrative business in India. I am reminded of what Prof. K.N. Raj, who was a member of Smt. Indira Gandhi's Economic Advisory Council, said. He said: "Poverty eradication schemes have become a lucrative industry giving the highest returns to those promoting them, hence the enthusiasm which poverty eradication has aroused."

Nani Palkhivala, in his book, *We, the People*, at page 38 said: "Our first concern must be to look after the weakest—the man who is bowed by the weight of centuries, stolid and stunned dead to rapture and despair, a thing that grieves not and that never hopes."

He further said: "Poverty is cruel, but it is curable. The only known cure is economic pragmatism instead of wooly ideology. In the field of economics, the tree of ideology has never borne any fruit. We have countless chances for development. Opportunities multiply when they are seized, they die when neglected. We have barely tapped our immeasurable potential for growth. Immense man-power, superb skills and enterprise are to India what oil is to the Middle East. The only difference is that the oil will be depleted one day, but our human resources will never be."

According to Palkhivala, there is one and only one way in which India can banish poverty, and that is by putting to the maximum productive use of millions of man-hours which fleet over India every day, never to come again. To every economic policy and legislation, we must apply the acid test—how far will it bend the talent, energy and time of our people for fruitful ends and how far it will dissipate them in coping with legal inanities and a bumbling bureaucracy.

Unemployment: Mahatma Gandhi had said that in a country of seven lakh villages, the problem of unemployment cannot be solved until and unless every village and every house is made centre of self-employment. But in India, youths, educated or uneducated want government or factory jobs, for which they are prepared to pay bribe money in thousands and lakhs. This is a curse to the youths who are seeking jobs and blessings to those who are providing jobs.

The problem of unemployment and poverty cannot be solved either by aspirations or by slogans. They are never solved by purblind ideology or by opaque ignorance masquerading progressive politics. They can be solved by realistic and pragmatic economic policies which can harness the immeasurable reservoir of the people's faith, response, energy and enterprise.

Farmers' Plight: The farmers, consisting of 87 percent of the total population of India, have been in perpetual poverty from time immemorial, mainly because they are not prepared to come out of the conventional farming practices. However, those who have switched over to modern farming methods have witnessed significant prosperity and growth.

Corruption: Prime Minister Narendra Modi, true to his vow, "*Na khaunga, na khane dunga*", has been making sincere efforts to weed out corruption, but the malady is so deep that his efforts have so far proved to be an exercise in futility.

Even though the government claims that it has brought down the incidences of corruption, allegations of crony capitalism and sweetheart deals involving the rich and the powerful in India continue to be made. In January 2015, a controversy broke out over Modi's wearing a fancy suit that had his name monogrammed along with its pinstripes. Opposition leaders derogatorily described his government as a 'suit-boot ki sarkar'. There was a swift reaction: the suit was put up for auction and it was stated that the proceeds from this auction would be used for a noble cause of cleaning the Ganga. The reserve price for the suit was kept at ₹ 11,00,000, but the final price at which the suit was auctioned was ₹ 4,31,31,311. It was later rumoured that the Surat-based trader Laljibhai Patel who bought the suit had been favoured by the Gujarat government by allotting government land to an entity with which he was associated, for building a private sports club.

Modi government has also been attacked by its political opponents for allowing particular private sector companies to partner with multinational defence giants for manufacturing equipment to help the foreign suppliers fulfil their offset/export obligations under the current defence procurement policy. Notable among such companies are those in the Reliance ADA Group, led by Anil Ambani, which has struck an association with a French group which supplies Rafael aircrafts to India. The position of Dassault, the Indian government and Reliance is that Dassault independently has chosen Reliance and not the Indian government. It has been further alleged that under the Modi government, sector regulators have been allowed to use discretionary powers to allegedly favour certain players, for example, Reliance Jio has been favoured in the telecom and Internet sector, which is a part of Reliance Industries Limited led by Mukesh Ambani. These allegations have been denied by these companies and government's spokes persons. (*Reforming India: The Nation Today,* edited by Niraja Gopal Jayal, Penguin Viking, pp 151-53)

Castes: India has been in the grip of castes for centuries and there is hardly any hope of coming out of it. Contrary, the castes are being cemented to derive political dividends. It is pertinent to recollect what Dr. Ambedkar said in this respect in the Constituent Assembly:

> "...I am of opinion that in believing that we are a nation, we are cherishing a great delusion. How can people divided into several thousands of castes be a nation? The sooner we realize that we are not as yet a nation in the social and psychological sense of the word, the better for us. For then only we shall realize the necessity of becoming a nation and seriously think of ways and means of realizing the goal. The realization of this goal is going to be very difficult – far more difficult than it has been in the United States. The United States has no caste problem. In India there are castes. These castes are anti-national. In the first place because they bring about separation in social life. They are anti-national also because they generate jealousy and antipathy between caste and caste. But we must overcome all these difficulties if we wish to become a nation in reality."

Religion/Communalism: At the time of Independence, both leaders and the masses were acutely aware of the grave consequences of intermingling politics with religion, as evidenced by the painful partition that the country had endured. As a result, there was a resolute determination to separate politics from religion and prevent any further turmoil.

The Constituent Assembly, in a resolution adopted on 3rd April, 1948, unambiguously stated:

> "Whereas it is essential for the proper functioning of democracy and the growth of national unity and solidarity that communalism should be eliminated from Indian life, this Assembly is of opinion that no communal organization which by its constitution or by the exercise of discretionary power vested in any of its officers or organs, admits to or excludes from its membership persons on grounds of religion, race and caste, or any of them, should be permitted to engage in any activities other than those essential for the bona fide religious, cultural, social and educational needs of the community, and that all steps, legislative and

> administrative, necessary to prevent such activities should be taken."

In spite of this solemn, unambiguous resolution, our post-Independence era proved that we have not stuck to the spirit of the wholesale Constituent Assembly resolution to eliminate communalism from our body-politic.

Here are the guidelines given by the consolidator and integrator of India, Sardar Patel, on the all-important minority-majority question:

"It is up to the majority community to create by its generosity sense of confidence in the minorities; and so also it will be the duty of the minority communities to forget the past and to reflect on what the country has suffered due to the sense of fairness which the foreigner thought was necessary to keep the balance between community and community."

"If they really have come honestly to the conclusion that in the changed conditions of this country, it is in the interest of all to lay down real and genuine foundations of secular State, then nothing is better for the minorities than to trust the good-sense and sense of fairness of the majority, and to place confidence in them. So also, it is for us who happen to be in a majority to think about what the minorities feel, and how we in their position would feel if we were treated in the manner in which they are treated. But in the long run, it would be in the interest of all to forget that there is anything like majority or minority in this country and that in India there is only one community."

The advice of Sardar Patel is most relevant in India today, particularly for the RSS.

Constitution: Our Constitution is the distilled essence of the consecrated, collective sadhana of the cream of the nation's noblest, wisest, most experienced, versatile and unalloyed patriots of the highest caliber who had, for decades, voluntarily and cheerfully undergone the baptism of fire in freedom's battle under Gandhiji's sublime moral leadership. Prime Minister Narendra Modi has often said that the Constitution is the only sacred document of India, not the *Gita,* the *Ramayana*, or the Vedas. However, his government's statements on the issue of the appointments of Supreme Court and High Court Judges seem to be going against the spirit of the Constitution.

Ashutosh Varshney, in his article in the book, *Reforming India: The Nation Today*, at pp 342-43, says: "Driven by an intellectual agnosticism, Modi government's relationship with the Supreme Court in particular, and the judiciary in general, has been an object of intense curiosity since his rise to power.

Normally trapped in confidentiality, the executive-judiciary tension burst out in the open in January 2018, when some of the senior-most Judges of the Supreme Court openly rebelled against the desire of the Chief Justice of the Supreme Court to placate the government. In March 2018, Justice Chelameswar's letter to the Chief Justice protesting against government interference became public. Here are the sections of the letter relevant to our discussion of the populist desire to tame the judiciary.

Lord Bingham in his book, *The Rule of Law*, said that there are countries in the world where all judicial decisions find favour with the powers that be, but they are probably not places where any of us would wish to live.

We, the judges of the Supreme Court of India, are being accused of being ceding our independence and our institutional integrity to the executive's incremental encroachment. The executive is always impatient, and brooks no disobedience even of the judiciary if it can. Attempts were always made to treat the Chief Justices as the departmental heads in the secretariat.

Let us also not forget that the bonhomie between the judiciary and the government in any state sounds the death knell to democracy. We both are mutual watchdogs, so to say, not mutual admirers, much less constitutional cohorts."

Varshney further says: "A public expression of what is normally shrouded in secrecy has made it evident that India's executive under Modi seriously tried to tame the independence of the judiciary."

Vice President Targeting Supreme Court's Basic Structure Ruling

Rekindling the debate over the doctrine of separation of powers, Vice President Jagdeep Dhankhar, citing the Supreme

Court's landmark judgement of 1973 in the Kesavananda Bharati case in which it ruled that Parliament had the authority to amend the Constitution but not its basic structure, has said it will be difficult to answer the question, "Are we democratic nation?"

In his inaugural address at the 83rd All-India Presiding Officers Conference in Jaipur, Dhankhar again raised the issue of the powers of the judiciary vis-à-vis the legislature, highlighting the 2015 judgement of the Supreme Court to strike down the National Judicial Appointments Commission (NJAC) Act.

On 7th December, 2022, presiding over Rajya Sabha for the first time on the opening day of the winter session of Parliament, Dhankhar called the striking down of NJAC Act a severe compromise of Parliamentary sovereignty and disregard of the mandate of the people. He had also said that Parliament, being the custodian of the ordainment of the people, was duty bound to address the issue and expressed confidence that it would do so.

At the Jaipur conference, Dhankhar, referring to the topic of the relationship between the judiciary and legislature, one of the topics of discussion, said, "we cannot have an ostrich-like stance". He further said, "Parliamentary sovereignty and autonomy cannot be permitted to be qualified or compromised as it is quintessential to survival of democracy". The legislature, he said, did not have the power to write judicial orders, and the executive and judiciary did not have the authority to legislate. He also cautioned against one upmanship and public posturing from judicial platforms which, he said, is prevalent today. This is not right.

In an apparent reference to the Supreme Court asking the Attorney General to advice government functionaries to exercise control in their comments on the Collegium, Dhankhar said that he did not entertain the Attorney General on the issue.

"I cannot be party to emasculating the power of the legislature," he said noting that he had been a "soldier of the judiciary," referring to his career as a lawyer.

The Vice President stressed on the importance of those occupying constitutional posts and remaining politically neutral. "People in the executive, legislature and holding senior political positions must take care that high constitutional offices are kept away from their political stance. We have noticed recently some serious observations that are transgressions," he said without elaborating.

Earlier, Lok Sabha Speaker, Om Birla spoke on the importance of the executive, legislature and judiciary respecting each other. He said that legislatures had always respected powers and authority of the judiciary, and the judiciary was expected to follow the separation of powers mandated by the Constitution. He further said that the three branches should work with mutual trust and harmony. (*Indian Express,* 12th January, 2023)

The confrontation between the government and the Supreme Court on Collegium, National Judicial Appointments Commission and the appointments of the Supreme Court and the High Court Judges, I am afraid, may lead to a breaking point. It would be premature to say who will be victor and who will be vanquished.

Patriots Arise! Awake!

Prime Minister Narendra Modi has been bitterly criticizing the leaders of the Congress and the leaders of other opposition parties ignoring that most of the leaders of his own party are no exception. The present situation of politics and politicians in the country is summarized below:

The debased, disconcerting and disastrous devaluation of values has come to full circle. The national scene is deeply distressing, grotesque, gloomy and grim. What is the outcome? Sky-rocketing prices, a steeply rising unemployment spiral, indescribable indiscipline and above all, corroding moral decay at all levels.

Naked forces, coupled with cunning and fraud, unscrupulous and unholy hotchpotch alliances with unprincipled factions and groups, and false promises and unabashed alibis to hoodwink the masses have become the methods of capturing and clinging to power.

The creed of majority of the politicians has become: disturbance is the best way to peace, hatred to love, and fraud to sincerity; suggesting that vilification and vindictiveness are short-cuts to grab and retain power.

The ideal of "Government of the People, by the People and for the People" has degenerated into "Government **off** the People, **buy** the People and **far** the People". Indeed, we have now "Government of the Politicians, by the Politicians and for the Politicians".

The commanding heights of national life—political, economic, industrial, educational and social—have come to be dominated by opportunists, devoid of moral scruples and largely motivated by self-interest. It has brought a schizophrenic dualism—double-think and double-talk, and paved the way for the era of politics without principles, commerce without morality, education without character, wealth without work, and social service without service motive, which Gandhiji considered sins.

Our politicians have become totally engrossed with silly and savage infighting, crafty and crude manipulations, arrent and obnoxious horse trading, unscrupulous and despicable engineering of defections, pulling down and putting up of governments as naughty children do with sand castles.

An analysis done by the Association for Democratic Reforms (ADR) shows that the 15th Lok Sabha had 315 crorepatis, which means that more than half of our members of Parliament belong to India's affluent class. Only 18 members of Parliament had declared assets less than ten lakh rupees.

In the 14th Lok Sabha, the number of crorepati members of Parliament was 156, which means that between 2004 and 2009 their number grew by a whopping 102%. What is more, the average assets of an MP too, have shown a quantum jump in this period from ₹ 1.86 to ₹ 5.33 crore, i.e., 186%.

The ADR's analysis of the affidavits of 304 persons who were MPs in 2004 and recontested in 2009 election shows that over this one term, their assets grew by mind-boggling 289%. The average assets of these MPs went up from ₹ 1.92 crore in 2004 to ₹ 4.8 crores in 2009. In the case of some MPs, the ADR found that their assets had gone up by 1000% over the period of five years.

Criminality among politicians has risen sharply. According to the ADR, 24% of the winners in the 2004 Lok Sabha election had a criminal background, which rose to 30% in 2009 general election, 34% in 2014 election and 43% in the 2019 election. Shockingly, 29% of those elected in 2019 had reported serious crimes including rape, murder, and culpable homicide. Between the two national parties, out of 303 winners from the BJP in 2019 election, 116 (39%) has a criminal record as against 29 (56%) out of 52 winners from the Indian National Congress. Such are the representatives of the masses of a poor country.

Dr. Ambedkar had said: "A time will come when I suppose unless we, in Parliament, realize our responsibilities and shoulder the task of looking after the welfare and good of people within a reasonable time, I have not the slightest doubt in my mind that this Parliament will be treated by the public outside with utter contempt. It would be a thing not wanted at all."

In the course of discussion on the Representation of Peoples Act, Dr. Ambedkar said: "Now it seems to me that education can hardly be the sole qualification for membership of this House. If I may use the words of Buddha, he said that man requires two things. One is *Gyan* and the other is *Sheel. Gyan* without *sheel* is very dangerous; it must be accompanied by *sheel,* by which we mean character, moral courage, ability to be independent of any kind of temptation, truthful to one's ideals. I did not find any reference to the second qualification in the speeches I have heard from Members who have supported Professor Shah. But even though I myself am very keen to see that no member enters this August Assembly, who does not possess sheel in adequate degree, I find it extremely difficult to find any means or methods to ensure that valuable qualification."

Our politicians seem to have ignored the caution given by Dr. Ambedkar: "If the political parties for their own political purposes, do not attend to this matter, people themselves in the course of time will attend to it. People are not going to allow persons who cannot discharge their functions properly in this House to be continued and returned for ever. They want result, they want their welfare to be attended to, and I am sure that they will realize that the only instrumentality through which they can achieve this purpose is to send good men to this House."

Again, in his speech on 26th November, 1949, in the Constituent Assembly, Dr. Ambedkar said: "Political power in this country has too long been the monopoly of a few and the many are not only beasts of burden, but also beasts of prey. This monopoly has not merely deprived them of their chance of betterment; it has sapped them of what may be called the significance of life. These downtrodden classes are tired of being governed. They are impatient to govern themselves. This urge for self-realization in the downtrodden classes must not be allowed to devolve into a class struggle or class war. It would lead to a division of the House. That would indeed, be a day of disaster. For, as has been well said by Abraham Lincoln, a House divided against itself cannot stand very long. Therefore, the sooner room is made for the realization of their aspiration, the better for the few, better for the country, the better for the maintenance of its independence and better for the continuance of its democratic structure. This can only be done by the establishment of equality and fraternity in all spheres of life."

He further said: "Times are fast changing. People including our own are being moved by new ideologies. They are getting tired of Government by the people. They are prepared to have Government for the people and are indifferent whether it is Government of the people and by the people. If we wish to preserve the Constitution in which we have sought to enshrine the principle of Government of the people, for the people, and by the people, let us resolve not to be tardy in the recognition of the evils that lie across our path and which induce people to prefer Government for the people to Government by the people, nor to be weak in our initiative to remove them. That is the only way to serve the country. I know of no better."

Dr. L.M. Singhvi, in his book, *Freedom on Trial*, published by Vikas Publishing House Pvt. Ltd, New Delhi, at pp 242-244 said: "Fortunately, for us our Constitution embodies an excellent statement of ends and means and provides a detailed route map for achieving a high degree of means-ends concordance. Perhaps, the reason for our country failing to achieve higher levels of effectiveness and excellence in implementing our constitutionally ordained goals in a constitutional manner is the enthronement of the new-found God of political power in our body politic and the failure of our citizenship. Failure of leadership and failure of citizenship in an institutional and operational sense have been our greatest impediment.

Institutionally, the failure of the party system in Indian politics is the most glaring shortcoming. Our party system is fractured and fragmented. It produces a very superficial and irresponsible attitude to political process. Our Constitution is often hamstrung by the strange working of our party system. There is too much shadow-boxing, too much vituperation and mud-slinging, too much hypocrisy and self-seeking, too much favoritism, corruption and arbitrariness, too much proximity of words and laxity of conduct to allow democracy and rule of law to work out an acceptable design of law and life. The situation often appears to be beyond repair, redemption or redress. Most of the political parties in India have, at one time or the other, suffered popular retribution at the polls, but like Bourbones, they tend to remember little and to learn nothing. The result is that we do not have healthy competition in our political system. Citizenship development has an important part to play in bringing about a change of climate and little institutional restructuring.

We have too many political parties and very little Intra-party democracy. We put little premium on talent within the parties. Party tickets are given, more often than not, on considerations which are alien to public weal. Tammany Hall methods are common in the working of parties and in electoral politics. No wonder that we lack an infra-structure leadership at all levels and therefore tend to lean heavily on charisma. Too much, too often, comes to depend on too few. Development of citizenship will help the emergence of credible and responsible leadership at different levels and will be a source of strength to higher echelons of leadership. Indeed, much-needed improvement in the quality of leadership at different levels is possible with only enlightened citizenship development and participation. We need men and women of integrity, ability, experience and stature in public life and we must find ways and means of securing and sustaining their induction into legislatures and other offices of responsibility. True, we cannot hope to have a surfeit of such outstanding men and women, but even a few such persons would be able to provide that mainspring of inspiration in a nation's life. It is not romantic rhetoric, but a way to conjure up a catalytic transformation of our nation which the example and inputs of such dedicated citizen-statesmen may set in motion. Truly has it been said by the poet:

> God give us men! A time like this demands;
> Strong minds, great hearts, true faith and ready hands;
> Men whom the lust of office does not kill;
> Men whom the spoils of office cannot buy;
> Men who possess opinions and a will;
> Men who have honour, Men who will not lie;
> Men who cannot stand before a demagogue;
> And damn his treacherous flatteries without winking!
> Tall men, sun-crowned, who live above the fog;
> In public duty and in private thinking."

Narendra Modi's compulsion in 2014 was to become Prime Minister and perform in such a way that he continued as Prime Minister in 2019 to consolidate his regime, which he has done.

Modi's considerable success in making India Congress and Opposition *Mukta* and the incapability of the Opposition parties to unite, suggests that Modi is destined to continue as Prime Minister in 2024, unless Rahul Gandhi's *Bharat Jodo Yatra* converts into a wave against him.

I believe that Narendra Modi has genuine desire to go by the principles of Mahatma Gandhi, Sardar Patel and Dr. Ambedkar, and he will sow the seeds to sprout in creating values and purity in public life and weed out the crop of politicians of the type mentioned above during his third term as Prime Minister.

Sheshrao Chavan

Acknowledgments

The thought of writing this book occurred to me after reading the speech of Prime Minister Narendra Modi delivered on 15th August, 2022, from the ramparts of the Red Fort.

I had to go through the following books to analyze the issues dealt with by the Prime Minister in his speech.

Reforming India: The Nation Today edited by Niraja Gopal Jayal, Penguin Viking (for the article of Smita Gupta and interview with Mark Zuckerberg); *We, The People*, Nani Palkhivala, UBSPD, New Delhi; *We, The Nation: The Lost Decades*, Nani Palkhivala, UBSPD, Newe Delhi; *Freedom on Trial*, Dr. L.M. Singhvi, Vikas Publishing House, New Delhi; *Democracy and Rule of Law: Foundations and Frontiers*, Dr. L.M. Singhvi, Oceans Books, New Delhi; *The Mind of Mahatma Gandhi*, R.K. Prabhu and U.R. Rao, Navajivan Publishing House, Ahmedabad; *What Millennials Want: Decoding the World's Largest Generation*, Vivan Marwaha, Penguin Viking; *Corruption*, John B. Monteiro, Manaktalas, Bombay; *Corruption and the Destiny of Asia*, Syed Hussein Alatas, Prentice-Hall (M) Sdn Bhd, and Simon and Schuster (Asia); *From Raj to Rajiv: Forty Years of Indian Independence*, Mark Tully and Zareer Masani, Universal Book Stall, New Delhi; *The Future of India: Politics, Economics and Governance*, Bimal Jalan, Penguin Viking; *The Constitution, Corruption, Pathological Casualties and Radical Remedies Reformatories*, Justice Krishna Iyer, Universal Law Publishing Co., New Delhi; *Post Centenary Silver Jubilee of Bombay High Court*; *On Balance: An Autobiography*, Leila Seth, Penguin India; *Law, Men of Law and Education*, Justice H.R. Khanna, N.M Tripathy Pvt. Ltd, Mumbai; *India from Curzon to Nehru and*

After, Durga Das, Rupa Publications, New Delhi; *The Story of My Life*, Morarji Desai, S. Chand & Co. New Delhi; *Resurgence of Rajiv Gandhi: Assassination of Indira Gandhi and After*, Rai Singh, A.B.C. Publishing House, New Delhi; *Through the Corridors of Power: An Insider's Story*, Dr. P.C. Alexander, Harper Collins Publishers India; *A Grain of Sand in the Hourglass of Time: An Autobiography,* Arjun Singh, Hay House India, New Delhi; *One Life is Not Enough: An Autobiography,* K. Natwar Singh, Rupa Publications, New Delhi; *The Accidental Prime Minister: The Making and Unmaking of Manmohan Singh*, Sanjaya Baru, Penguin Books; *A Judiciary Made to Measure*, M.C. Setalvad, edited by N.A. Palkhivala; *Our Constitution Defaced and Defiled*, Nani Palkhivala, Macmillan; *Sharana Revolution and Indian Constitution*, edited by K.M. Marula Siddayya, Akhila Bharatha Sahithya Parishad, Mysore; *The Spirit of The Constitution*, Justice J.M. Shelat, Bharatiya Vidya Bhavan; and *The Indian Triumvirate: A Political Biography of Mahatma Gandhi, Sardar Patel, and Pandit Nehru,* V.B. Kulkarni, Bharatiya Vidya Bhavan.

The articles written by the following persons in *The Indian Express* were of great help to me: Ashutosh Varshney, Mohmad Salim, Prashant Bhushan, T.R. Andhyarujina, Veerappa Moily, Arvind P. Datar, Sriram Panchu, and P. Chidambaram; so also, articles written by Anil Divan; Sruthisagar Yamunan; and Justice Ajit Prasad Shah in *The Hindu* were also of great help to me.

I have also made use of the editorials in *The Hindu* and *The Indian Express* as well as their news at appropriate places.

I must make a special mention of the statements and the observations of Jagdeep Dhankhar and Kiren Rijiju, Vice President and Union Law Minister, respectively, on the appointments of Supreme Court and High Court Judges. I thank them.

I offer my thanks to the authors of the books and their publishers as well as the writers of articles in *The Indian Express* and *The Hindu*.

I have had the benefit of consultation with Justice A.S. Bagga, Hon'ble retired Judge of Bombay High Court and Shri Ankushrao Kadam, Chancellor of MGM University, Aurangabad. They are constant source of inspiration for me. I would fail in my duty if I do not complete formality of thanking them.

I thank all those who have directly or indirectly encouraged me to write this book. At the end I thank Shri Harjeet Singh of Atlantic Publishers and Distributors (P) Ltd., New Delhi, who assured me to publish the book within three weeks. There can be no greater joy for the author to see his book published in such a short period.

Sheshrao Chavan

1
Dedicated and Committed to Mahatma Gandhi

From the rampart of Red Fort, on the occasion of the 76th Independence Day on 15th August, 2022, Prime Minister Narendra Modi said: "I have dedicated myself to fulfill Mahatma Gandhi's vision of inclusion. I have committed myself to his vision of empowering and uplifting the person sitting at the last mile. I can see the fruition of this mission in the past eight years because of the experience gained over several decades of independence."

It is an open secret that all the development that is claimed to have been brought about during the last seventy-five years, does not appear to have made even a dent on the basic problems faced by the masses. People are even today steeped in ignorance, and groaning under the weight of poverty, unemployment and ill-health. In this context, the legendary Sudama, the poor Brahmin and the ashram-mate of Sri Krishna, is the true representative character of the majority of our countrymen, even today.

On 15th August, 1947, India had the immortal hour of her tryst with destiny. On that day, great national leaders of India were in Delhi. But, the greatest of them all, Mahatma Gandhi was not there. The bugles were sounded and the trumpets were blown, but he was not there to take the salute. A thousand cameras clicked and the limelight beat fiercely on the political stage, but he was not there to take the bow. At that time, he was working among the poor of Bengal.

The reason for his absence was simple. He had two dreams in his life. His first dream was fulfilled, but the second was not; and according to him, the true time for the celebration would be when his second dream would be fulfilled. His first dream was liberation of India from British rule. His second dream was liberation of Indians from oppression and injustice, from inequity and inequality, from discord and disharmony. To quote his own words:

> I shall work for an India, in which the poorest shall feel that it is their country in whose making they have an effective voice; an India in which all communities shall live in perfect harmony. There can be no room in such an India for the curse of untouchability, or the curse of the intoxicating drinks and drugs. Women will enjoy the same rights as men. Since we shall be at peace with all the rest of the world, neither exploiting, nor being exploited, we should have the smallest army imaginable. All interests not in conflict with the interest of the dumb millions will be scrupulously respected, whether foreign or indigenous. Personally, I hate distinction between foreign or indigenous. This is the India of my dreams. I shall be satisfied with nothing else. (*Young India*, 10-9-1931, p. 255)

Every Prime Minister right from Jawaharlal Nehru to Narendra Modi has been pledging to eradicate poverty, but every one of them miserably failed. This is evident from the Global Hunger Index. India's score of 29.1 in the Global Hunger Index 2022 falls under the 'serious' category in the hunger meter. It ranked 107 out of the 121 countries analyzed even below Rwanda (102) and Ethiopia (104). In Asia, Afghanistan with a rank of 109 is the only country behind India. Neighboring countries, Pakistan (99), Bangladesh (84), Nepal (81) and Sri Lanka (64) have all fared better than India.

No less a person than General Secretary of RSS, Dattatreya Hosabale, in a webinar organized by RSS-affiliate Swadeshi Jagran Manch as part of its Swawalambi Bharat Abhiyan, said: "The poverty in the country is standing like a demon in front of us. It is important that we slay this demon. Top 1% of India's population has one-fifth (20%) of the nation's income. At the same time, bottom 50% of the country's population has only 13% of the country's income." He also highlighted the widespread unemployment in the country. He further stated: "There are 4 crore unemployed people in the country. The labour force survey says that we have an unemployment rate of 7.6%".

What is the status of poverty, inequality and unemployment in India?

Poverty

Officially, India used to estimate poverty rate by looking at the consumption expenditure of people in relation to the official poverty line. The last revision of the poverty line was done by Prof. Suresh Tendulkar-led committee more than a decade ago. The Tendulkar poverty line was a consumption expenditure of ₹ 29 per day per person in urban areas and ₹ 22 per day per person in rural areas. Before Tendulkar's revision, India's poverty line was ₹ 12 for rural areas and ₹ 17 for urban areas.

In 2019, two academics, Santosh Mehrotra and Jajati Parida, used the consumption expenditure data from Periodic Labour Force Survey (PLFS) to estimate the status of poverty level in the country.

Using only the Tendulkar poverty line, we find that the total number of poor people fell by 137.4 million between 2004 and 2011 and then rose by 76.5 million between 2011 and 2019.

Even after 75 years of independence, we are still plagued by two basic problems—poverty and unemployment. In the Second Nehru Memorial Lecture, Lord Mountbatten referred to his first interview with Nehru on 24th March, 1947, when he asked Nehru what he thought was the greatest problem confronting India? At that time Nehru replied: "The Economic Problem, the problem stubbornly refuses to go away" (*We, the Nation: The Lost Decades,* Nani Palkhivala, p. 9).

An economist has rightly remarked in January 1987 that Socialism as practiced in India has been a fraud. Our brand socialism did not result in transfer of wealth from rich to the poor but only from the honest rich to the dishonest rich (*Ibid.*, p. 6).

Perspective observers in foreign countries, where Indians work and prosper are baffled by one question, "How does India with its great human potential and natural resources, manage to remain poor?" The answer is that we are not poor by nature but poor by policy. You would not be far wrong if you called India the world's leading expert in the art of perpetuating poverty (*Ibid.*, p. 9).

Viewed from the right perspective, even our poverty can be harnessed as a tremendous driving force in fulfilling great national purposes. Let us not forget that while several civilizations have perished through affluence, no civilization has ever died of adversity (*Ibid.*, p. 319).

Nani Palkhivala, almost two decades back said: "By voting ignorant professional politicians to power, we have kept a singularly gifted and enterprising country in the ranks of the poorest country on the earth". He further said: "It appears cynical, but it is true that for portly politicians, goodly in girth, poverty is a good business. They talk continually about *Garibi* without having the will, the expertise or the imagination to eradicate it" (*Nani Palkhivala: Selected Writings,* L.M. Singhvi and S.R. Pai, p. 51).

Duty of the Rich

Gandhiji said: "The rich should ponder well as to what their duty is today. They who employ mercenaries to guard their wealth may find those very guardians turning on them. The moneyed classes have got to learn how to fight either with arms or with the weapons of non-violence. For those who wish to follow the latter way, the best and the most effective mantra is: Enjoy the wealth by renouncing it."

Expanded, it means: "Earn your crores by all means. But understand that your wealth is not yours; it belongs to the people. Take what you require for your legitimate needs, and use the remainder for society."

Gandhiji further said: "I see coming the day of the rule of the poor, whether that rule be through force of arms or of non-violence. Let it be remembered that physical force is transitory even as the body is transitory. But the power of the spirit is permanent, even as the spirit is everlasting" (*Harijan*, 01-02-1942, p. 20).

Gandhiji's advice was: "Moneyed men may earn their crores (honestly only, of course), but so as to dedicate them to the service of all is perfectly sound. It is the surest method to evolve a new order of life of universal benefit in the place of the present one where each one lives for himself without regard to what happens to his neighbor" (*Harijan*, 22-02-1942, p. 49).

Grinding Poverty

Gandhiji said: "The grinding poverty and starvation with which our country is afflicted is such that it drives more and more every year into the ranks of the beggars, whose desperate struggle for bread renders them insensible to all feelings of decency and self-respect. And our philanthropists, instead of providing work for them and insisting on their working for bread, give them alms" (*An Autobiography,* M.K. Gandhi, p. 320).

He further said: "My *ahimsa* would not tolerate the idea of giving a free meal to a healthy person who has not worked for it in some honest way, and if I had the power, I would stop every 'Sadavrat' where free meals are given. It has degraded the nation and has encouraged laziness, idleness, hypocrisy and even crime. Such misplaced charity adds nothing to the wealth of the country, whether material or spiritual, and gives a false sense of meritoriousness to the donor."

"How nice and wise it would be if the donors were to open institutions where they would give meals under healthy, clean surroundings to men and women who would work for them. I know that it is easier to fling free meals in the faces of idlers, but much more difficult to organize an institution where honest work has to be done before meals are served. To people famishing and idle, the only acceptable form in which God can dare appear is work and promise of food as wages" (*The Mind of Mahatma Gandhi,* R.K. Prabhu and U.R. Rao, pp. 193-95).

Prime Minister Narendra Modi's scheme of giving free foodgrains to eighty crore Indians is against the philosophy of Mahatma Gandhi.

Unemployment

On 4th January, 2019, *The Washington Post* reported a story that has become too familiar to most Indians. When opening for 63000 jobs came out in the country's railways, 19 million people applied. The *Post's* story followed another galling report by *The Economic Times* on how 93000 people, including 3700 Ph.D. holders, 28000 post graduates, and 50000 graduates applied for 62 vacancies of government messenger's position in Uttar Pradesh. The messenger position required a minimum education of class five and a hard-to-find skill of riding a bicycle.

Similarly, when the Mumbai Police began a recruitment drive in 2018 to hire approximately 1100 constables, the junior most officer in the police force, more than 200,000 people applied including three doctors, five lawyers, 167 MBAs and 423 engineers.

The minimum qualification required was completing higher secondary schooling, or the 12th standard. Arup Patnaik, who had served as the city's Commissioner of Police in 2012 told the *Mumbai Mirror* that had reported the story: "During my time as the CP, there were no applications from the engineers or lawyers or doctors." He added: "There were few post graduates. The youth in Maharashtra are keen on government jobs. With the 'Make in India' push, it is a sad reflection of our times that engineers are applying for this post, especially when there are so many infrastructural projects like the Metro and Coastal Road" (*What Millennials Want,* Vivan Marwaha, Penguin Viking, pp. 40-41).

Recently, in Maharashtra, for 18000 posts of police constables 18,00,000 applications were received.

In December 2018, former RBI Governor and Chief Economist at IMF, Raghuram Rajan cited an incident in which 25 million people applied for 90,000 jobs in railways as evidence for the fact that India was not simply creating enough jobs for its young. A month later, in January 2019, the *Business Standard* broke an explosive story. It published a leaked report by the National Sample Survey Office (NSSO), a government body, which found that unemployment in India had reached at 45-year high.

The report also contained an alarming finding: "Youth unemployment was much higher compared to the overall population. It also found that the labour force participation rate, or the share of the population either employed or available for employment had fallen to 49.8% in 2017-18, down from 55.9% in 2011-12. This means that an entire half of India's working age population (15 years and above) was not contributing to any economic activity."

The NSSO and its annual survey, considered as the gold standard of employment data in India, soon came under attack from the ruling BJP. That he would create millions of jobs was one of the signature promises of Narendra Modi in his 2014 election, and any data that showed he was not succeeding became a political problem which needed to be neutralized. Two non-government members of the National Statistical Commission resigned from their positions, claiming that the government had sidelined them and was trying to suppress the release of the data. The Vice Chairman of the NITI Aayog, Dr. Rajiv Kumar called a press conference, seeking to discredit the study by casting doubt on its methodology.

On 31st May, 2019, merely days after Prime Minister Modi's re-election, the Ministry of Labour and Employment quietly released its employment data. Its figures matched those of the leaked NSSO report which the *Business Standard* published and also showed that unemployment was at 45-year high. The irony was lost on no one (*Ibid.*, pp. 52-53).

Azim Premji University's 'State of Working India, 2018' report found that the rate of unemployment among the educated has reached to 16%. These numbers likely underestimated the actual unemployment rate given the prevalence of large-scale disguised unemployment across the economy and how most economic activity in India takes place in the informal sector (*Ibid.*, p. 63).

Educated unemployment is a crisis that defines millennials more than any other demographic group in the country. In

January 2018, Prime Minister Modi sat down for a televised interview with ZEE News anchor Sudhir Chaudhary. In response to a question about the job crisis in India, Modi asked his interviewer, "If a man selling *pakoras* outside ZEE TV office takes home ₹ 200 at the end of the day, is that not employment?"

Modi, a measured and calculated speaker, was completely off the mark, and in response, the Congress Party said that if frying *pakora* is classified as employment, begging should be included as well.

Modi's answer was obviously disrespectful towards India's aspirational and educated millennials, but also more alarmingly made clear that India's so-called 'demographic dividend' could become a demographic disaster if not treated correctly. If the leader of the nation believes that frying *pakoras* for ₹ 200 daily qualifies as the sort of employment that the country ought to create for its youth, it will never breakout from poverty.

And that is because the maths simply does not add up. If a young Indian is to open a stall for frying *pakoras* and make ₹ 200 a day working every single day, he will make ₹ 6000 a month. It does not even include his operating cost. Even if it does and he makes ₹ 6000 in absolute profit, that will still not be enough to survive, let alone thrive, in modern India. It is simply not sufficient for a single man, even if he lives with his parents, and it is certainly not enough to support a wife and children.

According to an estimate of the United Nations Development Programme (UNDP), India needs to create nearly 300 million jobs between 2015 and 2050 to capitalize on its demographic dividend. But these jobs cannot include frying *pakoras* by the road side or begging. They must be generated in labour intensive and stable sectors of the economy, largely in the formal manufacturing sector.

India experienced severe working-hour and employment losses in 2020 and 2021 and Indian youth employment deteriorated in 2021 compared to 2020, according to the Global Employment Trends for Youth 2022 report released by the International Labour Organization. The recovery in youth employment is still lagging globally, the report says confirming that COVID-19 has hurt young people more than any other age group.

In India, according to surveys conducted by the Centre for Monitoring the Indian Economy (CMIE), the youth employment participation rate declined by 0.9 percentage points over the first nine months of 2021 relative to its value in 2020, while it increased by 2 percentage points for adults over the same time period.

Ten Lakh Jobs in 18 Months

Prime Minister Narendra Modi, in June 2022, announced that his government would be recruiting 10 lakh personnel within the next 18 months in a 'mission mode,' a major drive after recruitment to government jobs was derailed following the COVID-19 pandemic.

In a tweet from his official handle @PMOIndia, Mr. Modi said: PM@narendramodi reviewed the status of the Human Resource in all departments and ministries and instructed that recruitment of 10 lakh people be done by the government in mission mode in next 1.5 years.

The announcement came on the day when Defence Minister Rajnath Singh and the three service chiefs announced the *Agnipath* scheme of recruiting youth between the ages of 17.5 and 21 years for a four-year stint in the armed forces with a provision of voluntary retention after this period, based on merit.

75,000 Jobs Provided

On 22nd October, 2022, new employees in thirty-eight Union ministries and departments were handed over appointment letters at functions in multiple locations across the country.

In his address via video conference, Prime Minister Modi said more recruitment letters would be handed over in coming days. He said NDA-ruled States and the UTs of Jammu and Kashmir, Andaman and Nicobar Islands, Dadra and Nagar Haveli, Daman and Diu along with central government institutions will organize similar *rozgar* melas and hand over appointment letters to eligible candidates.

On the pandemic's fall out on employment and the economy, Prime Minister said that no one in the world expects to recover from the impact of the biggest crisis in 100 years within just 100 days. "But we have been able to shield the impact so far with everyone's efforts. And that has been possible because over the last eight years, we have removed the economic shortcomings that created hurdles," he said.

Due to its economic policies over the last eight years, he said, India has jumped five places from being the world's 10th largest economy to the 5th largest. He listed various schemes that generated jobs, including the Pradhan Mantri Mudra Yojana and Mahatma Gandhi National Rural Employment Guarantee Act, and said that to generate employment, government is working on multiple fronts.

Over the last few years, 20 lakh crore worth of credit, he said, has been availed through the Mudra Scheme. Over 7.5 crore beneficiaries started their business for the first time with Mudra loans. Seventy percent of the beneficiaries are women. Over eight crore women connected with self-help groups, are now selling what they make, he said.

He said innovators, entrepreneurs, farmers and people from fields of manufacturing and services have a crucial role in making India self-reliant. Highlighting the importance of *Sabka Prayas,* the Prime Minister said that everyone's effort is critical and *Sabka Prayas* is possible only when all important amenities reach everyone.

Prime Minister Modi said that the Employment Provident Fund Organization (EPFO) data indicates the success of employment policies. "In the month of August 2022 alone, 17 lakh people joined the EPFO, in the formal economy. In that, around eight lakh are in the age group of 18-25 years," he said. He linked the NDA Government's push for infrastructure projects with job creation, saying that globally it is accepted that infrastructure creates jobs. "Thousands of kms of roads are being built; rail lines are being doubled, converted and electrified; and airports are being constructed. The government is working with a target of ₹ 100 lakh crore investment in infrastructure. All this will create lakhs of local jobs and will also develop the tourism sector," he said. "Through Digital India, five lakh Common Service Centers alone have provided jobs to lakhs of youth," he said. "With the expansion of 5G, employment opportunities are going to increase even more in the digital sector," he said.

Identifying manufacturing and tourism as the two big creators of jobs, Prime Minister Modi said that processes are being simplified for global companies to come to India, set up their factories and fulfil global demands. The Production Linked Incentive (PLI) Scheme has been started to encourage investments in India. More the production, more the incentive will be. The benefits of this policy have started showing in many sectors, he said.

On the recruitment drive, Prime Minister Modi said that it is meant to provide basic services to people faster. He said the drive itself is an example of the changing times. "Eight years ago, applying for a government job itself was the start of many problems. Over the years, we have removed those problems and simplified the processes. We have abolished interviews for Groups C and D," he said.

The posts for which appointment letters were handed over included central armed force personnel, sub-inspector, constable, lower division clerk, steno, personal assistant, income tax inspector and multi-tasking staff. Prime Minister Modi urged the new employees to always remember their *kartavya path* (duties) towards people while doing their jobs. Those being given appointment letters joined at various levels in Group A and B (Gazetted), Group B (Non-Gazetted) and Group C.

Vacant Posts

As of March 2020, 8.8 lakh jobs were vacant in various departments of the Union Government. In 2019, the number of vacant posts was around 9.2 lakh (23% of the sanctioned posts) and in 2018, there were 6.8 lakh such vacancies (17% of sanctioned posts).

The unemployment rate saw a decrease of 0.6% and fell to 4.2% in 2020-21, compared with 4.8% in 2019-20, according to the Periodic Labour Force Survey (PLFS) for 2020-21 released by the Ministry of Statistics and Programme Implementation. This means that only 4.2% of adults who looked for jobs could not get any work in rural and urban areas of the country in 2020-21. Rural areas recorded an unemployment rate of 3.3% and urban areas recorded an unemployment rate of 6.7% (*The Hindu,* 15th June, 2022).

Inequality

India is one of the most unequal countries in the world. The income of the top 10% of India's population is 22 times that of the bottom 50%. An annual income of ₹ 11.5 lakh would place an individual in the top 10% of earners, because the country's average is just ₹ 2 lakh. The top 1%, however, have an average annual income of well over ₹ 44 lakh.

Gandhian Way to Eradicate Poverty and Unemployment

Mahatma Gandhi said: "There is no doubt in my mind that in a country like ours, teeming with millions of unemployed, something is needed to keep their hands and feet engaged in order that they may earn an honest living. It is for them that Khadi and cottage industries are needed. It is clear to me as day light that they are badly needed at the present moment. These little things add substantially to the income of the poor villagers. If you can ensure them three Annas instead of the three pice that they get today, they will think that they have won Swaraj. That is what Khadi is trying to do for the spinners today" (*Harijan,* 02-01-1937).

Dangers of Mechanization

In the *Harijan* of 16th November, 1934, Gandhiji wrote: "Mechanization is good when the hands are too few for the work intended to be accomplished. It is an evil when there are more hands than required for the work, as is the case of India. The problem with us is not how to find leisure for the teeming millions inhabiting our villages. The problem is how to utilize their idle hours, which are equal to the working days of six months in the year...I am quite safe in saying that every mill-hand does the work of at least ten labourers doing the same work in their villages. In other words, he earns more than he did in his village at the expense of ten fellow-villagers. Thus, spinning and weaving mills have deprived the villagers of a substantial means of livelihood. It is no answer in reply to say that they turn out cheaper, better cloth, if they do so at all. For, if they have displaced thousands of workers, the cheapest mill cloth is dearer than the dearest Khadi woven in the villages. Coal is not dear for the coal miner who can use it there and then, nor is Khadi dear for the villager who manufactures his own Khadi."

With regard to the poverty, Gandhiji, in the *Harijan* of 11th May, 1935, wrote: "The reason of our poverty is the extinction of our industries and our consequent unemployment. Some years ago, India's agricultural population was said to be 70 per cent. Today, it is said to be 90 per cent. It does not mean that 90 per cent are agriculturists, but that, instead of 70 per cent who depended on land, 90 per cent are now driven to depend on land. In other words, whereas there were industries and crafts enough to feed the 20 per cent, some time ago, these are no longer there and the people have, thus, been thrown on land. They, thus, steal their living, not because they want to, but because there is no more land."

Pattern of State Assistance

In the *Harijan* of 25th January, 1946, Gandhiji wrote: "It is possible to clothe today the whole of India in Khadi on the smallest outlay and in the shortest time possible. Each provincial government has to tell the villagers that they must manufacture their own Khadi for their own use. This brings in automatic local production and distribution. And there will be undoubtedly a surplus for the cities at least to a certain extent which, in its turn, will reduce the pressure on the local mills. The latter will then be able to take part in supplying the want of cloth in other parts of the world."

Gandhiji as back as 1920 said: "I feel convinced that the revival of hand-spinning and hand-weaving will make the largest contribution to the economic and moral regeneration of India. The millions must have a simple industry to supplement agriculture. Spinning was the cottage industry years ago, and if the millions are to be saved from starvation, they must be enabled to introduce spinning in their homes, and every village must repossess its own weaver" (*Young India,* 21st July, 1920).

In the *Young India* of 8th December, 1921, Gandhiji wrote: "I claim for the *Charkha* the honour of being able to solve the problem of economic distress in a most natural, simple, inexpensive and business-like manner. The *Charkha,* therefore, is a useful and indispensable article of every home. It is the symbol of the nation's prosperity and, therefore, freedom. It is a symbol of not of commercial war but of commercial peace. It bears not a message of ill-will towards the nations of the earth but of good-will and self-help. It will not need the protection of a navy threatening a world's peace and exploiting its resources, but it needs the religious determination of millions to spin their yarn in their own homes as today they cook their food in their own homes. I may deserve the curses of prosperity for many mistakes of omission and commission, but I am confident of earning its blessings for suggesting a revival of the *Charkha.* I stake my all on it. For every revolution of the wheel spins peace, good-will and love. And with all that, in as much as the loss of it brought about India's slavery, its voluntary revival with all its implications must mean India's freedom."

In the *Young India* of 21st August, 1924, Gandhiji wrote: "What is claimed for spinning is that:

1. It supplies the readiest occupation to those who have leisure and are in want of a few coppers.
2. It is known to the thousands.
3. It is easily learnt.
4. It required practically no outlay of capital.
5. The wheel can be easily and cheaply made. Most of us do not yet know that spinning can be done even with a piece of tile and splinter.
6. The people have no repugnance to it.
7. It affords immediate relief in times of famine and scarcity.
8. It alone can stop the drain of wealth which goes outside India in the purchase of foreign cloth.

9. It automatically distributes the millions thus saved among the deserving poor.
10. Even the smallest success means so much immediate gain to the people.
11. It is the most potent instrument of securing co-operation among the people."

In the *Young India* of 19th February, 1938, Gandhiji wrote: "I have often said that if seven lakh of the villages of India were to be kept alive, and if peace that is at the root of all civilizations is to be achieved, we have to make the spinning wheel the center of all handicrafts. Thus, my faith in the spinning wheel is growing everyday and I see it more and more clearly that the Sun of the wheel will alone illumine the planets of other handicrafts. But I go a step further and say that just as we go on discovering new stars and planets in the vast solar system, even so we shall go on discovering fresh handicrafts every day. But for the sake of this thing, we have to make the spinning wheel the really life-giving Sun."

Other Village Industries

Gandhiji suggested the following cottage industries to be set up in the villages to provide employment to the village people: tanning, dairying, gur and khandsari, compost manure, hand-made paper, machine oil and ghani oil, bee-keeping and hand-pounding of rice.

The governments have been implementing most of the above cottage industries. The Modi Government has created opportunities for rural and urban youth through *Kaushalya Vikas Kendras* to set up their own small industries and business and become employer rather than employees.

2
Gandhiji's Views on Religion

The views of Mahatma Gandhi on religion, communal harmony, especially Hindu-Muslim relations, unity of India, purity in public life and welfare of last man have been summarized here for the introspection of Narendra Modi as to how far he agrees with them vis-à-vis RSS ideology and how far he will be able to implement them.

Religion

Gandhiji believed that the essence of religion is morality and that the true religion and true morality are inseparably bound up with each other.

"I would not make a fetish of religion and condone evil in the sacred name," Gandhiji said in 1927. He again said in the same year, "My belief in the Hindu scripture does not require me to accept every word and every verse as divinity inspired. I decline to be bound by any interpretation, however, learned it may be, if it is repugnant to reason or moral sense." Nor did he look upon Hinduism as the only religion. He said: "I do not believe in the exclusive divinity of the Vedas. I believe in Bible, the Quṛan and Zend-Avesta to be as divinely inspired as the Vedas. All religions are but different paths, leading to the same goal. All have one father and all are his children, in this thought alone all religious differences can cease to exist. I see in every religion my own religion and my own religion in every other religion."

Gandhiji further said: "In reality, there are as many religions as there are individuals, but those who are conscious of the spirit of morality do not interfere with one another's religion. If they do, they are not fit to be considered a nation. The Hindus, the Muslims, the Parsis and the Christians who have made India their country are fellow countrymen and they will have to live in unity. In no part of the world are one nationality and one religion synonymous terms; nor has it been so in India."

Gandhiji believed that the religion had been and has continued to be one of the most powerful influences on the lives of men and women on the earth. And no government or king or leader who did not take this into serious account, understand it and make provision for it, could be said to have an integrated view of the welfare of the people of that country.

There was not a single aspect of Gandhiji's life which was not permeated by religion in its widest and richest sense combining both ethical and spiritual values as well as deeply emotional faith. To Gandhiji, God was not communal leader; He was universal phenomenon and a personal master. Gandhiji believed that the individual was an indivisible vanity, body, mind and spirit.

Gandhiji promoted the precept and practice of a kind of universal religion among the people. He conducted prayers in public. He quoted scriptures often not as a philosopher does to prove a theological or metaphysical point, but as a practicing devotee to explain an ethical proposition. His everyday life had the disciplined austere routine of a sanyasi living in an ashram. His inflexible moral sense, which illumined his every thought, word and deed was derived directly from his intense, abiding faith in God.

"One should appear to be as one really is and should act accordingly is not the last, but the first step to practical religion. The building up of a religious life is impossible without such a foundation," Gandhiji said.

Gandhiji wanted unreserved reverence for all the religions in the world. Reverence is much more than tolerance. Gandhiji asked much more than tolerance among the greatest religious systems. He pleaded for deep mutual understanding of the humility to learn from each other. He described his own religion which transcends Hinduism, Islam, Christianity, etc.; and does not supersede them. Gandhiji at one stage made it clear that his religion has no geographical limits. He said, "religion must help humanity toward its ethical goals on earth." He saw the ethical aspect as consisting of three conditions—(i) behavior of man to man, (ii) behavior of man towards property and (iii) behavior of man to woman.

Gandhiji said: "A religion which takes no account of practical affairs and does not help them is no religion." With Gandhiji the supreme consideration was man. He often said: "With me man comes first." He wanted the Kingdom of God, but it was to be established not in heaven but here on this earth as Kingdom of righteousness. He demonstrated in his life and work that it is possible for human beings to close the gap between ideal and the practical, and he proved that religion properly understood could become a tremendous revolutionary force for changing life into something better, nobler and greater. He tried to make his religion a vital part of his life and applied it to the different problems he faced.

For Gandhiji religion was a personal encounter with the Divine. He struggled hard to get that insight into reality over 40 years. In the spirit of Hindu religion, he looked upon the Divine not only as a transcendental Absolute but as a personal God. He was truly a 'Bhakta' with an unflinching faith in God. Yet his concept of religion had nothing to do with any dogma or custom or ritual. He had told the federation of International Fellowship in 1928 that, after long study and experience, I have come to the conclusion that (a) all religions are true, (b) all religions have error in them and (c) all religions are almost as dear to me as Hinduism.

"No man can live without religion," Gandhiji wrote, "there are some who in the egotism of their reason declare that they have nothing to do with religion, but that is like a man saying that he breaths but that he has no nose."

Gandhiji looked upon politics as a branch of ethics and religion. It is not a struggle for power or wealth, but a persistent and continuous effort to enable the submerged millions to attain the good life to raise the quality of human being, to train them for freedom and fellowship, and for spiritual depth and social harmony. A politician who works for these ends cannot help being religious.

Gandhiji introduced spiritual and moral values in politics. By his application of the traditional moral weapons of fasting, self-suffering and prayer, he kept the spirit of religion alive in himself and in his followers, and largely succeeded in maintaining the purity of his methods even when applied on mass scale.

Religious Unity

Gandhiji tried to unite all religions and races. He respected all religions—Hindus, Muslims, Parsis, Christians and Jews, and believed if we wish to live as a nation, the interest of anyone of us must be the interest of all. The only deciding consideration should be the justice of a particular cause. Gandhiji continued more and more actively his campaign for the unity of India. He called Hindus and Muslims to form a solid alliance. The relations between the Hindus and Muslims were continuously embittered by prejudices, mutual fear and suspicion. The British had always taken advantage of the mutual enmity between Hindus and Muslims. Gandhiji accused them of even fostering it. This is evident from what J.T. Sutherland recorded in his book, *India in Bondage*. In the words of Sutherland: "Before the British came there seems to have been little hostility between Hindus and Muslims. Everywhere they seemed to have lived together for the most part peacefully and harmoniously. Hindus lived in security and peace under Muslim rulers. Hindu princes appointed Muslims to high posts, sometime to the very highest and Muslim princes were as generous in placing responsibilities and conferring honors on Hindus. In the native States today where there are few British, there are very few riots and very little enmity to be seen."

"What succeeded in dividing Hindus and Muslims is not religion, but politics," Gandhiji said, "Hindus and Muslims have fought wars, but they have stayed together. This is politics—politics disturbs much more than any other aspect. There is harmony in Hindu-Muslim cultures, spirituality, painting and music, but it is politics which divides countries."

The concept of theocratic state was developed by politicians. Theocracy is bad whether it is of the Islamic type or of the Hindu type. There is no verse in the *Quran* which speaks of *Jihad* or holy war against non-Muslims. In the *Quran*, the *Jihad* refers to the war against evil. A true Muslim fights the war against evils.

Gandhiji devoted himself to bring the two communities into harmonious collaboration and without advocating or desiring an impossible fusion between the two. He tried to unite them in friendship. When his voice proclaimed the identity of Hindu-Muslim cause it awoke with a start. He said, for India unity is truth and division evil. Unity is that which embraces and understands everything; consequently, it cannot be attained through negation.

India is a pluralistic society. She exemplifies the adage 'unity in diversity.' This emotional oneness was described by Gandhiji as "Soul of India," by Jawaharlal Nehru as "Spirit of India," and Bankimchandra personified it as "Mother India." There are a number of geographical, historical, social, cultural, religious and other events and developments that contributed to the evolution of a pluralistic and yet homogeneous society in India during the last five thousand years. But, India of today is a country without Indians. Nehru once remarked, "this is an India, but where are the Indians?" We have millions of Bengalis, millions of Gujaratis, millions of Tamils, but very few Indians. India has become a land of every narrow and unhealthy 'ism' except nationalism and patriots. "My patriotism is subservient to my religion," Gandhiji said, "I cling to India like a child to its mother's breast, because I feel that she gives me the spiritual nourishment I need."

Diametrically Opposite Views

The views of Rashtriya Swayamsevak Sangh (RSS) and Mahatma Gandhi are diametrically opposite, which can be seen from the following statements of Sarsanghchalaks of the RSS.

Dr. Keshav Baliram Hedgewar, the first Sarsanghchalak of RSS, denounced Muslims as Yavan-snakes. He said: "From the ancient times, India is the country of Hindus, therefore, the national life shall be made rich by them only, and nobody shall have the courage to attack or shock it." He believed that *Hindutva* is *Rashtriyatva*. The nation belongs to Hindus. He, in his last speech before his death in 1940, said: "I see before my eyes today a miniature Hindu *Rashtra.*"

In 1939, M.S. Golwalkar, the successor of Hedgewar, said: "Minorities must live by the grace of majority; only a Hindu could be a true Indian. Those whose faith did not originate on this subcontinent are foreigners. Muslims, Christians, Jews and Parsis would have to adopt the Hindu culture and language, must learn to respect and hold in reverence Hindu religion, must entertain no idea, but the glorification of the Hindu race and culture. They may stay in the country, wholly subordinated to the Hindu Nation; claiming nothing, deserving no privileges, far less any preferential treatment, not even citizens' rights. In this country, Hindus alone are nation and the Muslims and others, if not actually anti-national, are at least outside the body of the nation."

Golwalkar further said: "So far as nation is concerned, all those who fall outside the five-fold limits can have no place in the national life unless they abandon their differences, adopt the religion, culture and language of the nation and completely merge themselves in the national race. So long as they maintain their racial, religious and cultural differences, they cannot but be only foreigners who may be either friendly or inimical to the nation."

Golwalkar also said: "There are only two courses open to the foreign elements either to merge themselves in the national race and adopt its culture, or to live at its mercy so long as the national race may allow them to do so."

Mahatma Gandhi, in one of his visits to the RSS camps, said: "If the Hindus feel that in India there is no place for anyone except the Hindus and if non-Hindus, especially Muslims, wish to live here, they will have to live as the slaves of the Hindus, they kill Hinduism."

Narendra Modi has been groomed at RSS right from his childhood and, therefore, it is hard to believe in his dedication and commitment to Mahatma Gandhi, unless he is convinced and in turn has convinced RSS bosses that no political party can survive in India without taking shelter of 'Father of the Nation'.

3
Congress and Opposition Mukta Bharat

In January 2014, while addressing the 'Vijay Sankalp Rally' in Goa, Narendra Modi called on the audience to vote for a 'Congress *Mukta* Bharat'. He said: "Be it dynasty politics, nepotism, corruption, communalism, division in society or poverty, getting freedom from all this is what I mean by a 'Congress *Mukta* Bharat.'" He reiterated the same thoughts in his speech on 15th August, 2022.

Stating the BJP's commitment to change the future of India, Modi said: "We need efforts to integrate the nation, not divide it."

The events that have unfolded in last eight years of Modi rule includes putting up and pulling down governments casting aside even elementary decencies and ignoring many urgent, vital and basic tasks; crafty and crude manipulations and despicable engineering of defection as naughty children do with sand castles. This is evident from the cases of Madhya Pradesh, Karnataka and recently Maharashtra. The selective arrests of opposition party leaders show that we are perhaps, heading towards an opposition *Mukta* Bharat as said by BJP President J.P. Nadda that there would be only one national political party and that will be BJP. All other political parties will vanish.

Amit Shah, the Home Minister of India, publicly declared that the next 30-40 years will be the era of the BJP. Encouraging defections from the parties in power in States will sound the death knell for democracy.

Democracy is the basic feature of the Constitution. Parliamentary democracy does not envisage a condition where a one-party government becomes permanent. The presence of a vigilant opposition is necessary not just for a vibrant democracy but for its very survival. When the opposition criticizes the government or carries on an agitation to arouse public opinion against a party's misdeeds, it is performing a duty that has been assigned by the Constitution. Without an effective opposition, democracy will become dull and legislature will become submissive. The public will perceive the legislature as ineffective and incapable of fulfilling its duties, potentially leading to a loss of interest in the functioning of Parliament.

During the Constituent Assembly debates, Naziruddin Ahmad, a member of the Constituent Assembly, said: "If you are not desirous of creating anti-Congress feeling, it is very necessary for you to create an opposition, if necessary, by some members volunteering to go to the opposition and making it healthy and strong."

Ramnarayan Singh, another member of the Constituent Assembly, went further and said: "A government which does not like opposition and always wants to be in power is not a patriotic but a traitor government."

Necessity and Importance of Opposition in Democracy

On 28th October, 1951, Dr. Ambedkar, in his speech at D.A.V. College, Jalandhar, Punjab, said: "There are two pillars on which the Parliamentary System of Government rests. These two pillars are—(i) an Opposition and (ii) Free and Fair Elections." Elaborating it, Dr. Ambedkar said: "For the last twenty or thirty years we are acclimatized to one single political party. We have nearly forgotten the necessity and importance of 'Opposition' for the fair working of Parliamentary Democracy. We are continuously told that opposition is an evil. Here again we are forgetting what the past history has to teach us. You know that there were Nibandhkars to interpret the Vedas and Smritis. They used to begin their comments on *Slokas* and *Sutras* by stating firstly the *Purva Paksha,* the one side of the question. They used to follow up by giving the *Uttar Paksha,* the other side. By this they wanted to show that the question raised was not an easy question; it is a question, where there is a dispute, discussion and doubt. Then, they used to give what they termed as *Adhikaran* where they used to criticize both the *Pakshas*. Finally, they gave the *Sidhant,* their own decisions. Here from we can find that all our ancient teachers believed in two party system of government.

One important thing in Parliamentary Democracy is that people should know the other side, if there are two sides to a question. Hence, a functional opposition is required. Opposition is a key to a free political life. No democracy can do without it. Britain and Canada, the two exponents of Parliamentary System of Government, recognize this important fact and in both countries the Leader of Opposition is paid salary by the government. They regard the 'Opposition' as an essential thing. People of these countries believe that the 'Opposition' should be as much alive as the government. The government may suppress the facts; the government may have only one-sided propaganda. The people have made provision against the eventuality in these two countries.

Now, the question arises as to whether there is any desire on the part of the party in power to permit any Opposition to be created. Congress does not want any Opposition. Congress is attempting to gather people of sundry views under one canopy. I ask whether this is a desirable trend in the political life of this country."

During Dr. Ambedkar's days, it was Congress that was ruling the country. The position of Opposition in BJP rule is no different. Narendra Modi as Prime Minister had earlier pledged to make Congress *Mukta* Bharat in which he considerably succeeded. Now, he has pledged to make 'Opposition *Mukta* Bharat' and his every move seems to be marching towards accomplishing the goal.

Opposition's Space Shrinking

Former Chief Justice of India, Justice N.V. Ramana, expressed concern over the transformation of political opposition into hostility, stating that there used to be mutual respect between the government and the opposition earlier. However, he observed that in recent times, the space for the opposition to function and voice their opinions has been shrinking.

Addressing an event in the Rajasthan Assembly, Justice Ramana said: "We must note that India was meant to be a Parliamentary democracy and not Parliamentary government, for the core idea of democracy is represented. Dr. Ambedkar cautioned that by Parliamentary democracy, we can never infer rule by majority. He said that the majority rule is untenable in theory and unjustifiable in practice."

"The framers decided to opt for a representative democracy. A representative democracy is about effective representation. It is where the minority is not overwhelmed by the majority," he said.

He further said: "In modern democracy the people expect the court to stand as a counterweight to Legislative and Executive excesses. This gains gravity, particularly whenever the Opposition is missing in action."

Emphasizing the importance of the Opposition space, he said: "The diversity of opinion enriches polity and society. Political Opposition should not translate into hostility, which we are sadly witnessing these days. These are not signs of a healthy democracy."

"Strong, vibrant and active Opposition helps to improve governance and corrects the functioning of the government and the Opposition which will lead to a progressive democracy. After all, Project Democracy is a joint effort of all the stakeholders," he added.

In his book, *Parliamentary Democracy*, published by Bharatiya Vidya Bhavan, Mumbai in 1971, Shri G.S. Pathak, the former Vice-President of India, at page 8 said: "It is not possible to correctly appreciate the functioning of Parliament without an idea of the part played by the Opposition. It is often said that the duty of the Opposition is to oppose, but really its functions are of a more varied character. Prof. Ronald Butt has said that the Opposition itself participates in the process of governing, because it helps to condition the contemporary climate of opinion through which the government of the day is itself influenced in the production of its policies. He observes that apart from the real, if indirect, effect it has on the evolution of Government policy, the Opposition can also, by a carefully fought and reasoned campaign, get the details of legislation amended. Prof. Jennings observes that in the House of Commons which is the focus of the whole apparatus, Her Majesty's Government is assisted by Her Majesty's Opposition. One permits the other to govern, because the second permits the first to oppose, and together they lead their parties in the operation of the constitutional machine. Prof. Jennings notes that the Government tends to regard the Opposition as brake on a car going up-hill, whereas the Opposition thinks that the car is going down-hill. Still, in the net result, the contribution of a responsible Opposition can be very constructive."

Pathak further wrote: "The Opposition's action can be described as one of enlightened self-interest. In appealing to public opinion, it appeals to the Government to rest its policy on public opinion."

To see a flock of members of the governing legislative party in a State, specifically in Maharashtra, being flown from one destination to another in chartered planes, housed in five-star hotels, and taken to States run by the party in power at the center is a sign of conspiracy.

Equally alarming is the recent trend of the use of powers, especially the Prevention of Money Laundering Act, ED and CBI raids against opposition members. Nobody can condone illegalities. Individuals, if guilty, must be proceeded with under the law. But, can one believe that such illegalities are committed only in the opposition? It raises a question whether dishonesty is the forte of only the opposition parties?

4
Nari-Shakti

Elaborating the achievements of women in various fields, Narendra Modi, in his speech expected that Nari-Shakti will take the country to new heights during the *Amrit Kaal* (a metaphorical term used by the Modi Government for a time of great opportunity and transformation). Prime Minister's pious intentions are laudable. He said: "Participation of women in leadership and decision-making positions in corporate sector is startling. The number of women in senior management positions in the corporate sector in India is 39%, which is higher than global average. Number of women CEOs in Fortune 500 companies is 15% while female board members in the management of private enterprises has been growing from 15% (2016), 16.9% (2018) to 19.7% in 2022. If this trend continues, near parity will be reached by 2045, according to a forecast made by Deloitte."

Narendra Modi spoke high of women working and shining in various fields, but he has to look to the ground realities about the women, which are as given below:

NCRB Data

The National Crime Records Bureau (NCRB) recorded 32,033 cases of rape in 2019, which means that 87 Indian women were raped every day. Of these, 15% were children. The statistics are shameful, but it is not the statistics that should worry us as much as the strenuous efforts made in the 'New India' to change the narrative at the behest of political leaders at the highest level.

The latest report released by the NCRB shows that 1,49,404 cases of crime against children were registered in 2021 of which 53,874 (36.05%) were under the Protection of Children from Sexual Offences Act (POCSO).

There were 47,221 POCSO cases out of 1,28,531 cases of crime against children in 2020, i.e., 36.73% and 47,335 of 1,48,185 such cases in 2019, i.e., 31.94%.

NCRB data on cases registered under POCSO show a steady increase in the rate (incidents per one lakh children:): 12.1 in 2021 (53,276 girls and 1,083 boys); 10.6 in both 2020 and 2019.

Crime against women rose by 15.3% in 2021 from previous year, according to the latest data released by the NCRB, with 4,28,278 cases registered in 2021 following 3,71,503 cases in 2020.

The NCRB report also shows that the rate of crimes against women (number of incidents per one lakh population) increased from 55.9% in 2020 to 63.3% in 2021. A majority of these cases (31.8%) fall in the category of cruelty by husband or his relatives, followed by assault on women with intent to outrage her modesty (20.8%), kidnapping and abduction (17.6%), and rape (7.4%).

According to the report, the highest rate of crime against women in 2021 was registered in Assam (168.3%), despite a marginal dip over the last three years. The state recorded over 29,000 such cases in 2020.

The other top states in this category include Odisha, Haryana, Telangana and Rajasthan. Rajasthan, like Assam, showed a marginal decrease in the actual number of cases while the remaining three states marked an increase.

The report places Uttar Pradesh on the top (with 56,083 cases) in term of actual number of cases registered in 2021, although the rate is lesser at 50.5%. The other states that recorded the highest number of crimes against women include Rajasthan, Maharashtra, West Bengal and Odisha.

Nagaland stood out with the lowest number of crimes against women registered in the past three years: 43 in 2019, 39 in 2020, and 54 in 2021. It also had the lowest crime rate against women in 2021 at 5.5%.

Among Union Territories, Delhi had the highest rate of crime against women in 2021 at 147.6%. It also topped in absolute numbers of cases registered, recording an increase over the past three years from 13,395 in 2019 to 14,277 in 2021.

The NCRB also collated data for crime against women in 19 cities across the country with a population over two million. Amongst these cities, the 2021 data shows that Jaipur had the highest rate over 194%, followed by Delhi, Indore and Lucknow. Chennai and Coimbatore, both in Tamil Nadu, had the lowest rate. In actual numbers among these cities, Delhi topped in 2021 (13,982) followed by Mumbai, Bangaluru and Hyderabad. Delhi also marked the highest number of actual cases in the past three years amongst these cities, with 12,902 in 2019 and 9,782 in 2020.

Rajasthan had the highest rate of rape in 2021 at 16.4% and topped in actual numbers with 6,337 cases registered last year. Uttar Pradesh, Madhya Pradesh and Maharashtra followed with over 2,000 registered cases in the last year. Rajasthan had also the highest number of minor girls raped in 2021 with 1,453 registered cases.

Overall, there were 30,016 registered cases of rape in the country last year, indicating a marginal decline over the past five years from 33,977 cases reported in 2018.

Cases of murder after gang-rape for which the NCRB has maintained records since 2017, have remained steady—278 cases in 2021, the same as in 2019. In 2020, there were 218 such incidents. The highest number of cases under the category was registered in 2018 with 291 cases. In 2021, the highest number of such cases took place in Uttar Pradesh with 48, followed closely by Assam with 46. Bihar, Arunachal Pradesh, Goa, Himachal Pradesh, Manipur, Mizoram, Nagaland and Uttarakhand did not register any case under this category last year.

According to NCRB data, murder after rape makes up less than one percent of the total rapes in the country annually. In these cases, the NCRB data between 2017 and 2021 show that Uttar Pradesh, Assam, Madhya Pradesh and Maharashtra had the highest number of cases in the country annually for the period 2017-20.

Over 27,000 women were abducted in 2021 to be compelled into marriage, including 12,000 minors, with the highest number recorded in Uttar Pradesh (8,599), followed by Bihar (6,589).

Only 502 cases were registered in the country under the Domestic Violence Act in 2021 which was 0.1% of the total cases of crime against women. The highest number of cases (270) were filed in Kerala. Meanwhile, 6,589 cases of dowry deaths were registered in 2021 with the highest number of such deaths registered in Uttar Pradesh and Bihar (*Indian Express,* 30th August, 2022).

The latest case is that of 19-year-old Ankita Bhandari from Uttarakhand. She was the daughter of a former security guard and an *Anganwadi* worker. She had completed class-12 and was keen to go to college. But then, with her father having quit his job years ago, she decided to sign up as a receptionist at a resort barely a month ago. She did not, however, live long enough to collect even her first salary.

The police recovered her body from a canal, six days after she went missing from a resort in the Lakshman Jhula area of Rishikesh, Uttarakhand. The police arrested Pulkit Arya, resort owner and son of a former state minister Vinod Arya, who confessed to pushing Ankita into the canal after an altercation.

Speaking to *The Sunday Express*, Uttarakhand DGP Ashok Kumar said that the police have found evidence suggesting that the accused were putting pressure on Ankita to provide "special services" to some of the guests and she was killed when she resisted.

DGP Ashok Kumar further said that police have recovered a WhatsApp chat between Ankita and a friend who lives in Jammu. "In the messages, she made it clear that they want her to provide 'special services.' That friend and the chat is major evidence for us. Also, we found the body from the same canal (Shakti canal near the Chilla power house) where the accused confessed to having pushed her," said the DGP (*Indian Express,* 25th September, 2022).

In the wake of massive protests following the murder of Ankita, BJP expelled the father and the elder brother of the accused from the party. Chief Minister Pushkar Singh Dhami ordered demolition of the resort owned by the accused. Pulkit Arya's elder brother was removed from the post of nominated vice-chairman of the State's OBC Commission. After the massive protests and outrage, the government formed a Special Investigation Team (SIT) and escalated the probe under the leadership of DGP P. Renuka Devi.

The Opposition targeted the BJP on the incident. "Will this bulldozer action solve the issue? By bulldozing the resort, you think our anger and the blot on our culture and society will fade away. Make the rules so stringent so that people will be scared to commit crime," former chief minister of Uttarakhand Harish Rawat said (*The Hindu,* 25th September, 2022).

For educated girls from rural areas, urban pockets are centers of hope with promised potential for social and economic independence and upward mobility. Many cannot make it to the metros, and for them, small towns are places to fulfill their dreams and aspirations. The murder of 19-year-old Ankita Bhandari has jolted the dreams not only of Ankita, but of many young girls all over the country.

Young girls of all strata aspire to move out of the social control, which combined with the lack of jobs in the local area, leads to their immigration to urban centers for employment. In many cases, their contributions to family incomes are critical for survival, especially at a time rural household incomes are dwindling. Migration to big cities is a hard task for those coming from the economically weaker strata, given the difficulties in finding jobs and places to stay. For such women, service sector jobs in small towns are the only possible option. Ankita was one such girl who took up her first job as a receptionist.

In most of the rape cases, the victims are usually Dalit and rapists are from upper caste. If rape cases manage to come to trial, more than 90% of rapists get away with their barbarous crimes.

On law and order and women's safety less said the better. Women's safety, a key promise in the BJP's election campaign, has been callously treated in Uttar Pradesh. An Alt News Analysis of national crime data placed Uttar Pradesh on top for custodial rapes and dowry deaths. Further, NCRB data show that the number of dowry deaths per one lakh people in Uttar Pradesh is the highest in the country. This is excluding the gang rapes that have regularly hit the headlines.

Rules are already there. Justice J.S. Verma Committee's recommendations are also there. And yet the rapes and atrocities on women are continuing, nay, they are on increase. The reason is that fear of law and order is dwindling. Besides, it is not only the BJP leaders who are involved in the crime, but the Congress and other political parties and big wigs are also seen involved.

Rulers must Protect Women

Former Chief Justice of India, N.V. Ramana, in his 40th Convocation address of Sri Sathya Sai Institute of Higher Learning, a deemed-to-be university, said: "The present-day rulers must honor and protect women and children and the weak. When a person becomes a king, he is likely to inherit 24 bad qualities that he must avoid and question himself every day if he is on the path of righteousness before he embarks on taking administrative decisions."

Quoting from *Mahabharata*, Justice Ramana said: "At a time when Narada asked Dharmaraja about how a king should conduct himself, the latter said the king should rule in such a way that it is beneficial to the majority of people and he must not take decisions that are unthoughtful."

"In Ayodhya Kand of the *Ramayana,* when a group of *vartakas* (businessmen) came to meet Lord Rama, he asked them if they were respecting and protecting the elders, women, children, and the weak," Ramana added.

Struggle for Women

The award-winning author, Githa Hariharan, in her introduction to Justice K. Chandru's book, *Listen to My Case! When Women Approach the Courts of Tamil Nadu,* has pointed out that the process of going to court is hard for women; it is even harder when women do not have financial or emotional support from their family, custom or the present reading of the law.

The representation of women in the Indian judiciary too is poor. For example, Justice Indira Banerjee, the senior most woman judge in the Supreme Court, highlighted how the top court since its inception in 1950 has seen only eleven women judges. However, during his tenure as the Chief Justice of Supreme Court, C.V. Ramana elevated three women judges of whom one may become the Chief Justice by the present order of seniority.

Faisal C.K., in his write up in *The Indian Express* of 30th August, 2022, says: "The inclusion of women in the judiciary would ensure that the decision-making process is more responsive, inclusive and participatory at all levels. But, this is only a dream. In the existing unsatisfactory jural environment, the occasional escape of the patriarchal cat from the judiciary's bag is quite expected."

Faisal further says: "For women, ensuring human dignity is still a broken promise. In *Bradwell* vs. *The State of Illinois,* 1872, the Supreme Court of the United States held that God designed the sexes to occupy different spheres of action and that it belonged men to make, apply and execute laws, and regarded it as an axiomatic truth." The fact of the case was that Myra Bradwell, residing in the State of Illinois, made an application to the judges of the Supreme Court of that State for a licence to practice law. The Supreme Court denied her the permission and was of the opinion that the "paramount destiny and mission of women are to fulfill the noble and benign offices of wife and mother. This is the law of the creator." "Is this antediluvian attitude that women are the children of a lesser God, still ruling the judicial roost in India?", Faisal asks.

Mahatma Gandhi's Views on Women

As early as 1921, writing in the *Young India*, Mahatma Gandhi said: "Of all the evils for which man has made himself responsible, none is so degrading, so shocking or so brutal as his abuse of the better half of humanity—to me, the female sex, not the weaker sex."

It is interesting to consider what was Gandhiji's concept of India's womanhood? He had the unique thought and understanding that a woman is also a person in her own right.

In a plan of life, he maintained that woman has much right to shape her own destiny as has man. Gandhiji recognized very early that to the impartial outsider, the legal and customary status of woman is bad enough throughout and demands radical alteration.

Gandhiji held that fundamentally man and woman are one, characteristically declaring that the soul in both is the same. The two live the same life and have the same feelings. However, he believed that while both are fundamentally one, difference in their vocations and roles are to be expected and accepted. But, it must be continually kept in mind that woman is gifted with equal mental capacities. She has the right to participate in minutest detail in the activities of man, and has the same right of freedom and liberty as he.

Gandhiji looked upon women as naturally entitled to the same rights as men. By his insightfulness he discerned many unworthy men enjoyed a superiority over women which they neither deserved nor should have been allowed by society, because of the sheer force of vicious custom. He regretted that many of the movements stopped half way because of the condition of our women, or did not yield appropriate results because women-power and the source of its strength were neglected.

Gandhiji said: "The men and women are a peerless pair being supplementary to one another; each helps the other, so that without the one the existence of the other cannot be conceived; and, therefore, it follows, as a necessary corollary from these facts, that anything that will impair the status of either of them will involve the equal ruin of them both." He recognized that as the members of the same humanity, the problems of man and woman must be one in essence, i.e., human problem.

Gandhiji saw the capacity of woman for suffering, especially in India, in her role as the silent worker for the well-being of the family; as the partner of man in the field at the time of sowing and reaping in rain and the Sun; as one who is oblivious of the pain in the joy of creating new life when life has been conceived; and finally, as one who has a greater power of endurance. He went to the extent of saying, without her, humanity could not be; and if non-violence is the law of our being, the future is with woman.

It is not surprising, therefore, to hear Gandhiji indignantly declare that it is a libel to call woman the weaker sex. Among the social evils he fearlessly exposed and vehemently condemned were the practices of purdah, dowry, child marriage, and the oppressive tradition of binding women to wear jewels due to social and family pressures. He also spoke out against the plight of widowed women, the system of devadasis, the double standards regarding chastity for men and women, and the heartbreaking circumstances faced by women forced into prostitution.

Gandhiji was pained and humiliated by the custom of purdah. He asked a very pertinent question: Why do our women not enjoy the same freedom that men do? Why should they not be able to walk out and have fresh air? He asserted that we must subject everything capable of being tested by the anvil of reason to rigorous examination and reject that which does not satisfy it, even if it may appear in an ancient grab. Speaking as early as 1927, he emphasized that humanity will remain diminished as long as women are caged and confined to their houses and little courtyards.

The phrases that Gandhiji used for the dowry system are revealing. For example, he called it the hateful system of dowry, marriage by purchase, and degrading practice. He saw inherent evil in the dowry system both for the giver and receiver because it creates a bondage, because it is like buying and selling, bargaining, and because this system turns human beings into 'things.' This subdues human relationship and distorts it; cripples it. It degrades the man for putting himself in the market and dishonors women because they are the silent observers in a matter of life-long relationship that should be uplifted and honorable. He believed that the remedy of this degrading custom lay in the hands of youth movements in the country. So, he said: "There are many youth movements in the country. I wish that these movements will deal with questions of this character." He called for the creation of strong public opinion so that no one would want to dirty their fingers with the giving and receiving of dowry. He even advocated excommunication for the young men who received dowry and urged that the parents of girls should ignore caste and provincial differences to counter this evil custom. In 1929, he shocked many by declaring: "If I had a girl under my charge, I would rather keep her a maiden all her life than give her away to one who expected a single pie for taking her for his wife."

In 1936, Gandhiji raised a very pertinent issue which is relevant even today: "How is that so many boys and girls who have even passed through colleges, are found unable or unwilling to resist the manifestly evil custom (compulsory marriage with dowry paid and received), which affects their future so intimately as does marriage?" He questioned what value education they had if they did not dare defy a custom which was wholly indefensible and highly immoral? He maintained that there was something radically lacking in the system of education that made the educated so insensitive to evil customs and ready to yield to them. He challenged the girls to remain spinsters if need be.

When Gandhiji spoke about widow remarriage and advocated for it, he was not only expressing his compassion for the child-widows who were victims of an oppressive custom and blind superstitions, but he was also upholding the fundamental principles of equity and justice. He firmly believed that widows should be granted the same freedom that widowers enjoy in society.

The Indian society's indifference to the plight of women, which compelled some of them to resort to prostitution, deeply troubled Gandhiji. He was practical enough to recognize that the men would be as fallen as the women if this profession spread and flourished as it did in India. He did not believe that the solution lies merely in finding for these women an honorable means of living. Rather with his deep insight into human character he maintained that it is a social disease (a moral leprosy, he called it) promoted by men of no moral or ethical standard. It is accepted by society as necessary evil with the dual standard it allows. Women themselves will have to rise to the task of eradicating it. Gandhiji hoped women leaders would emerge to take active leadership in abolishing this degrading profession. Laws alone could never be effective. His whole being rebelled against the custom of devadasis, which insulted God. He said: "In the name of religion we commit a double crime by dredging women and involving worship of God along with it. We have this moral leprosy in today's India also and along with it we have the responsibility of indirectly encouraging it by indifference and perhaps, lack of interest."

Gandhiji put the primary responsibility of ridding the society and family of some crippling customs such as child marriage, objections to widow remarriage, lack of women's education, purdah, dowry system and so on, on the shoulders of the educated class, and more specially, on those of the educated women. The questions arise: Why have they not gone further? Why do our women not enjoy the same freedom that men do? I believe that the educated women of India will need to answer these questions seriously and take some kind of a pledge to do something right away even if that is quite late in the day.

Gandhiji advocated for both men and women to employ reason and, through this, shape social and public opinions in order to reject customs and social compulsions that are unreasonable, inhuman, degrading and restrictive, even if they have been sanctified by time and considered time-honored. He challenged the young girls and warned them against copying the modern girl because modern girl has a special meaning for him as he wrote in the *Harijan* of 4th February, 1939, when some students complained to him about the misbehavior of students towards the women students. The phrases used by Gandhiji are revealing and fundamental to the Gandhian way. Expressions like 'crusading', 'God helps only those who help themselves', 'steadfastness', 'faith in one's own self', 'spiritual strength', and 'leading dignity to a cause' are at the core of Gandhiji's principles.

Mahadev Desai lists some clichés that India helped to grow in his time, and they are by no means obsolete in our time. For example, the husband is like a God; son is preferable because he continues the family name and must inherit; and the wife remains faithful even if the husband is unjust because that attitude is her *dharma*.

Gandhiji was far advance of his time in recognizing that men and women were equal. He said many a time, "I admit no distinction between man and woman except such as has been made by Nature and can be seen with human eyes."

In his own life he never underestimated *Nari-Shakti*. As a matter of fact, the major force which acted as a catalyst in the achievement of political equality of women in India was Gandhiji's preaching and practicing his faith in the equality and ability of women.

The massive participation of women in the national movement under Gandhiji's leadership had a direct impact on the then social and political India. It is significant that when the government rejected women's demand for equal franchise, at the Karachi session, the Indian National Congress in 1931 under Gandhiji's guidance accepted unconditionally women's right to vote without any discrimination based on sex. The country redeemed this pledge politically after independence. The Constitution of India pledges the principles of equality and dignity of the individual, and proclaims the fundamental right of women to political, economic and legal equality.

5

Corruption: Incurable Disease

Prime Minister Narendra Modi focused on corruption, nepotism and dynastic system. His intentions to weed out all the three from India are pious. But, the million-dollar question is whether he will succeed given the current situation, the character of our politicians and the prevailing mindset of corruption. The pertinent inquiries are who these corrupt individuals are and where they can be found. Those whose purpose of life is to amass wealth and thrive on it will create, I am afraid all sorts of hindrances to defeat his efforts. There was a time when India was considered the land of future, a nation of tremendous potentialities, faced with enormous problems, but striving to solve them.

Today, India has become a land of scams after scams carried by rank corrupts, be they from political herd or business magnets or corporate houses, or burcaucrats. The insatiable lust for money and thirst for power, combined with the self-serving nature and relentless pursuit of position among political bigwigs, remains unquenched.

Different groups seem to prowl about like hungry wolves waiting for their prey. The very conception of freedom has taken the shape of a large-scale jobbery. The democratic practices have been sent to winds. The increasing statism, the criminalization of politics and politicalization of criminals are complete negation of democratic principles. Politics has become the short cut to make fortune. Rank political opportunism has become the order of the day.

Corruption, bribery, swindling of funds, fraud, scams, dishonesty, immorality, lack of respect for elders, vices becoming virtues, indiscipline, disregard for law and order have become a way of life. The honest are branded dishonest and the dishonest are proclaimed not only honest but men of status. The upright is victimized, corrupt and inefficient are encouraged and installed on coveted positions which demand only custodians of moral values to occupy them.

Expressing his views on corruption, C. Rajagopalachari, the first Indian Governor-General of India, said: "The worst form of corruption which power breeds is the desire for more and more power and for its perpetuation."

The public money is lost to crooks who have taken loans from banks and have salted away the millions of rupees somewhere safe. Corruption seems to have been institutionalized. Immorality is often taught in the name of morality.

There is no serious attempt to weed out corruption. Gandhiji had said: "There is so much of corruption today that it frightens me. Everybody wants to carry so many votes in his pocket because votes give power." He had come to realize that the Congress rank and file were as corrupt and greedy in power as they had been idealistic and self-sacrificing out of power. He said: "I know that if I survive the struggle for freedom, I might have to give non-violent battle to my own countrymen, which may be as stubborn as that in which I am now engaged."

"Corruption is the outcome of selfishness, wants lie at the root of it. Slash your wants, corruption will disappear," Gandhiji said. On another occasion Gandhiji said: "I can retain neither respect nor affection for a government which has been moving from wrong to wrong to defend its immorality. Such a government must be moved to repentance."

In 1946, when the Indian Independence Bill was being piloted by Labour Prime Minister Clement Atlee in the House of Commons in England, Sir Winston Churchill angrily gave the grim warning that "the governance of India would slip into the hands of men of straw, rascals, rogues and freebooters of whom no trace would be found in a few years. Not a bottle of water or a loaf of bread shall escape taxation, only the air will be free; the blood of hungry millions will be on the head of Mr. Clement Attlee."

How prophetic are these words of Sir Winston Churchill? What are the social and economic situations the country facing today? It is nothing but spiraling price rise, heavy taxes, and scarcity of essential commodities. All these have resulted in popular discontent taking the shape of strikes, bandhs and demonstrations, often resulting in violence. Terrorism, riots, communalism and casteism getting rampant has made the lives of millions unbearable. Often, public property like buses and trains are set on fire. Innocent people are put to difficulties and death.

Santhanam Committee Report

The high-water mark of corruption reached in India during the period of the Second World War. Before the war, according to the Santhanam Committee Report, corruption was prevalent among the low-level officials. The higher ranks were comparatively free of it. Lack of fluid resources set limits to the opportunities and capacity for corruption. After the transfer of power at the time of independence, there was patriotism and high ideals. Attempts were made to check the spread of corruption. In 1962, Santhanam Committee gave following preamble on corruption: "Yet, various factors have operated to nullify in some measure the anti-corruption drive. The sudden extension of the economic activities of the government with a large armoury of regulations, controls, licenses and permits provided new and large opportunities. The quest for political power at different levels made successful achievement of the objective more important than the means adopted. Complaints against the highly placed in public life were not dealt with in the manner that they should have been dealt with if public confidence had to be maintained. Weakness in this respect created cynicism and the growth of the belief that while the governments were against corruption they were not against corrupt individuals, if such individuals had the requisite amount of power, influence, and protection."

The rapid urbanization brought about the weakening of rural values. Social controls resulting in the maintenance of frugality and simplicity of life were replaced by those encouraging materialism, impersonalism, status craving, greed for money and power, and an unwillingness to adhere to moral values. In this climate, the business and commercial classes, whose ranks were swelled by speculators and adventurers of the war period, exerted their corruptive influence. The large part of these classes belonged to government service. All these formed a fertile soil for corruption.

There were also a cumbersome and dilatory procedures and practices in the working of government offices. This gave rise to the 'speed money' type of corruption. Generally, the bribe giver did not wish, in these cases, to get anything done unlawfully, but wanted to speed up the process of the movement of files and communications relating to decisions. Certain sections of the staff concerned were reported to have got into the habit of not doing anything in the matter till they were suitably persuaded.

Deposing before the Santhanam Committee, a secretary said that even after an order had been passed by a higher authority this was not communicated to the applicant until he had paid appropriate gratification to the subordinate concerned. Besides being the most objectionable corrupt practice, this custom of 'speed money' has become one of the most serious causes to delay and inefficiency.

The scope and incentives for corruption were greatest at the points where important decisions that would substantially affect the fortunes of interested groups or individuals, were taken such as in the assessment and collection of taxes, obtaining licenses, contracts, or in orders of supplies.

The Santhanam Committee Report sheds light on the involvement of businessmen and industrialists as major corrupting influences on an organized scale. According to the report, corruption serves as a convenient tool for these individuals to acquire substantial unearned profits while also maintaining their competitive edge in their respective industries. Their corrupt practices include tax evasion and avoidance, accumulating unaccounted wealth through various means such as using fake firms and individuals to obtain licenses, engaging in license trafficking, manipulating accounts to suppress profits and avoid legitimate taxes and claims, accepting money for unaccounted transactions, and undervaluing transactions involving immovable property. Additionally, these individuals possess significant financial resources, allowing them to spend lavishly on entertainment and maintain a network of liaison and contact personnel, some of whom lead extravagant lifestyles.

The report further mentioned the activities of these contact persons to subvert the integrity of government servants. The tendency to subvert the integrity in the public services instead of being isolated and aberrative is growing into an organized and well-planned racket. In addition to such attempts there is the offer of employment to retired government servants by the commercial and industrial sector. It is generally believed that such employment is secured in many cases as a quid pro quo for favours shown by the government servant while in service. The fact that some of these retired government servants who have accepted employment with private firms live in Delhi and perhaps operate as "contact men", has further heightened these suspicions.

Of the judiciary, the Santhanam Committee Report said that the committee was informed by responsible persons, including Vigilance and Special Police Establishment Officers, that corruption existed in the lower ranks of the judiciary all over India and in some places, it had spread to the higher ranks also. The rapid increase of corruption in India gave smuggler and other criminal gangs a foothold in Indian society. The money they had illegally acquired was transformed into legitimate assets through lawful business practices.

The black marketers also had significant influence in Indian politics. They joined political party, became office bearers, and eventually controlled the party. They donated to the parties which did not have independent sources of income. Once entrenched, the black marketers would exploit any available opportunity, engaging in illegal activities such as selling goods produced illicitly, theft of relief food or other materials, hoarding and selectively releasing commodities, and engaging in money trading. Black marketing operations were more significant apparently in iron, steel, cotton yarn, man-made fibres, cement, fertilizers, aluminium, sugar, molasses, motor vehicles, coal and paper.

Scarcity of goods, coupled with dishonest industrial practices to perpetuate the scarcity, was the main cause of the black-market operation which assumed staggering heights after the mid-1960s.

In the transportation and construction industries, corruption has one of the most fertile soils. Here, the corrupt elements in the opposition parties also share the spoils. "Hush money" is paid to the opposition not to expose violation of the laws by the industries. A whole network and organizations are set up for the huge corruption syndicate. Bureaucratic positions favorable to corruption are referred to as 'wet posts.' An officer is supposed to stay not more than three years in such a post. However, some stay much longer because they can function as stooges for councilors or bureaucrats.

In a society totally gripped by corruption, everything that is possible to corrupt is seized for the purpose. The forms and manifestations of corruption are beyond description. New ideas are continually added. Corruption has become an industry. Like an industry it seeks to create a public demand. Hence, new rules and legislations are added to existing ones for the purpose of corruption. Whenever a new rule or law is introduced, and the public becomes dependent on officials to enforce it, there is a risk of potential corruption (*Corruption and the Destiny of Asia,* Syed Hussein Alatas, Prentice Hall (M) Sdn. Bhd. and Simon and Schuster (Asia) Pvt. Ltd, pp. 52-55, 57, 93-94).

The Santhanam Committee, set up in June 1962, due to pressure in Parliament, by the then Home Minister, Mr. Lal Bahadur Shastri, was charged to review existing instruments for combating corruption and to advise on practical measures to make anti-corruption measures more effective.

The committee, consisting of seven members—five members of the Parliament and two senior officials of the Union Home Ministry, with K. Santhanam, M.P., as Chairman—was ostensibly given a very broad mandate. Its terms of reference were to examine the functioning of the vigilance units in the ministries and departments of Government of India, as well as the Special Police Establishment. The primary objective was to suggest measures to enhance and optimize their performance further.

The committee was asked to consider and suggest steps to be taken to emphasize the responsibilities of each department for checking corruption. The objective was to suggest changes to the Government Servants' Conduct Rules, ensure the expeditious trial of cases related to bribery, corruption and criminal misconduct, and take necessary steps to garner public support for implementing various anti-corruption measures. These actions aimed to create a favorable environment for enhancing public morals and fostering ethical governance.

Yet, the mandate fell short in some important spheres. For example, corruption among ministers was excluded from the Santhanam Committee's investigation by the Government of India. On 20th February, 1963, in a reply to a specific question in the Parliament, the then Home Minister explained that Ministers were not top executives but executives of the Parliament, and it was open to the Parliament to deal with them directly. This explanation was most unsatisfactory. In fact, in taking up the question of corruption among its employees, Government began at the wrong end. If there is corruption in the administration, the ministers are primarily and ultimately responsible for it. They know, and have the means to know, who among their colleagues and subordinates are corrupt. If they take no action against their colleagues, it is not because of lack of knowledge but because of lack of will. Their philosophy, as a well-known publicist has pointed out, seems to be: touch one, touch all, therefore touch none. If ministers are above board, they can prevent corruption among the services. As it is widely believed that their reluctance to tackle corruption is either because their hands are not clean or they are so inefficient at their jobs that they play into the hands of the officials.

The results of Nehru's Fabian Socialism were certainly not disastrous. But, the jungle of laws, regulations and controls that sprang up in the name of socialism gave it a bad name and provided a happy hunting-ground for corrupt politicians and bureaucrats. One such example is of an Indian industrialist who said that there were no less than thirteen government inspectors who could close his factory down. But, none of them were apparently interested in inspecting the safety, quality, pollution levels, or whatever else they were supposed to inspect. All that they were interested in was collecting their pay-offs. L.K. Jha, a veteran economic adviser to the Government of India in 1960s, candidly acknowledged that the system had given rise to corruption. However, he firmly asserted that in an economy facing severe shortages, there seemed to be no viable alternative to exerting control as a measure. For all his idealism, Nehru accepted the fact that there was no simple answer to corruption (*From Raj to Rajiv: 40 Years of Indian Independence,* Mark Tully and Zareer Masani, Universal Book Stall, New Delhi, p. 33).

Dr. Radhakrishnan, former President of India, said: "In our country, moral life is shaken to its foundations. Love of wealth and power has gained wide acceptance. Most of us live on the surface of life with no moral earnestness. There is hardly any corner of Indian life which has not been defiled by corruption."

The then Governor of Bihar, Mr. Madabhushi Ananthasayanam Ayyangar while inaugurating Bihar Lawyers' Conference on 3rd April, 1963, said: "I am afraid, in some cases people have become persona designata with the judges. You just appoint this lawyer because he is a son-in-law or he belongs to this community, or if the case is transferred to some other judge, he gives up one lawyer and appoints the other. It is a disgrace to the lawyers. It is a disgrace to the judges. People were persona grata with this man or that man. Not only here, the cancer has spread to the districts also. As I have heard, some boy became a lawyer and wherever his father is a subordinate judge, this boy is taken. Another case has come to my notice of a sub-divisional officer having a satellite wherever he goes. It is a disgrace" (*Corruption: Control of Maladministration,* John B. Monteiro, Manaktalas, Bombay, p. 52).

It is sad, to say the least, that a country with such a rich cultural heritage and profound political history is now being ranked among the most corrupt countries in the world, earning the unfortunate epithet of a nation plagued by corruption. Former Governor of the Reserve Bank of India, Bimal Jalan, in his book *The Future of India*, writes: "Regrettably, there is also widespread public acceptance of corruption as an unavoidable aspect of Indian life. High corruption is associated with the wrong choice of high-cost public projects, low maintenance expenditure and poor quality of essential public infrastructure which, in turn, increases the cost of production of goods and services by business enterprises, both public and private.

An important finding of empirical research is that the adverse effects of corruption are more on small enterprises and growth of employment in the economy. Thus, a survey of 3000 enterprises across twenty transition economies, covering all regions, found that corruption and anti-competitive practices were perceived as the most difficult obstacle by start-up firms. For small enterprises, such practices raised costs and reduced profits because they had to make payment that did not contribute to productivity or output but were necessary for survival. In order to avoid undue harassment, bribes amounting to substantial portion of the operating costs had to be paid to meet the demands of a host of inspectors working in concert with each other."

Jalan further writes: "The most repugnant aspect of corruption in India is not that it is there, nor that it is so pervasive, but that it is widely accepted as an unavoidable feature of Indian life. At the political level, corruption among parties and politicians is believed to be unavoidable as elections have become expensive and funds have to be raised, by whatever means, to contest them. Similarly, in defence of the high incidence of bureaucratic corruption, it is argued that civil servants in India are not paid well or that such corruption is a 'universal phenomenon'.

Corporates in India, large and small, also choose to survive and thrive by participating actively in corruption on the grounds that it is the only way to get their business done. Interestingly, corruption in businesses in India is perhaps as internal as it is external. The common man or woman also has to participate in corruption because there is simply no other option if he or she has to get a ration card, a license, permission or registration.

In addition to its wide acceptance as a necessary evil, another area of grave concern is the interlocking or 'vertical integration' of corruption at various levels of the government hierarchy—elected politicians, higher bureaucracy and lower bureaucracy. Along with vertical integration of corruption at various levels of the executive branch, there is also horizontal spread of corruption to other public institutions, including legislatures, parts of judiciary, media as well as independent professions. This has made the prevention and control of corruption even more difficult. As if all this were not enough, another unfortunate development has been the politicalization of corruption. Interestingly, cases of corruption are being given a political colour without any serious intent to tackle the problem. This has facilitated the entry into politics of persons with a track record of corruption. The public no longer knows whom to trust—the accuser or accused."

"Prime Minister Rajiv Gandhi had pointed out that 'out of ₹ 100 crore allocated to an anti-poverty project, I know only ₹ 15 crore reaches the people. The remainder is gobbled up by middlemen, power brokers, contractors and the corrupt'."

Referring to the Santhanam Committee Report, Bimal Jalan says: "Since then, a number of other committees have been set up for the reform of the governance and administrative structure. Various other agencies including the Comptroller and Auditor General (CAG), the Central Vigilance Commission (CVC), the Central Bureau of Investigation (CBI) and the Pay Commissions have also submitted countless reports expressing their anguish over rising corruption and suggesting measures to combat it. Unfortunately, most of the actions taken by the various governments over the last forty years to launch new programs have had the effect of increasing both the demand and the supply of corruption rather than reducing them. The demand for and the supply of so-called 'speed money' has increased.

There are multiple investigating and prosecution agencies at the centre and in the states to fight corruption and convict the guilty. Yet the legal provisions and judicial processes are so cumbersome that cases of successful prosecution of corrupt civil servants or politicians are negligible.

The corruption in India is now so entrenched that a serving member of India's administrative service (Das 2001) has observed that: 'the corruption network in India is so perfectly orchestrated that there is a thriving internal economy linking principals and agents. The principals (ruling politicians) provide the opportunity and protection, while the agents (civil servants) pay for their spoils by sharing the bribe. All the actors involved—ministers, civil servants, anti-corruption functionaries—have stake in protecting corruption and increasing its proceeds, and also, in freezing out the critics of corruption.'

While the number of agencies involved in collecting information, conducting researches and taking the necessary action to bring civil servants and politicians to book have multiplied over time, the quantity of corruption as well as the impunity with which it can be carried out has also expanded. The judiciary has passed severe edicts against the executive authority in corruption cases, but in most cases of importance, the investigation either remains incomplete or the evidence is weak. According to data collected by Das (2001), on cases referred to the CBI, the number of civil servants who have been punished for corruption or have lost their employment as a result of its investigation is negligible. In few cases, where punishment has been awarded, the penalty has been relatively weak, with the result that the necessary deterrence is non-existent. The record of other central and state agencies is equally dismal if not worse. As for powers of the judiciary and its role in anti-corruption cases, the following observation of Justice J.S. Verma (2004), a former Chief Justice of India, is noteworthy: 'The monitoring by the Supreme Court in the (Jain) Hawala case provided full autonomy to the CBI in the conduct of investigations by it, with the authority to prosecute all those found guilty by it. In spite of this freedom, the level of its performance can be gauged from the fact that chargesheets filed did not make out a prima facie case to frame the charge in any case, and all the accused were discharged by the court. The impression is that the purpose of filing half-baked chargesheets was only to get rid of the monitoring by the Supreme Court led by me.'

There are multiple causes for the relative ineffectiveness of India's judicial system in checking the incidence of corruption or disposal of even the most outrageous cases of corruption. These have been analyzed in considerable details by a number of committees, including the High Court Arrears Committees of 1949, 1972 and 1992, as well as several law commission reports. However, despite much soul-searching, debate and recommendations emanating from these high-level committees, the position in disposal of cases has become progressively worse. According to the Malimath Committee report, between 1968 and 1989, the number of pending cases multiplied almost four-fold. The multiple levels of appeals available to the accused also ensure that a powerful person, particularly with a political background, can remain free for even two decades or more."

Although the Constitution of India sought to combat corruption, the conduct of general elections, periodically held as a symbol of democracy, unfortunately, became tainted by corruption. Consequently, corruption continued to pervade public life, public offices and public administration, impeding genuine efforts to eradicate this issue. The Executive at every level is the victim of bribery, so too the Legislature where Houses have seized to be functional because of controversies which have marred the operation of the ministers. Even judiciary, a refined organization with a sublime reputation, is being tainted by huge sums of money polluting governance. The issue of corruption and its unfortunate entanglement with illicit activities has deeply affected the sanctity of Indian culture. Thus, the trinity of instrumentalities of Indian Constitutional administration is so nauseating that the integrity of government is a casualty. When India won *Swaraj* expectations were great. But expectations darkened into anxiety, anxiety into dread and dread into despair. To rid this calamity of widespread corruption is the major crisis that challenges the destiny of India and what Jawaharlal Nehru told in his historic speech on 15th August, 1947, remains the tremendous task before 'we, the people of India.' That task has many dimensions and the Preamble to the Constitution gives eloquent expression to this extra-ordinary problem faced by every patriot of the nation (*The Constitution, Corruption, Pathological Casualties and Radical Remedies Reformatories,* Justice V.R. Krishna Iyer, Universal Law Publishing, New Delhi, p. 22).

Justice Iyer, at a Convocation address in the University of Burdwan, said: "I concede the grave degeneracy, aggravation of communalism and ubiquitous corruption which have shockingly escalated since independence. It is no serendipity that abuse of public power victimizing the have-nots, insatiable gold rush invading the heart and soul and infatuation with materialist pleasures as the summum bonum of existence have become universal. Unconscionable abuse of political power, unchecked yen of bureaucrats and tycoons to amass fortunes, invisible accumulation of unaccountable riches by the proprietaries and pauperization and privation of the proletariat have created the Frankenstein's monster of Almighty Corruption at once omnipresent, omniscient and omnipotent. When a fragment of the truth of these lies came out through the court's invigilation in horrendous hawala litigation, people beheld the spectre of boundless abuse by supremos in several walks of life. Corruption is a national distortion of development and robbery of hungry people's hopes of progress."

Advising the students, Justice Iyer said: "Student power is a symbiosis of patriotic ideals and irrepressible energy. You must therefore carefully but dauntlessly investigate these dangerous trends and cleanse the country of this miasmic malady festering the body politic. Corruption bombs can be defused not so much by the C.B.I. and the Supreme Court as by the intelligent, investigative, pervasive exposure by the conscientize alumni of houses of learning."

Justice Krishna Iyer further advised the students: "When you see fraud and scam do not be silent. Silence is guilt where there is a duty to speak. Who can protest but does not is an accomplice in the act. Remember, there are no passengers on Spaceship Earth. Everybody, you and I included, is crew. So, please fight on for a New just World Human Order" (*Ibid.*, pp. 92, 94).

Justice Krishna Iyer, in his article "A Creative Critique of Indian Democratic Policy—A Project Panchsheel" published in the book mentioned above at page 106 writes: "The greatest menace to Bharat has been Corruption, so vast that the soil of the country has been sordidly poisoned. What is our basic democratic structure and man power? There shall be franchise for every little Indian freely to be expressed through a national General Election compulsorily held every five years where the free vote of the humble Indian human shall decide the mould. The country's fundamental policies are constitution of the Executive, composition of the Legislature and the sublime stature and power of the Judiciary within the framework of thc constitutional provisions.

This perspective takes us to an identification of the worst villain which has damnified Indian public life, namely corruption, administrative organization and every other instrumentality which we may call the Governance of India. True, to a large extent our founding fathers have made certain structural basics unalterable. To that extent the rule of law and of life retain its Vedic cultural character.

From the days of Kautilya's *Arthashastra* down to the guns of Godsey which shot Gandhi dead, corruption, poverty and violence have been the triple vices which make the great country of India ever sublime but never achieving *Purna Swaraj*.

The moral greatness of our Vedic days and collapse of values have reached a new low when even some of the celebrated cricketers are bowled out of all sportsmanship morality. The challenge of today is a bitter battle for life with human values. Once money has made its way to the head everyone surrenders to the commercial syndrome."

Justice Iyer further writes: "A whole volume can be written on Indian corruption if one has the time and the facility to do research on this sordid subject. But I have neither and so do not propose to write more on corruption in public life."

Corruption has become such a large-scale racket only because we in India tend to honour a man who has acquired his wealth illegally as a man of exceptional intelligence and turpitude. A society that does not attach any stigma to the corrupt man can hardly be rid of such ignoble men.

6

Judiciary not Free from Corruption

I have written a biography of Justice Chandrashekhar Dharmadhikari, which has been published under the title, *Rule of the Heart: The Justice of Chandrashekhar Dharmadhikari* by Global Indian Foundation, Singapore; Gandhi Smriti and Darshan Samiti, New Delhi; and Institute of Gandhian Studies, Wardha. It was released by the then Chief Justice of India, Justice R.C. Lahoti at Aurangabad and Justice Dalbir Bhandari, Judge, International Court of Justice, Hague at Jodhpur.

Justice Dharmadhikari expressed his views on Judges and Judiciary as mentioned in the book, which are reproduced below:

In the past, a person who made allegations against a Judge of the High Court was regarded as a potential inmate of a lunatic asylum. Today, most regretfully, he is listened to without disbelief.

In the first two decades of our Republic, it was the compulsion of veracity, not the fear of law relating to contempt of court, which was responsible for the fact that no charges of corruption were leveled against the judiciary. Now the compulsion of veracity dictates such charges in defiance of the contempt of Courts Act. The Lawyers Association of Bombay passed resolutions a few years back, virtually charging some judges of the High Court with corruption. The Chief Justice Chittatosh Mukerjee had to take an extreme step of not allotting any cases or judicial powers to three judges of Bombay High Court for some years. The three judges told Mukerjee that his action is beyond his powers and jurisdiction, on which they were advised by Justice Mukerjee to file writ petition and get his order set aside. The three judges dare not file writ petition. It was only a threat. The said judges continued in office till their retirement, enjoying the office and remuneration without doing any judicial work.

The question is: Which is the best way of dealing with a corrupt judge in the higher courts without creating a crisis of public faith in the judiciary?

Justice Chandrashekhar Dharmadhikari said: "The corruption existing in the courts cannot be justified by clever arguments. There is a dictum in Sanskrit, which means, if you commit a sin anywhere else, it can be washed in the holy land, but if you commit sin in the holy land itself, it is stuck diamond-hard, where will you wash it."

Justice Dharmadhikari further said: "The question of corruption is not limited to lower courts only, but the higher courts are also infected by it and the very prestige of judiciary is vanished into thin air. It is said that corruption is a global phenomenon. If the very spring and soul are defiled, how can we expect pure water from it? Judges connive at corruption by accepting it as inevitable evil. They say that the corruption is present in social life, it is trickling in judiciary too. To say such a thing is to shirk responsibility."

With regard to the appointments in the judiciary, Justice Dharmadhikari said: "While making appointments in the judiciary, we do not appoint any Tom, Dick and Harry. It is said that these appointments are made by selecting persons from the cream of society. The milk gets spoiled but the cream rarely gets spoiled. It is earnestly believed that a judge is the ideal before society. If his hands are unclean, where can society look to find an ideal? If corruption is excusable, because it has become very common and if such an impression is created, then the money earned by corrupt means could be treated as white. It is indeed a matter of great frustration that no one seems to give any serious thought to it."

Another argument is put forth that good and capable people are not attracted to judiciary because salary paid to judges is too low for decent standard of living. This gives scope for corruption. It is quite surprising, painful and unjust to say that in a country where 83 crores and 60 lakhs, that is 87% of the total population live below poverty line, 27% of which live under the Sun wherever they find place, the salaries of judges are considered low.

Today, a High Court judge receives a monthly salary of approximately ₹ 2,25,000, inclusive of various allowances. Additionally, the government provides a chauffeur-driven car with the expenses for petrol covered. The judge enjoys the benefit of residing in a rent-free furnished bungalow spanning 3200 sq. ft. The government also covers the costs of telephone, electricity, water, medicine, and health services. Moreover, the government provides essential electronics such as TV, computer, and laptop. Twice a year, the judge and his/her entire family receive air travel expenses borne by the government. Furthermore, servants are made available at government expense. In addition to all these benefits, the judge receives ₹ 25,000 per month as a sumptuary allowance. "If this is considered low income," Justice Dharmadhikari said, "we will have to think about the integrity of those who enter judiciary keeping an eye on the salary."

Justice Dharmadhikari said: "I can tell with my own experience, that the salary and perquisites are adequate. Of course, only if you do not have luxurious habits, addiction for races, squandering money on drinks and holding parties in clubs or five-star hotels. It would be inhuman if all these luxuries and habits are gratified only at public and government money. There are two words, 'need' and 'greed.' Salary is for fulfillment of need. Greed is never satisfied."

In an annual meeting of the judges of the Supreme Court and Chief Justices of High Courts two main demands were made, one of them was increase in salary to the extent of three lakh rupees per month and the other was to increase in the retirement age. This is mind boggling.

In earlier days, the salary of the High Court judges ranged between ₹ 3000 and ₹ 4000 per month. Due to limited resources, two or three judges would share a car that they personally owned, and many of the facilities available to judges today were not accessible back then. Yet, they laid the foundation of the judiciary on a solid footing. Their judgments were considered as classic in the English literature. They were conscious that they were occupying the Chairs once occupied by King Vikramaditya and Ramshastri Prabhune and tried their best to come up to their level or stature.

During a discussion relating to the Federal Court of India, Gandhiji observed before the Federal Structure Committee, "So far as the salary is concerned, you will laugh, naturally, but the Congress believes that it is an impossible thing for us who, in terms of wealth, are a Nation of dwarfs, to vie with the British Government, which represent today giants in wealth. India, whose average income is 3 shillings per day, can ill afford to pay the high salaries that are commanded here. I feel that it is a thing which we will have to unlearn if we are going to have a voluntary rule in India. It is very well so long the British bayonet is there to squeeze out of the poor people, taxes to pay the salaries of ₹ 10,000 a month, ₹ 5000 a month and ₹ 20,000 a month."

When the question was raised that competent people would not be available on low salaries, Gandhiji said: "I do not consider that my country has sunk so low that it will not be able to produce sufficient men who will live somewhat in correspondence with the lives of the millions and still serve India nobly, truly and well. I do not believe for one moment that legal talent has to be bought, if it is to remain honest."

In this connection Gandhiji made a mention of Motilal Nehru, Chittaranjan Das, Manmohan Ghosh and Badruddin Tyabji, and said that these persons earning lakhs of rupees, for the sake of national work, honestly and without the least expectation, offered their services. At the call given by Gandhiji, when these senior lawyers earning lakhs of rupees left practice and participated in freedom movement, what did they get except imprisonment and distressing and miserable conditions?

Gandhiji could never believe that good men can be purchased with money, nor that money can make people good. Referring to the colossal expenditure on courts, Gandhiji observed about the entire system of judiciary: "There is something sinful in the system. It is an expensive luxury." Here is an observation from Oscar Wilde: "Cynic is a person who knows the price of everything and value of nothing."

A Clean Conscience alone can Enshrine Sacredness

In the opinion of Justice Dharmadhikari, "The basic question in democracy is: Who will watch the watchman? By appointing a watchman, the work is not over. We have to keep a vigil whether he is awake or otherwise. A strong and vigilant Citizens' Forum has to be evolved. The Hindus who are idol worshippers always face a typical dilemma: How to hit the scorpion on an idol of Shiva, without meaning to hit the idol? A rational approach can alone solve such dilemma. A clean conscience alone can enshrine sacredness. The corrupt has no caste, creed or religion. We cannot forget that one who protects corruption, helps and protects a corrupt person is, also, in a way stamped as a corrupt. Prestige of judiciary does not depend on monuments or traditions. It has certain eternal values. Judiciary represents the democratic values and culture of our country. It is not mere adornment of values but an expression of fundamental values. This awareness has gone into oblivion. This, indeed is a great tragedy."

As the Prime Minister of India, Dr. Manmohan Singh, addressing a conference of the Chief Ministers and Chief Justices of the States in Delhi, said: "Corruption is another challenge that we face both in the government and the judiciary." Supporting a call from the Chief Justice of India to set up a designated Special Courts for trying cases under the Prevention of Corruption Act, Dr. Manmohan Singh said: "I agree that there is urgent need to do so. This will instill greater confidence in our justice delivery system at home and abroad."

This is the history and degree of corruption in India. Before independence, the Kings and after independence, none of the Prime Ministers has been able to weed out corruption. Narendra Modi as Prime Minister has been expressing his good intentions to wipe out corruption, but how far he will succeed is a million-dollar question. The corruption has gone into the blood of Indians, which will be next to impossible even for Brahmadev to remove.

7
Need for Judicial Reforms

Judiciary is considered as the sovereign sway of Vasishtha Rishi. No king or emperor ever ruled or wielded power over the ashram of Vasishtha Rishi. Independent judiciary is the soul of democracy. Justice is God's gift. Therefore, we use the words "*Nyaya-mandir*" and "*Nyaya-murti*".

The saint Eknath described *Nyaya-murti* by saying:

Janachiye Netri Deese to Sansari
Pari to Antari Sphatik Shuddha

The definition of a good judge reads like that of sainthood. A good judge is compassionate but firm. His robes and all the trappings of the court room can make a judge rise above himself, and that is the reason why common man wants judicial enquiry whether it is an accident or a fire. The common man's confidence is the foundation of judiciary.

For a citizen, court of law is the only last resort, '*Sharan Teertha*'. As often said, the main question before the rule of law and the democracy is, who will watch the watchman, and it is firmly believed that a person who believes in true judicial concepts, spirituality and morality alone can act as such watch dog or watchman.

It is a general feeling amongst the public that there is no justice in any other department and the only forum left is the court of law. Therefore, all questions, whether they are educational, political or even spiritual, ultimately become legal problems and the judiciary is expected to resolve them.

Emergency

After the declaration of Emergency on 25th June, 1975, the Fundamental Rights of citizens enshrined in Article 21 of the Constitution came to be suspended. Meaning thereby that a citizen had no right to life and even if government killed him illegally, he had no right to approach the court for relief, because that right also stood suspended.

ADM Jabalpur's Case

At the early hours of 26th June, 1975, numerous detentions had taken place all over India under the Maintenance of Internal Security Act. As a result, Habeas Corpus Petitions were filed in various High Courts.

The government raised a preliminary objection in all these cases. It contended that in asking for release by the issuance of a writ of Habeas Corpus, the detenues were, in substance, claiming that they had been deprived of their personal liberty in violation of the procedure established by law. This plea was available to them only under Article 21 of the Constitution. But, since the right to move for enforcement of that right had been suspended by the Presidential Order of 27th June, 1975, the petitions were liable to be dismissed at the threshold.

The preliminary objection, despite the proclamation of Emergency and the various Presidential Orders and Ordinances that were passed to keep ahead of the courts, was rejected by the High Courts of Madhya Pradesh, Allahabad, Bombay, Delhi, Karnataka, Punjab and Rajasthan for various reasons. The State Governments and the Government of India filed appeals in the Supreme Court.

All the governments' appeals against the Habeas Corpus rulings were clubbed together, which came to be known as ADM Jabalpur's Case. The hearing started on 15th December, 1975. The case went on for 37 days and the hearing concluded on 25th February, 1976. On 28th April, 1976, the judges held, by a four to one majority, that a detention order could not be challenged on any ground during the Emergency. In coming to this conclusion, they obviously overruled all those High Courts which had decided in favour of the detenues.

The bench of five included some of the brightest judges. They held that no citizen had standing to move a High Court for a writ of Habeas Corpus in view of the Presidential Order dated 27th June, 1975. They also held that detenues could not challenge detention order as either factually illegal or mala fide in law and that the provision for not revealing the grounds of detention was valid. Further, they held that Article 21 was the sole repository of the Right to Life and Personal Liberty against the State, and this Article had been explicitly suspended. However, Justice Y.V. Chandrachud, who was then Chief Justice, expressed 'a diamond-bright-diamond-hard hope' that reported misdeeds of whipping, stripping, starving or even shooting detenues would not tarnish the record of Free India. And Justice Beg astoundingly pronounced that "the care and concern bestowed by the State authorities upon the welfare of detenues who are well-housed, well-fed and well-treated, is almost maternal. Even parents have to take appropriate preventive action against those children who may threaten to burn down the house they live in".

As a senior advocate and jurist, H.M. Seervai said: "While the High Courts rose to the occasion, the Supreme Court sank. The Supreme Court in the supreme moment failed to discharge its duty. It delivered a judgment which in substance said that anyone of us could be picked up and shot, and our widows may have the comfort of filing a criminal prosecution for murder after the Emergency was over." That judgment has few defenders now. Two of those who wrote it were ashamed of it, and one has said that the order was incorrect and did not conform to the judgment (*Post Centenary Silver Jubilee of Bombay High Court,* p. 49).

Though in a different context, Mahatma Gandhi had said about such a judgment that "my condolence and pity go out to the judges who have delivered a judgment which, let me hope, in their cooler moment they will regret."

It was left to a single courageous judge, Justice H.R. Khanna, to dissent and uphold the Right to life and liberty. While doing so, he reiterated the observations of Chief Justice Hughes: "A dissent in a court of last resort is an appeal to the brooding spirit of the law, to the intelligence of a future day, when later decision may possibly correct the error into which a dissenting judge believes the court to have been betrayed."

Attorney-General Niren De argued that the Rule of Law existed only within the four corners of the Constitution and that natural rights did not exist outside it. Justice Khanna, referring to Article 21 which deals not only with liberty but also with life, asked him, if a policeman killed a person for reasons of enmity and not of State, was there to be no remedy? Niren De replied that consistent with his argument, as long as the Emergency lasted, there would be no remedy, and added: "It shocks my conscience and may shock yours."

Justice Khanna held that Article 21 could not be held to be the sole repository of the right to life and personal liberty. In fact, it was an essential postulate and basic assumption of the Rule of Law in every civilized society. He added that Article 226, which empowered the High Courts to issue writs, was an integral part of the Constitution and could not be bypassed by the Presidential Order; and that rights created by statutes which were not Fundamental Rights could also be enforced during the period of Emergency. Further, there was no contradiction between the power of the government to detain a person under preventive detention and the power of the court to examine the legality of such a detention.

In 1999, Dr. L.M. Singhvi, who was High Commissioner of India to U.K. and a member of Parliament, in his first Golden jubilee lecture under the auspices of the Supreme Court Bar Association at the Indian Law Institute, said: "Permit me now to temper my commemorative panegyrics with sad and somber note for we must not forget or condone the Himalayan failure of the Supreme Court of India in the Habeas Corpus case of A.D.M. Jabalpur, which put the nation's diamond-bright and diamond-hard hope on human right and fundamental rights in an archival glass case. That was when freedom was on trial and our widely admired and much adored Supreme Court failed us. The grim tale tragedy the darkness at noon should never be forgotten. The court developed a strange amnesia schizophrenia in the majority judgment in that case and forgot its legal legacy of enlightened liberalism and form of many judgments including that of *Makhan Singh* vs *Punjab* (AIR 1964 SC 381) and in form of a case decided by a Special Bench of seven judges on which the Bench could have built. It forgot its mission and its trusteeship in the matter of fundamental rights. It ignored the resonant reverberation of Lord Atkin's famous dissent in *Liversidge* vs *Anderson* (1942 AC 206). It remained for that solitary sentinel of time liberty on the qui vive at that troubled time in our history, Justice H.R. Khanna to hold the flame heroically as did Lord Atkin, but in a different society and a different combination of circumstances. That dissenting judgment is the glory of the Supreme Court's jurisprudence and reminds us of the moving words of Chief Justice Hughes whom Justice Khanna also quoted: 'A dissent in a court of last resort is an appeal to the brooding spirit of the law, to the intelligence of a future date, when a later decision may possibly correct the error in which a dissenting judge believes the court to have been betrayed.' Let our vigilant custodian never again be betrayed into enormity of such an error so that our mind is without fear and our head is held high. Let our vigilant custodian be a true trustee of that tryst with destiny on which the constitutional pilgrimage of India embarked forty-nine years ago" (*Democracy and Rule of Law,* Dr. L.M. Singhvi, Ocean Books, New Delhi, pp. 219-20).

Needless to say, Justice Khanna had to pay for his views. He was superseded by Justice Beg and not made Chief Justice of the Supreme Court, when he should have been by virtue of his seniority. But, he was applauded in India and abroad and his photo was installed in the Supreme Court after the Emergency.

The *New York Times* wrote in its 30th April, 1976, editorial: "If India ever finds its way back to the freedom and democracy that were proud hallmarks of its first 18 years as an independent nation, someone will surely erect a monument to Justice Khanna of Supreme Court."

I have had the honour of having 'Foreword' of Justice H.R. Khanna to my book, *Makers of Indian Constitution: Myth and*

Reality. When I handed over the manuscript of the book to him, he asked me, "Why do you want my 'Foreword' to the book?" I told him that I have dealt with a very sensitive issue in the book and you are the only person in India today who can write without fear or favour. He smiled and agreed to write the 'Foreword'. Within a fortnight, I received his 'Foreword' for my book.

Concluding his 'Foreword', Justice Khanna said: "Mr. Sheshrao Chavan, in preparing this book, has taken great pains and has come out with a very valuable and authentic piece of Constitutional literature. He has not dealt with the matter in a superficial manner but has delved deep into the record of these historic events and focused light on them. I have no doubt that this publication would create fresh awareness of a very significant period of India's history and the process of Constitution-making."

The book was published by Bharatiya Vidya Bhavan under Bhavan's Book University.

Three Cs: Caste, Corruption and Cost

Senior Lawyer Nariman, in his speech on the occasion of 125th Anniversary of Bombay High Court, said that judiciary is suffering from three Cs—Caste, Corruption and Cost. This appears to be very telling and bold but true statement.

Smt. Leila Seth, Chief Justice of Himachal Pradesh High Court, revealed startling facts with regard to the appointment of Smt. Fathima Beevi to the Supreme Court. In her words: "Justice Fathima Beevi had been in judicial service since 1958 and had been elevated to the Kerala High Court in 1983. She had retired in April 1989 at the age of 62. Since she had retired more than five months earlier, it was quite unusual—perhaps unique—that her name should have been put up for the Supreme Court. A couple of Supreme Court judges told me that she had lobbied for the position on the grounds that she would be the first Muslim woman in the world to be a judge of a Supreme Court, and that there was at the time no Muslim judge in the Supreme Court of India. When it was pointed out to her that Justice Ahmadi was a Supreme Court judge, she had responded that he was not a Muslim, merely an Ahmadi, and even Pakistan did not treat Ahmadis as Muslims."

Smt. Leila Seth further said: "Many people knew that her brother-in-law was a prominent local politician and believed that the Congress government had been assured that they would get the Kerala Muslim votes in the forthcoming elections if she were made a Supreme Court judge. The Law Minister at the time, Mr. Shankaranand, had been pressing for either Justice Fathima Beevi or Justice Padma Khastgir for some time. Chief Justice Pathak had written back to him to say, I find myself unagreeable to their appointment in the Supreme Court, and that I was the appropriate choice among the women judges of the High Court at that juncture."

Leila Seth continued: "Though I had heard some stories and gossip about Justice Fathima Beevi being appointed to the Supreme Court, I did not give them much credence. As a result, when her appointment was actually announced and she was sworn in on 6th October, I felt terribly upset, both for the system and for myself. It showed that lobbying worked. It showed that politics worked. It showed that the misuse of religion worked. Above all, it showed that every decent convention could be broken and that merit was no consideration."

"Fathima Beevi's judicial record was quite ordinary. When some people pointed this out to Chief Justice Venkataramiah, he only stated that she was going to be very junior in the Supreme Court, would retire in two and half years and would therefore not be heading a bench, so it did not matter. When his words were reported in the newspapers, lawyers and judges were shocked. Women lawyers were particularly dismayed, as she was the first woman judge of the Supreme Court and this was adding insult to injury first by appointing a retired and not so competent woman judge, and secondly by making such disparaging remarks" (*On Balance: An Autobiography,* Leila Seth, pp. 316-18).

It was widely rumoured that one young lawyer, who was son of a Chief Justice of India (Y.V. Chandrachud) was appointed as High Court judge over people who were his seniors in age and competence. The then President of India was not inclined to sign his appointment order, but he reluctantly did on persuasion saying that he knew that he was signing the warrant for the future Chief Justice of India. True to the words of the President, this Judge has become Chief Justice of India on 9th November, 2022. He is D.Y. Chandrachud.

During the tenure of P.V. Narsimha Rao as Prime Minister, the caste considerations had become so acute that it was said that three ministers of his Cabinet refused Brahmins for the post of a judge of the Supreme Court. This was disclosed by Narsimha Rao himself to Justice Chandrashekhar Dharmadhikari in a private talk at Hyderabad. What a pity that the Prime Minister was made helpless by his powerful anti-Brahmin colleagues.

Justice Y.V. Chandrachud after his retirement as the Chief Justice of India, in one of his speeches, said: "Political friendship has become a convenient shortcut, almost a password for achieving personal ambitions like appointments, transfers and promotions. Why read Seervai on the Constitution if an out-of-court friendship with someone in the corridors of power can fetch you a seat from where you can deliver sermons on the Constitution without knowing what that great document means and contains."

In a democracy like ours, we have a legislature, we have executive and we have judiciary. If there were no independent judiciary, political democracy would be impossible. Persons who have money power or muscle power can get their jobs or work done by following some well-known methods. But, the common man who is the very foundation of our Constitution cannot get his work done anywhere and has merely to suffer injustice at all levels. He has only one place open to get justice, that is, the court of law, temple of justice.

The present judicial system is, perhaps, the most expensive luxury; the biggest purse stands to win in it. Basically, there is something sinful in a system that allows for a professional to earn lakhs of rupees per month or per day. The result is that the profession has remained noble but the professionals are not necessarily noble. Generally, the legal talents are being bought. The lawyer's profession has become a speculative business and the best talent is not available to the poor at a reasonable rate or fee.

Justice H.R. Khanna, in his book, *Law, Men of Law and Education*, published by N.M. Tripathi Pvt Ltd., Mumbai, at page 65, said: "It would certainly be a melancholy reflection if the benefits of the constitutional and legal provisions were availed of only by the rich and well-to-do and if the poor and the indigent because of lack of funds could not get those benefits. Such a depressing state of affairs is bound to give rise to a big question mark as to who were the people for whose benefit the Constitution was primarily enacted." In the words of Justice Vivian Bose, "What was the point of making all this pother about fundamental rights? I am clear that the Constitution is not for the exclusive benefit of government and states, it is not only for lawyers and politicians and officials and those highly placed. It also exists for the common man, for the poor and the humble, for those who have business at stake, for the butcher, the baker and the candlestick maker. It lays down for this land, 'a rule of law,' as understood in the free democracies of the world."

In the present system there is equality before law but with unequal opportunities. Equality without equal opportunity in the true sense is inequality. Here, everybody wants to be more equal than others on the basis of caste, creed, religion, money power or mafia power. The judicial system should be such where a common man and society can participate. It should be a participatory judicial system.

If all organs of the State act impartially and judiciously, it will not be necessary to approach a Court of Law. Because, people are not getting justice anywhere else, they have to go to the court which has become the last resort, a *Sharan Teertha,* for a common man.

Delay

The greatest drawback of the administration of justice in India is 'delay'. There are inordinate delays in the disposal of cases. Dr. Nani Palkhivala had said: "We as the nation have some fine qualities, but a sense of the value of time is not one of them. Ancient India had evolved the concept of eternity and infinity. So, what does it matter if thirty years are wasted in a litigation against the backdrop of eternity? Further we believe in reincarnation. What does it matter if you waste this life? You will have many more lives in which to make good."

Dr. Palkhivala further said: "I am not aware of any country in the world where litigation goes on for as long a period as in India. Our cases drag over a length of time which makes eternity intelligible. The law may or may not be an ass, but in India it is certainly a snail and our cases proceed at a pace which would be regarded as unduly slow in a community of snails. Justice has to be blind but I see no reason why it should be also lame: here it just hobbles along, barely able to walk."

He continued: "A charitable trust with which I am concerned, filed a suit to recover possession of its building. It took thirty years to get the final decision of the Supreme Court. Even after that, the trust has been unable to recover full possession, because there are obstructionists' notices in the Small Causes Court in respect of some floors, which would take another decade to dispose of. If litigation were to be included in the Olympics, India would be certain of winning at least one gold medal."

"The fault is mainly of the legal profession. We ask for adjournments on the flimsiest grounds. If the judge does not readily grant adjournments, he becomes highly unpopular. I think it is the duty of the legal profession to make sure that it cooperates with the judiciary in ensuring that justice is administered speedily and expeditiously. It is the one duty of which we are totally oblivious."

"Sometimes judges are asked to intervene on humanitarian grounds, e.g., in the case of encroachments on public property. Courts of law are there to enforce the law. But, in matters relating to encroachments and similar cases the courts are expected to prevent enforcement of the law. Lawyers who would not allow homeless persons to stay with them in their own houses or build a hutment next to the wall of their own building, act as great champions of the downtrodden in such disputes. Double standards have become shamelessly common in the legal profession."

"We take cases in mind-boggling numbers to the court of law. Small wonder that we have colossal arears in courts. Do we not have to blame ourselves as members of the legal profession for this state of affairs? Lawyers are entitled to earn their living, but not at such an unbearable cost to society" (*We, the Nation: The Lost Decades,* Nani A. Palkhivala, UBS Publishers and Distributors, New Delhi, pp. 215-17).

Today, the court is not for the poor. One often hears the rich saying to the poor that he would drag him to the court and torture him—*Tuze Adalat Men Khich Kar Tang Karunga*. Rich people sometimes use the court as their means to achieve their goal of harassing opponents.

The Guinness Book of World Records gives its longevity award to a suit that was filed in Pune in 1905 and remained unsettled till 1966. When editors of Guinness made an inquiry from the officials in New Delhi, they were told that there was no record of the extraordinary litigation, but it was admitted that in our High Courts we have more than 50,00,000 cases pending which are ten to thirty years old. In the present adversary judicial system one side always wants to delay because that helps to protect and preserve their vested interests. It is, therefore, necessary to have participatory judicial system.

Soli Sorabjee, an eminent lawyer, in his keynote address delivered on the occasion of the celebration of 125 years of the Bombay High Court, said: "The time has long past for compiling statistics of arrears in courts and setting up Commissions to go into this problem. A parallel extra-legal or paralegal agency, whose first tenet is contempt for the rule of law and judicial process has been set up and is doing well. It is notorious fact that the common man has become utterly cynical, almost contemptuous about courts and administration of justice. He prefers to seek justice by taking the law in his own hands or relying upon socialized agencies which promise prompt results by recourse to extralegal means. The reason is the unbearable burden of litigation, the excruciating delays, the crushing cost and the general harassment involved in doing a lawyer."

In conclusion of his keynote address Sorabjee said: "Delay in the disposal of criminal appeals and the continued incarceration of the appellant, because the court has no time to hear their appeals, is a hideous mockery of justice. When the person succeeds how is he to be compensated for the slice of his life taken away from him? The monstrosity of the situation is evident yet we have got so used to it so as to become apathetic and indifferent" (*Post Centenary Silver Jubilee of Bombay High Court*, pp. 113-14).

Speaking of litigation, Smt. Leila Seth in her book, *On Balance: An Autobiography*, at page 349, writes: "Shaw Wallace & Co. at one time owed Primo (her husband) a substantial sum of money and were not paying, despite repeated reminders. He was angry and wanted to sue them. I begged him to settle. I said: 'Take half, take one-third, even take one-fifth, but settle. You have a good case, but if you take them to court, you certainly won't get anything now; if you have grand-children, they might. Apart from that, you will lose sleep and get high blood pressure when you will hear lies being treated as truth and frivolous adjournments being taken by the other side to delay the matter. I know that I will have to bear the brunt of it, as you will keep telling me what a frustrating and useless exercise the whole process is?' I badgered him to settle and settle he did. It was over in a few days and, though he got mere fifth of what he should have, he had to call his own. It was practical *tatkaal* justice, if very imperfect."

Smt. Seth further writes: "I often think about how litigation or the threat of litigation affects people. It takes over one's whole life. The fear of the lawyers and the courts, the delay, the tension when you have to appear and all too often, the complete lack of reasonableness of the prosecutor or opponent is horrible realities. It is time-consuming, expensive and nerve-racking. And the result is so unpredictable. You can be called upon to pay damages even for something for which you are not responsible. If that is what I faced as a judge owing to an objurgate bureaucracy, if that was what I as a judge, advised my husband to do rather than battle an obstructive large company, what must be the lot of the common man, who is totally bewildered by the language and the trappings of the law, has no access to the levers of power or the ears of the influential, has little to fall back on during the years of expense and delay, and lacks even the knowledge of what he should do or to whom he should go in order to redress an injustice or assert a just claim."

Justice H.R. Khanna, in his book, *Law, Men of Law and Education*, at page 12, writes: "The delay in the disposal of cases is a standing stigma on our judicial system. Not only ordinary cases but even those which call for prompt and speedy disposal linger on in courts for years. This understandably creates enchantment and causes anguish to all; those who knock at the door of courts to seek prompt relief. Justice delayed in a large number of cases is as good or bad as justice denied. Where is the justice if a young wife or husband seeks matrimonial relief and gets it after ten or fifteen years by which time the period of youth becomes a matter of the past. Of what avail is the acquittal of a person who has to spend years as an undertrial prisoner in jail. Instances like these can be multiplied *ad infinitum*."

In the same book at pages 43 and 44, Justice Khanna writes: "Long delay has also the effect of defeating justice in quite a number of cases. As a result of such delay, the possibility cannot be ruled out of loss of important evidence because of the fading of memory or death of witness. The consequences, thus, would be that a party with even a strong case may lose it not because of any fault of its own but because of the tardy judicial process entailing disappearance of material evidence. When a person knocks at the door of the court, he does so because he feels that he has a grievance and the court would grant him the necessary relief within a reasonable time. As it is, we find that cases linger on in courts for years and years, bringing disillusionment to all those who, at one time, set high hopes in courts. The problem of delay and huge arears stares us all and unless we can do something about it the whole judicial system would get crushed under the weight of it. For long have we taken the patience of the people for granted. The need today is for some effective measures consistent with demands of justice, equity and fair play to accelerate the disposal of cases and clear the arears."

As a common man, I think, we are all responsible for this. Khalil Gibran has said: "As a single leaf turns not yellow but with the silence knowledge of whole tree." This can be said about our judicial system. I fail to understand why judges speak about changing the system after their retirement. Are not those who speak about the system responsible for this malady?

Craving for Other Jobs

No less a person than the Chief Justice and the Vice-President of India, Justice Hidayatullah said in his address on the occasion of the celebrations of 125 years of the Bombay High Court: "The craving for other jobs in the judiciary is increasing. These are Law Minister-ship and membership of Parliament. One Chief Justice resigned from the Supreme Court, contested election and failed. Two retired judges of the Supreme Court contested Presidential election and also failed miserably and one Chief Justice escaped by a whisker to fail also. If the opposition had not had a beating in the Presidential election and was not prepared to face another, one more retired Chief Justice would have joined the band of failures."

Justice Hidayatullah further said: "One Supreme Court judge and one High Court judge resigned from the courts and got into Parliament. They canvassed for this with the Executive. Before these judges working for short spell resigned, entered politics and became Law Ministers. The others did not accept judgeship even after being nominated. All this degrades the office of a judge, but, of course the lure is there" (*Post Centenary Silver Jubilee of Bombay High Court,* p. 78).

Unfortunately, the craving for political positions is seen on increasing returns rather than diminishing returns in terms of law of economics. When a judge, who is a sitting judge craves for post-retirement assignment, it is obvious that he must be preparing for it before his retirement.

8
Appointments of Supreme Court and High Court Judges

Article 124 of the Constitution provides that every judge of the Supreme Court shall be appointed by the President by the warrant under his hand and seal after consultation with such of the judges of the Supreme Court and of the High Courts in the States as President may deem necessary for the purpose and shall hold office until he attains the age of 65 years.

Provided that in the case of appointment of a judge other than the Chief Justice, the Chief Justice of India shall always be consulted.

Provided further that

(a) A judge may, by writing under his hand addressed to the President, resign his office;

(b) A judge may be removed from his office in the manner provided in clause (4).

Similar power is given by Article 217 to the President in consultation with the Chief Justice of India, the Governors of the States and the Chief Justices of the High Courts for the appointment of judges to High Courts.

For forty-three years after the Constitution came into force, successive Prime Ministers and their Cabinets have been recommending to the President names of persons considered eligible for appointment after consultation with the Chief Justice, and no one had disputed the legitimacy of this role of the executive.

Collegium System

In 1981, in what is known as the first Judges' case, the Supreme Court held that the power of appointment of judges of the Supreme Court resided solely and exclusively in the President subject to full and effective consultation with the Constitutional functionaries referred to in Articles 124 and 217. However, in 1992, the Supreme Court, in the second Judges' case, professing to safeguard the independence of the judiciary, reversed the first verdict and rewrote the Constitutional provision to hold that the primacy in the appointment of a judge of the Supreme Court was with the Chief Justice of India, who would make his recommendation to the President after consultation with two of his senior judges. The President might accept or return the recommendation. If the recommendation was reiterated, the President was obliged to make the appointment.

In a later judgment, known as the third Judges' case, the Supreme Court diluted the primacy of the Chief Justice of India, and gave the power of appointment to the Collegium of the Chief Justice of India and four of his senior-most colleagues.

Perhaps, after 1993, India has become the only democracy in the world (after Japan) where the head of the government has no decisive say in the appointment of judges of the High Courts and the Supreme Court. Of course, the Prime Minister is still the authority to send proposals for appointment of judges to the President, but his role has now been practically reduced to one of endorsing the names proposed by the Chief Justice of the Supreme Court, who does so after consultation with his senior colleagues.

The Governors and Chief Ministers of the States have to be consulted by the Central Government under Article 217 before recommending the names of persons to be appointed as judges of the High Courts. Now, consultation is made by the judiciary, but this has become a mere formality as the actual selection of the persons to be appointed is with the judiciary after 1993. The judiciary seems to be keen to have the de facto power to appoint judges as it seems to be of the view that such a power is indispensable for preserving its independence.

For and Against Views on Collegium System

The legal luminaries and judges have been ventilating their views on Collegium system which are for and against.

Justice V.R. Krishna Iyer, a judge of the Supreme Court, said: "Today, the Supreme Court has interpreted the method of choosing the higher judiciary in a judgment where with a majority of one the Collegium has been created by the court. No plan, no commission, no Parliamentary debate, no national symposium but mere single vote who made a majority in a single judgment. The ad hoc accident is what governs the choice of judiciary. The Collegium is the senior most three or five judges of the High Court or the Supreme Court which constitutes the Collegiums. Their ideology, their class character, their antecedents nor performance nor their social milieu is considered. The whole process is arbitrary and naturally their perfunctory selection has come up for criticism. Indeed, the present Collegium at the Centre or the State in India answers the semantics of that word which according to the website means: 'A group whose members pursue shared goals while working within a frame work of mutual trust and respect.' It is a pity that despite the Constitution infallibility of the Supreme Court its appointments have been disappointments" (*The Constitution, Corruption, Pathological Casualties and Radical Remedies, Reformatories*, V.R. Krishna Iyer, Universal Law Publishing Co. Pvt Ltd., New Delhi, pp. 134-35).

Justice Krishna Iyer also said: "There is no constitutional sanction for this instrument except the pronouncement of the Supreme Court. The whole process of the Collegium is secret. The Bar has no voice. The public has no chance to speak, no institution is consulted" (*Ibid.*, p. 142).

Justice A.P. Shah as Chairman of the Law Commission of India, in his interview to the *Sunday Express*, said: "In my opinion, the Collegium system is not a democratic institution; there are no checks and balances in it. If you let the same system continue without any meaningful voice to the executing civil society, even if you make it a little more transparent and a criterion is laid out, it may not improve the system itself."

Justice Shah further said: "The problem is that most judges till they are in the Collegium defend the Collegium system because it is very difficult for a serving judge to criticize it. Nobody honestly believes that this system works well. Many retired judges, barring the exception of former Chief Justice Altamas Kabir, and a few others, believe that this system has not worked."

Mohammed Salim, a CPM member of Lok Sabha, in his write up in the Indian Express of 14th August, 2014, said: "The present system of appointment suffers from many infirmities. There is neither any scope for scrutiny nor transparency. This method of appointment also does not address the diversity in Indian society. Moreover, it leads to the appointment of judges who hold similar views and have the same broad orientation. It is also prone to encourage nepotism in the judicial system."

Anil Divan, a senior Counsel, in his article in *The Hindu* of 7th August, 2014, wrote: "The present secretive process followed by the Collegium excludes public scrutiny, violates the citizen's right to know and leads to diminishing respect for the judiciary. Some bad appointments produced by this system are also notorious."

Prashant Bushan, a distinguished lawyer, in his article in *The Indian Express* of 11th August, 2014, wrote: "The system of appointment of judges by the judiciary did lead to the depoliticization of the judiciary to a large extent and did substantially improve its independence. But, the process of appointments was still shrouded in secrecy and keeping the control over appointments with sitting judges, who had little time from their judicial work, coupled with the lack of transparency in such appointments. No criterion for selection was laid down, nor was any system devised to evaluate various candidates in the zone of consideration on any criteria. No system of inviting any applications or nominations was devised either. Thus, the quality of appointments did not substantially improve even in this system. Even late Justice J.S. Verma, the author of the original judgment, came to say that he did not anticipate that his judgment would lead to such poor appointments by the judiciary."

T.R. Andhyarujina, former Solicitor General of India, in his write up in *The Indian Express* of 9th August, 2014, said: "Unfortunately for 20 years Collegium system has not worked satisfactorily. In the first instance, the Collegium system lacks transparency and is secretive. The public is not aware of the selection of a judge until his name is forwarded to the government by the Collegium. Second, there have been instances of judges being selected or not selected due to favoritism or prejudice of members of the Collegium. Third, selection of competitive merit of the appointees is discarded and judges are generally appointed to the Supreme Court on the seniority in ranking in the High Courts."

Rumi Pal, a former Supreme Court judge, has said that the process by which a judge is presently appointed to the High Court or the Supreme Court is one of the best kept secrets in the country.

V.N. Khare points out that prior to 1993, when the primacy vested with the executive, eminent judges were still appointed to the High Courts and the Supreme Court.

National Judicial Appointments Commission

M. Veerappa Moily, who was Union Minister from 2009 to 2011, in his article in *The Indian Express* of 19th August, 2014, writes: "The issue of appointment and removal of judges was examined by the National Commission to review the working of the Constitution chaired by Justice M.N. Venkatachaliah. The Commission recommended the constitution of a National Judicial Commission, which would have the elected participation of both the executive and the judicial wings of the State as an integrated scheme for the machinery for appointment of judges."

The government introduced the Constitution (98th Amendment) Bill in the Lok Sabha in 2003. This Bill sought to create a National Judicial Commission headed by the Chief Justice of India with two judges of the Supreme Court next to the Chief Justice in seniority, the Union Minister for Law and Justice and one eminent citizen to be nominated by the President in consultation with the Prime Minister as members.

The second Administrative Reforms Commission was of the view that the appointment of judges to the higher courts should be with the participation of executive, legislature and the Chief Justice, and should be bipartisan process above day-to-day politics. Therefore, the proposed National Judicial Commission should comprise representatives of all three organs of the state—the legislature, the executive and the judiciary. Such a body can devise its own procedures in identifying and screening candidates for the higher judiciary.

Parliament passed a Constitutional Amendment Bill to provide for the National Judicial Appointments Commission (NJAC), which proposed to radically change the process of appointment of judges by giving both the Judiciary and the Executive equal say and veto power. The NJAC was mandated to appoint the judges of the Supreme Court and the Chief Justice and judges of the High Courts. It was also empowered to initiate transfers of the High Court judges.

The six-member NJAC will consist of the CJI, the two senior most judges of the Supreme Court, the Union Law and Justice Minister and two eminent persons. The choice of eminent persons will be made by a high-powered committee composed of the Prime Minister, the CJI and the leader of the Opposition or the leader of the largest party in Opposition. The two eminent persons will have a tenure of three years, and one will be a woman, or from the Scheduled Caste, Scheduled Tribe, or minority community.

In an important improvisation on earlier drafts of the NJAC, the Bill provides that no name opposed by two or more of the six-member body can go through. A name recommended for appointment as judge to the Supreme Court or the High Courts can be returned to the NJAC by the President for reconsideration. The Bill also provides for wider consultation with Bar bodies, senior advocates and eminent persons by the Collegium of the High Court before recommending a name for consideration by the NJAC in appointments to the High Court. In an important addition, the Bill also requires that the NJAC, before recommending a name for appointment as a judge in

High Court, takes the views of the concerned State Governor and Chief Minister in writing.

On 16th October, 2015, the Supreme Court struck down the Constitution (99th Amendment) Act, 2014 and with it the National Judicial Appointments Commission Act also perished.

Sruthisagar Yamunan, doctoral candidate in Comparative Constitutional Law at Central European University, in his article in *The Hindu* of 2nd December, 2022, said: "The court's central argument was that by removing the primacy of the judiciary in the new appointment process, the NJAC subverted the independence of the judiciary, a key component of the court's conception of the Basic Structure of the Constitution.

At the same time, the court acknowledged that there were problems with the Collegium system that required intervention. This led to separate proceedings by the same Bench in which the court appointed a two-member committee of senior lawyers, one of whom was a government Law Officer to compile suggestions received from the legal community. The government also put its suggestions in writing. After deliberations, viable inputs were to be incorporated into a new Memorandum of Procedure (MoP) for judicial appointments.

However, the Union Government, through Attorney General Mukul Rohatgi, took the position before the Bench that the right and power to frame the MoP was squarely in its field, going by the court's judgments that created the Collegium system. The court accepted this position and closed the proceedings, providing the Union government broadlines on what the MoP may focus on—eligibility, transparency, formation of secretariat, and complaints redressal during the process. What happened to the 11,500 pages of suggestions received by the committee is anybody's guess. Media reports indicate and the court and the government could not find a common ground over these reforms to the MoP. Thus, the process went into cold storage.

In the meantime, government's response to the striking down of the NJAC was in action—it began to stall appointments. While Mr. Rijiju took exception to criticism from the court that the government was sitting on recommendations, this is exactly what the government did. It belligerently opposed names it did not like and even ignored reiterations by the Collegium, which, as per the law, are binding on the government. An important case was that of Justice K.M. Joseph in 2018. When he was eventually appointed, he lost the seniority he would have got with the original recommendation as the names were split by the government for appointments.

On the other hand, the Union government made no attempts to revive the NJAC through Parliament by filling the gaps that the Supreme Court had pointed out in its 2015 judgment."

Arvind P. Datar, who practices in the Supreme Court and had appeared in the NJAC case, in his article in *The Indian Express* of 9th December, 2022, wrote: "Very few critics understand that the constitutional amendment and the NJAC Act 2014 was so badly drafted that the NJAC would have collapsed under its own contradictions. All the counsels who argued against the amendment, including Fali Nariman, the Late Anil Divan, the late Ram Jethmalani and this writer, had repeatedly informed the Supreme Court that they had no objection to the NJAC replacing the Collegium provided judges, sitting or retired, were in a clear majority in the Commission. But, the Union of India refused to relent and the 99th Amendment was eventually struck down as being violative of the basic structure.

A simple analysis of the appointment process shows that it was unworkable. Under Article 124 (A), the NJAC oddly had an even number of six members but the Chairperson, the Chief Justice of India, had no casting vote. What would happen if there was a tie and, therefore, a deadlock? No answer.

The Chief Justice and the next two senior judges represented the judiciary. The Law Minister and two eminent persons were the other three. One of the eminent members had to be nominated from persons belonging to Scheduled Castes, Scheduled Tribes, Other Backward Classes or should be a woman. In as many as 67 Central Acts, the eminent persons who have to be appointed as part of a committee or a commission, must have expertise in the subject that the statutes cover."

Strangely, to select Supreme Court or High Court judges, the eminent person needed no connection with the law. In fact, during the argument, the response of the Union of India was categorical: The eminent person need have no knowledge of law or the functioning of the courts. It was stated that even M.S. Swaminathan, the renowned agricultural scientist, could be a member. Thus, one-third of the NJAC could be constitutionally and blissfully unaware of the functioning of the Supreme Court or the High Courts and yet decide the destiny of our higher judiciary.

The NJAC Act, 2014, which prescribed the procedure for appointment and transfer of judges, was riddled with contradictions and absurdities. Section 5(1) required the NJAC to recommend the senior-most judge of the Supreme Court as the Chief Justice of India if he is considered fit to hold the office. Neither the 99th Amendment nor the NJAC Act had any prescribed criteria of what constituted fitness to hold office. On what ground the senior-most judge becomes unfit? No answer.

A shocking provision was the veto power. No recommendation could be made by the NJAC if any two of the six members disagreed. There could not be a more blatant method of frustrating the appointment process and enabling the executive to completely dominate the judiciary.

The selection procedure for the High Court Judges was even more bizarre. The Chief Justice and two senior-most judges of every High Court had to nominate persons to the NJAC for appointment as High Court judges. Simultaneously, the NJAC could also nominate persons for appointment as High Court judges. What would happen if the two sets of nominees were different? No answer. Further, the NJAC had to elicit in writing the views of the Governor and the Chief Minister. What would happen if the two took opposite views? Whose view would prevail? No answer.

And now comes the worst blow. The NJAC had the power to frame regulations laying down the criteria of suitability and the procedure of appointing judges of the Supreme Court and the High Courts. These regulations had to be tabled before both Houses of Parliament. Under Section 13, Parliament had the power to nullify these regulations or modify them. This single fatal section made a complete mockery of the appointment process. The present Collegium system, despite its drawbacks, is a far better method of selecting Supreme Court and High Court judges.

The repeated and orchestrated attacks on the Collegium and the Judiciary will, to borrow the words of Justice Douglas, "set in motion a subversive influence of our own design that destroy us from within."

Heading to Scrap Collegium

In an interview at the Times Now (an English Indian news channel), Law Minister Kiren Rijiju said: "Never say that the government is sitting on the files, then don't send the files to the government, you appoint yourself, you run the show." Describing the Collegium system as "alien" to the Constitution, Rijiju said: "You tell me under which provision the Collegium system has been prescribed."

When referred to the related news reports, Justice S.K. Kaul of the Supreme Court, without naming the Union Law Minister, said: "Let them give the power. We have no difficulty. I ignored all press reports, but what he says, that when somebody high enough says let them do it themselves, we will do it ourselves, no difficulty. It came from somebody high enough, should not have. All I can say is, should not have happened." Kaul was sharing the bench with Justice Oka.

Solicitor General Tushar Mehta urged the court not to go by media reports, to which Justice Kaul said: "It is an interview. With an interview, it becomes difficult to deny what you have said yourselves. I am not saying anything. I am just expecting both the Attorney General and Solicitor General to play the role of a Law officer to advice the government to ensure that the law of the land as laid down by this court is observed."

The bench of Justice Kaul, Justice Vikran Nath and Justice A.S. Oka was hearing a contempt plea by the Advocates Association, Bengaluru which said that the government was yet to approve eleven names reiterated by the Supreme Court Collegium in violation of the norms laid down by the top court.

Earlier on 11th November, 2022, while hearing the matter, the bench had noted that "keeping names pending is not acceptable," and also issued a notice to the Secretary (Justice) of the Central Government.

Taking it up, the bench sought to know if the Centre was not clearing the names because the National Judicial Appointments Commission (NJAC) had not passed muster. "How will the system work if the names are not cleared? We have expressed our anguish. It appears that the government is not happy that the NJAC has not passed muster. But, can that be the reason to not clear names?" asked Justice Kaul.

To sort out problems, a three-judge bench had laid down timelines to be followed by the government in case of appointing judges, Justice Kaul said, emphasizing that the timelines must be adhered to. Timelines having been laid down, those timelines have to be adhered to unless there is some exceptional circumstance, some one or two cases. This much time period, not 20 cases pending like this, Kaul said.

As the Attorney General remarked that things have to move in a certain way, Justice Kaul responded: "Attorney, when things have to move, they move in a day. When they don't have to move, they don't move in months. This is the problem."

Venkataraman, Additional Solicitor General in Supreme Court, said: "It is both a question of principle and policy, high consideration, also strategy, so many things are involved." Responding Justice Kaul said: "Maybe you have reservations on the law. But, till the law stands, it is the law of the land, tomorrow somebody else may say something like this about another portion of the law. You must look at a larger picture" (*The Indian Express*, 29th November, 2022).

The bench said the judgment by its Constitution Bench on the Collegium system must be adhered to. "In the meantime, the Collegium system coupled with the Memorandum of Procedure (MoP) must work as it exists, subject to any changes to be made," the bench said.

It is a fact that the Supreme Court remains obstinately committed to the Collegium system of appointing judges with little regard for criticism from within and outside the legal fraternity. In interviews to the media after his retirement, CJI, Justice U.U. Lalit categorized the Collegium system as the perfect system to protect the independence of the judiciary.

"We do not want to comment on anything said by former members of the Supreme Court Collegium. We do not want to say or comment on them. Now a days it has become a fashion to comment on earlier decisions when they were part of the Collegium," Justice M.R. Shah, leading a bench, said.

Setting the stage for confrontation with the judiciary on the appointment of judges, the government had returned 19 of the 21 pending recommendations by the Supreme Court Collegium for appointment of High Court judges. The recommendations were returned hours before the Supreme Court hearing on judicial appointments on 28th November, 2022. These include 10 names that were pending after they were reiterated by the Collegium, and nine names pending after the first recommendation.

Two recommendations had been accepted. They were for the appointment of advocates Santosh Govind Chapalgaonkar and Milind Manohar Sathaye as judges of the Bombay High Court. The Collegium had recommended their names on 12th September, 2022.

Of the 10 names returned after the Collegium's reiteration, five were for Allahabad High Court, two for Calcutta High Court, two for Kerala High Court, and one for Karnataka High Court (*The Indian Express,* 30th November, 2022).

The Collegium's decision of 26th September, 2022, recommending Justice Dipankar Datta, Chief Justice of Bombay High Court, as a judge of the Supreme Court, which was pending with the government had been cleared on 11th December, 2022.

Dismissing concerns of the government, the Supreme Court Collegium, headed by Chief Justice Chandrachud, recommended two advocates and six district judges for appointment as judges of the Rajasthan High Court. From the Bar, the Collegium recommended advocates Anil Kumar Upman and Nupur Bhati.

From district judiciary, the Collegium recommended Rajendra Prakash Soni, Ashok Kumar Jain, Yogendra Kumar Purohit, Bhuwan Goyal, Praveer Bhatnagar and Ashutosh Kumar (*The Indian Express,* 26th November, 2022).

The Hindu in its editorial of 1st December, 2022, wrote: "The Union government appears determined to turn its conflict with judiciary over judicial appointments into something unseemly. The sources of friction are two-fold. One is the daily diatribe by Union Law Minister Kiren Rijiju, who appears to have been given an assignment to target the Collegium system with trenchant criticism of its known, but uncorrected flaws, and top it with unwarranted remarks such as asking the Court not to send any files, if it felt that it was sitting on them. The second is the government's strategy of delaying appointments recommended by the Collegium as a counterblast to its loss of primacy in the matter. A Supreme Court Bench, hearing a contempt petition against the government for not approving names reiterated by the Collegium, has wondered whether the government is not acting on the files because the Court did not permit the implementation of the National Judicial Appointments Commission. There will be many takers for Mr. Rijiju's central point that the Collegium system is opaque. However, his adverse comments fail to hide the perception that the aim may be to delegitimize the Court. The government is also violating the prevailing legal position that a recommendation reiterated by the Collegium, after due consideration of its objections, is binding on it.

The Court has a valid point when it says the uncertainty over the fate of a recommendation for appointment is resulting in eminent lawyers withdrawing their consent or declining invitations to join the Bench. There are instances of the government ignoring even two or three reiterations, and of the absence of any communication of objections or reservations, if any, that the government may have about particular candidates. If the current trend continues, it is not difficult to conceive of a situation in which a major verdict that may go against the government is portrayed by the political leadership as stemming from the hostility of the judiciary and not one on merits."

In conclusion *The Hindu* suggested: "One way of stopping further deterioration is for the government to clear pending recommendations with due dispatch. Another way is for the judiciary to begin or agree to a process of reforms in the way of the Collegium functions, especially with regard to expanding the range of consultation and widen the zone of consideration so that the superior judiciary and those it consults, are more diverse and representative of all sections. It is also not beyond the realm of possibility for the government to bring about a new constitutional mechanism to make appointments without undermining judicial authority."

Sriram Panchu, a senior advocate of Madras High Court, in his article in *The Indian Express* of 13th December, 2022, suggested: "The judiciary would do well to realize that the opacity of the Collegium is a genuine cause of concern and criticism. One remedy for that with multiple benefits is to co-opt a senior independent member of the Bar, such as the president of the Supreme Court Bar Association in its deliberations. The Bar's views on prospective judges are valuable; lawyers often know more than reclusive senior judges about the desirability and its lack of prospective judges. And it will rid the Collegium of its tag of insularity. The best of all, the Bench and the Bar ally on working the Collegium, and politicians will be kept at bay; a bunch of judges is an easy target but avoiding tangle with the collective of judges and lawyers is ancient political common sense. And so, till a better system is forthcoming after some years, this jugaad method can chug along quite nicely."

P. Chidambaram, a former Cabinet Minister in Dr. Manmohan Singh Government, in his column in *The Indian Express* of 4th December, 2022, wrote: "In my column (The NJAC Conundrum, *The Indian Express*, 1st November, 2015), I criticized the judgement vehemently, but also suggested a common ground to make a new law. The strongest argument on the side of the Executive is that in no other country of the world do judges select new judges and the Executive is best placed to assess the character and suitability of the potential judge. The strongest argument on the side of judiciary is that serving judges know best about the practicing lawyers and serving district judges who alone are qualified to be elevated to the Bench. There is a large dose of truth in both arguments."

Chidambaram further wrote: "If the standoff continues, the situation will get only worse. There will be more vacancies. More vacancies will mean more, not less, difficulty in filling them. There will be more 'declines' and 'withdrawals'. The legal system, already under considerable strain, will collapse. None will be sadder than the judges, none will be happier than the Executive. The losers will be the people of India, especially those knocking on the doors of the courts seeking justice."

Possible Solution

In the conclusion of his column Chidambaram wrote: "I believe that the Executive cannot be totally excluded from the process of selecting potential judges. I also believe, given the current state of partisan, vindictive and majoritarian politics, the Executive cannot be entrusted with the sole power to select potential judges. Both Judiciary and Executive must find a place in NJAC 2.0. In my column, I had suggested that the Collegium may have the exclusive power to propose/nominate candidates, the NJAC may have the power to select and recommend, and the Executive may have the power (coupled with a duty) to appoint. The procedure can be refined further if the task is entrusted to a few non-judge legal luminaries."

Chidambaram further wrote: "The rising number of vacancies in the courts—and commonsense—requires that the Executive and the Judiciary must display a degree of statesmanship to resolve the issue. Absence of statesmanship, hard words will become harsh words, the wounds will continue to fester and justice will be the casualty."

The Attack on Last Bastion: Judiciary

Justice Ajit Prasad Shah, former Chief Justice of Delhi High Court and Madras High Court and former Chairman of Law Commission, in his article in *The Hindu* of 14th December, 2022, wrote: "Recent comments by the Vice-President, Jagdeep Dhankhar, and Law Minister, Kiren Rijiju, can be read as a concerted attack on the Collegium system, the Supreme Court of India, and even the Basic Structure Doctrine (conveniently forgetting that it is this doctrine that has kept the Indian Constitution intact). Clearly, the present government continues and try to undermine judiciary, which it has been doing since it first came to power in 2014. As a long-standing critic of the Collegium system, I might have joined the chorus that called out the problems with judicial appointments. But, this onslaught from the government has been particularly disturbing the wholly unwarranted."

"The present move—of attempting to undermine and to discredit the judiciary, is part of the larger mission to make the executive the most powerful entity. Today, executive accountability is a thing of memory, for no one raises any question about its actions. Since 2014, the government has undertaken a well-crafted, deliberate take down of various institutions and mechanisms that could hold the executive accountable. Its efforts may not be as brazen as the Indira Gandhi-led government, but the same ends are being achieved—the state is rendered practically comatose, and the executive, most often, has the upper hand."

"Parallels can be drawn with 'elected autocracies,' where elected governments use the very institutions integral to democracy to kill democracy itself and destroy civil liberties. We have heard nothing of the Lokpal since. The National Human Rights Commission has been made dormant. Investigation agencies are misused at the slightest opportunity, with action against activists, journalists, students, political opponents, or anyone who protests against the government. The Election Commission of India appears to have been clearly compromised. The Information Commission is almost non-functional. Others who can hold the executive accountable—academia, the press, and civil society—have also been systematically emasculated. Universities are under attack. An unbiased mainstream fourth estate in India no longer exists, and the media operates mostly as a propaganda machine. Civil society, too, is being slowly but surely strangled."

A Resurgent Judiciary

Justice Shah further wrote: "Since the Supreme Court's decision in 2015 on the National Judicial Appointments Commission (NJAC) Act, arguably, from the court under the Chief Justices of India (CJI) Dipak Misra onwards, through the tenures of notably Justice Ranjan Gogoi and Justice S.A. Bobde, the judiciary has remained passive, and even submissive, to the executive. Consequently, not even a whisper emerged against the Collegium. However, with the last three CJIs, i.e., Justice N.V. Ramana, Justice U.U. Lalit, and Justice D.Y. Chandrachud, the court is being more assertive and speaking in a non-aligned and confident voice. The executive seems to have recognized that the judiciary is the last bastion and final protector of civil liberties which it must overcome to claim the position as the most powerful entity in India."

"History tells us that in the early years of modern India, decisions on judicial appointments were usually made on the advice of the CJI. Even if concurrence was not contemplated, for our founding fathers, an independent judiciary was non-negotiable. B.R. Ambedkar was unambiguous that appointments should have no political pressure and considerations, but that 'consultation with persons who are well-qualified to give proper advice' would be appropriate. This was followed through the Nehru-era."

"Both the Indira Gandhi and Rajiv Gandhi governments attempted to manipulate the process. The Collegium was created as a historical response to contemporaneous challenges, and succeeded in preventing the executive from hijacking judicial appointments. However, I maintain that 'judges appointing judges' is never a good idea, and a formal, structured appointment commission, with rules and accountability mechanisms, is the ideal way forward."

"The NJAC law could have fixed this problem, it had many flaws, structured to undermine judicial independence, including giving a veto to so-called 'eminent persons.' The court could have read down these flaws and at least set up a body that could incrementally improve with every selection round. But, the government refused to accede to any change or modification in the law. Eventually, the court was forced to strike down the law completely, leaving us, once again, with the Collegium system."

Fixing the System of Appointments

Justice Shah said: "For better or worse, the Collegium system is currently the law of the land, which everyone, including the Executive must adhere to. Instead, we see a defiant government refusing to cooperate, let alone consult, with the Supreme Court. Names proposed by the Collegium are left pending for years, only to be eventually returned unceremoniously."

Justice Shah suggested: "Pending a clear, rule-based system, even the existing Collegium system can be improved, e.g., through well-defined criteria for appointments, transparency and accountability in selection, better methods of assessing candidates for elevation, and improved ways of ensuring diversity and representation. CJI Chandrachud, with two years in office, has a wonderful opportunity to make these changes, even as, in the long term, we strive for a well-structured and balanced legislation on judicial commission that brings in transparency without compromising judicial independence."

"We can rest assured that the leadership at the Supreme Court appears to be in good hands now and is resisting the pressure and attacks in a dignified and restrained way. If the government continues to stonewall, perhaps the judiciary should find ways to persuade or even compel the government to follow the law of the land. This is the best that the Supreme Court can do to protect democracy, and for the sake of Indian citizens."

Chief Justice D.Y. Chandrachud has called for 'balance and harmony' from lawyers. He has also urged the government and Judiciary to work together rather than find fault with each other.

Last Nail in Camel's Back

Vice-President Jagdeep Dhankhar, in his very first speech in the Rajya Sabha as its Chairman, said: "In any democracy, Parliamentary sovereignty is inviolable." He chided the two Houses for not taking cognizance, over the past seven years, of the Supreme Court Judgment setting aside the Constitution

Amendment to constitute the National Judicial Appointments Commission (NJAC) in 2015.

Dhankhar further said: "The amendment had been passed with unprecedented support by both Houses and approval by 16 Assemblies. However, on 16th October, 2015, the Supreme Court ruled by 4:1 majority that it was not inconsonance with the Basic Structure of the Constitution and scrapped the legislation."

Dhankhar said there was no parallel to such a development in democratic history as a duly legitimized Constitutional prescription had been judicially undone. He called it a "glaring" instance of a severe compromise of Parliamentary sovereignty and disregard of the mandate of the people.

The Basic Structure, Dhankhar said, is the prevalence of primacy of the mandate of the people reflected in Parliament.

"It is disconcerting to note that on such a momentous issue, so vital a democratic fabric, there has been no focus in the Parliament, now for over seven years. This House, in concert with the Lok Sabha, being custodian of the ordainment of the people, is duty bound to address the issue, and I am sure it will do so," he added (*The Hindu,* 9th December, 2022).

The Supreme Court said nobody is stopping the government from bringing a new law on judicial appointments, but till then the Collegium system and its Memorandum of Procedure is the final word.

The Court's remarks to the government came after Vice-President Jagdeep Dhankhar criticized the striking down of the National Judicial Appointments Commission Act by a Constitution Bench in October 2015.

"Yes, Parliament has the power to enact laws. The government can ask the Parliament to lay down a new law. Nobody can prohibit it. You want to bring a new law, gather consensus, you can always do that. However, then you may have to stand the scrutiny of a challenge. The scheme of the Constitution requires the Court to be the final arbiter on the position of a law as enacted by the Parliament," Justice S.K. Kaul, leading a three-judge Bench, addressed to Attorney General R. Venkataramani, for the government.

The Court said that the law on judicial appointments to the High Courts, as it stands now, is the Collegium system evolved by the Supreme Court in the 'Three Judges Cases.'

"Our job is to enforce the law as it exists now. When you (government) lay down a law, you expect the Supreme Court to enforce it. Similarly, if a law (Collegium system) is laid down by the Supreme Court then the government is equally bound to follow the law. Till the law of Collegium is prevalent, it should be followed to the 'T'," Justice Kaul admonished.

The Court said that comments made by high authorities about the Collegium were not "well taken." "We have to follow the Collegium system no matter what people would speak of the Collegium rightly or wrongly at the right place or the wrong place. If every person or section of the society decides what law to follow, there will be a complete breakdown," Justice Kaul said.

Law Minister Kiren Rijiju had been attacking the Collegium over the past days for its 'opacity' even as the government remained incommunicado over Collegium's recommendations of names to fill up judgeships. Supreme Court Bar Association president, senior advocate Vikas Singh, urged the Court to issue contempt action to bring the government in line. He said the comments made by the government directly attacked the court's constitutional power of judicial review.

The Court said it cannot engage in ping-pong battle or blame game over Collegium's recommendations. "You are sending back names twice over, thrice over. How many times? That is, if you don't find a name palatable, you will not appoint. Once a name is reiterated by the Collegium, there is no other passage for you but to appoint the person as judge," Justice Kaul said.

Die is Cast

Linking the huge pendency of cases in courts to vacant posts of judges, Union Law Minister Kiren Rijiju, referring to the Supreme Court's Collegium system of appointments to the higher judiciary, told Rajya Sabha in its winter session that this issue will not be resolved until a new system of appointments is evolved.

Rijiju also said: "There is a feeling among people of India that the long vacations which the courts avail is not very convenient for justice-seekers and it is his obligation and duty to convey the message or sense of this House to the judiciary."

Rijiju's remarks in the House came days after he criticized the Collegium system as being 'opaque' and the Vice-President Dhankhar called the Supreme Court's 2015 judgment of striking down the National Judicial Appointments Commission Act a severe compromise of Parliamentary sovereignty and disregard of the mandate of the people.

Replying to a question by Congress MP Rajeev Shukla in the Rajya Sabha on the number of working days of courts, Rijiju said that the number of pending cases in the country was nearing five crore, having reached 4.90 crore. He said that there were many reasons for this, but the primary one was the appointment of judges and vacancies in the sanctioned strength.

Rijiju's written reply stated that the sanctioned strength of the Supreme Court, High Courts, district and subordinate courts was 25,011 and working strength was 19,192 as on 12th December, 2022. He said 46 judges had been appointed to the Supreme Court from 1st May, 2014 to 5th December, 2022. The reply stated that 69,598 cases were pending in the Supreme Court as on 1st December, 2022, as per the Court's own website, and 59.56 lakh cases were pending in High Courts.

"At this point, the government has limited powers to reduce vacancies. I do not want to comment much on the courts as it sometimes looks like the government is trying to interfere with the court's powers. If you look at the provisions of the Constitution, the process of appointments was the right of the government with the consultation of the court. This changed after 1993. We are giving our support to end pendency of cases, but till we do not set up a new system for appointments, questions on appointment of judges will keep being raised," he said.

Citing the National Judicial Appointments Commission Bill, 2014, Rijiju said that Parliament had unanimously passed the Bill, but it was struck down by the Supreme Court in 2015. He said that the current system of appointment of judges—the

Collegium system—did not reflect the feelings of the public and the House. He said that many retired judges, including the members of the Constitution Bench that struck down the NJAC, have since stated publicly that striking down a Bill passed by Parliament was not right.

In a written reply, Rijiju told the Rajya Sabha on 22nd December, 2022: "The government had sent suggestions for supplementing the Memorandum of Procedure (MoP) for appointment of judges to the High Courts and the Supreme Court. The MoP is a document which guides the appointment and transfer of judges in the higher judiciary."

The Law Minister made these remarks in response to a question by CPI(M) member John Brittas, who asked if the government was planning to reintroduce the National Judicial Appointments Commission (NJAC).

Rijiju said that the government had brought the Constitution (97th Amendment Act, 2014) and the NJAC Act on 13th April, 2015, to make the Collegium system of appointments of judges 'more broad-based, transparent, accountable and bring objectivity in the system.' However, both the Acts were challenged in the Supreme Court, which eventually declared both the laws unconstitutional and void on 16th October, 2015. On 8th December, 2022, in response to a written question by Brittas and leader of the Opposition in the Rajya Sabha, Mallikarjun Kharge, Rijiju said that there was no plan to bring back the NJAC with suitable modifications.

Apart from regularly targeting the judiciary, Rijiju told the Rajya Sabha recently that the issue of vacancies in the higher judiciary would linger till a new system of appointment was created.

Bid to Delegitimise Judiciary

Congress leader Sonia Gandhi on 21st December, 2022 said: "BJP is scheming to delegitimize the judiciary which is in line with its bid to undermine the institutions that stand in its way."

"Ministers and even a high constitutional authority have been enlisted to make speeches attacking the judiciary. It is an effort to reduce the standing of the judiciary in the public's eyes", she said.

Sonia Gandhi's criticism is the strongest from the Opposition on the issue that has been dubbed as BJP's bid to relitigate the judicial appointment process, which had appeared settled after the striking down of the NJAC.

Speaking in the Rajya Sabha, its Chairman Dhankhar said that the UPA Chairperson's statement was far distanced from his reflections as delegitimizing the judiciary was beyond his contemplation. The observations were severely inappropriate, indicating a lack of faith in democracy. He was reflecting to the statement made by Sonia Gandhi at the Congress Parliamentary Party meeting and quoted her statement: "A troubling new development is the calculated attempt underway to delegitimize the judiciary. Ministers and even a high constitutional authority have been enlisted to making speeches attacking the judiciary in various grounds."

Dhankhar read out a portion of his speech in the Rajya Sabha, in which he said: "In any democracy, Parliamentary sovereignty is inviolable. We all here are under oath to preserve it. The power of the Parliament of the day to act in exercise of its constituent power to amend by way of addition, variation or repeal, any provision of this Constitution in accordance with the provision is unqualified and supreme, not amenable to executive attention nor judicial intervention, except for the purpose of deciding any case involving a substantial question of law as to interpretation of the Constitution envisaged in Article 145(3) of the Constitution." He further said: "Parliamentary sovereignty is quintessential to democracy and is non-negotiable."

"Subscribing to this is not optional if democracy has to sustain and blossom. I had emphasized that democracy blossoms and flourishes when its three facets, the legislature, judiciary and executive, scrupulously adhere to their respective domains. The sublimity of the doctrine of separation of powers is realized when the legislature, judiciary and executive optimally function in tandem and togetherness, meticulously ensuring scrupulous adherence to respective jurisdictional domains. Further I had indicated that this House is eminently positioned to take affirmative steps to bring out congeniality amongst these wings of governance," he said.

No Previous Government Interfered with Judiciary

In a letter to Dhankhar, Congress General Secretary in-charge (communications) Jairam Ramesh alleged "that no previous government, since the introduction of the Collegium system, has interfered as excessively and thoroughly in the functioning of our judiciary. Mr. Chairman, you call upon us to avoid taking partisan stance on constitutional offices. We also point out that this entire debate was initiated entirely, and without provocation, by the Law Minister, adding that the argument that the judiciary cannot do more than interpret the laws was incorrect."

He further said: "The power of judicial review is part of the basic structure of our Constitution. It vests the courts with the authority to strike down legislation that is in violation of the Constitution or executive action that is simply mala-fide. It is precisely these checks and balances under the Constitution which are not being adhered to by the government that has resulted in the current state of unease."

In his letter, Jairam Ramesh pointedly asked Dhankhar if it was not a fact that despite the Collegium's recommendation, the government has delayed important judicial appointments on multiple occasions, knowing fully well that such delays are effectively a denial. Is it not a fact that this government attempted to amend the qualifications and manner of appointment to various judicial and Quasi-Judicial Tribunals, such as the NGT, and had those choices struck down by the Supreme Court?

Senior advocate at the Supreme Court, Dushyant Dave, in his write up in *The Indian Express* of 26th December, 2022, says: "The controversy over the appointment of judges to the Supreme Court and High Courts is not a straight forward as it appears. The executive wants to take complete control of the last bastion of democracy, the judiciary."

"The judiciary under recent Chief Justices has shown remarkable resilience and is pushing back. Questions are being asked by judges on sensitive matters to sub-serve public purpose. Judgments and orders have been passed to protect the civil liberties and fundamental rights of citizens."

"Thus, the not-so veiled attacks by the Law Minister, followed by the Vice-President, himself a respected lawyer, are calculated to send a chilling message to the judiciary: Fall in line or we will take away your powers to appoint and transfer judges. They need to be reminded of Articles 141 and 144 of the Constitution, which make Supreme Court judgments the law of the land."

"...I am convinced that if the executive were to start appointing judges to the higher judiciary, they will end up making disastrous and subjective appointments as being done for other constitutional offices. And that will be the death knell of democracy in India. Citizens will be deprived of their fundamental rights and civil liberties will be jeopardized."

"Rule of law and an independent judiciary are basic features of our Constitution. The two are deeply connected. Constitution framers were quite clear in their resolve that 'No executive should be able to have any influence upon Judges.' But, as Dr. Ambedkar had feared, 'I feel, however, good a constitution may be, it is sure to turn out bad because those who are called to work it, happens to be a bad lot'."

In conclusion of his write up Dushyant Dave says: "Let us hope the executive does not prove Dr. Ambedkar wrong. If it does, let us pray that the judiciary will step in to defend the Constitution in letter and spirit."

History may be Repeated

Kumaramangalam, a senior member of the Bar, boldly and categorically asserted in the Lok Sabha in the year 1973 that it was the government's right and privilege under the Constitution to select for the office of the Chief Justice a person who is, in his words, "Forward-looking" and not "Backward-looking", a person who according to him, shares the philosophy of the government and not any other philosophy.

Let us understand what his statement means, in effect and in practice. It means that when it comes to the appointment of the Chief Justice, the government will select a person who shall uphold the government's view of the Constitution, not the philosophy in fact underlying the Constitution, but the government's understanding of that philosophy. We all know that when a judge takes office, including the Chief Justice, he takes an oath of office and his oath pledges him, among other things, to decide cases in accordance with the Constitution. Now, if he looks at the Constitution and feels that its interpretation is, according to him, in a particular direction or it has a particular meaning, he has not to give that direction or meaning to the words of the Constitution, contrary to his own understanding, the philosophy of the government.

Let us analyse what the philosophy of the government would, in ordinary practice, mean. The philosophy of the government would mean the philosophy of the ruling party. Today, it may be the philosophy of the ruling Congress, tomorrow it may be the philosophy of another party—it may be the Jan Sangh, it may be the Swatantra. Therefore, the judge or the Chief Justice has to keep track, when he is sitting on the Bench, and interpreting the Constitution, not of the language and the words of the Constitution, but of the philosophy of the ruling party which may change from time to time. So, you have not to have an impartial Chief Justice but a judge or Chief Justice who will bear in mind what, in effect, the government thinks the Constitution means. If the judge thinks the contrary, he is not sufficiently "forward-looking"; and must be discarded for the office of the Chief Justice.

The doctrine laid down so openly by Kumaramangalam is clearly a doctrine subversive of the independence of the judiciary (*A Judiciary Made to Measure,* M.C. Setalvad, ed. N.A. Palkhivala, published by M.R. Pai, pp. 7-8).

Judiciary Made to Measure

The judgment in the Fundamental Rights case (*Kesavananda Bharati* vs. *State of Kerala*, A.I.R. 1973, S.C. 1461) was delivered on 24th April, 1973. Chief Justice S.M. Sikri retired the next day. The unbroken convention of the Supreme Court's existence had been to make the senior most judge succeed to the office of the Chief Justice. But, on 25th April, 1973, the three senior most judges of the Supreme Court—J.M. Shelat, K.S. Hegde and A.N. Grover who had decided the monumental case against the government—were superseded, with the result that they immediately resigned. It was the saddest day in the history of our free institutions.

During the hearing of the Fundamental Rights case, the Attorney General appearing for the Union of India and the counsel for some States expressly referred in open court, both orally and in writing, to the alternative of "political action" if Supreme Court's rulings did not find favour with the government.

The passing over of the three senior most judges raised issues that extended far beyond considerations of injustice merely to three individuals. It evoked a sharp reaction from the Bar which was as unprecedented as the government's action itself. With the exceptions of lawyers who were involved in politics, there was a near unanimous vote at the meetings of the various Bar Associations in Delhi and in various States, strongly condemning the government.

For the government to rely upon the 14th Report of the Law Commission (1958) amounted to compounding the public wrong with public deception. That very Report totally destroyed the government's case. The Chairman of the Law Commission, and other three signatories to the Report—M.C. Chagla, S.M. Sikri and N.A. Palkivala—made public statements condemning the government's decision. If the government had followed the recommendations in the Report, the three judges would not have been superseded.

Law Commission's Report

The following quotations from the Law Commission's Report leave no doubt as to the role of courageous protector of the citizen's rights, which the Law Commission expected the Supreme Court to play in our nascent democracy:

"It (Supreme Court) was called upon to stand as a protector of the fundamental rights of the citizen against executive and legislative action. The importance of the court as the upholder of the rule of law and as the bulwark of the citizen's rights in a democratic Constitution containing a bill of rights was emphasized by Chief Justice Kania at its inaugural sitting. The court must consist of judges who taken as a body are, as lawyers and men of vision, superior to the body of judges manning the High Courts. Such a result can be achieved and maintained only by the exercise of courage, vision and imagination in the selection of judges made with an eye solely to their efficiency and capacity."

Justice Shelat, Hegde and Grover distinguished themselves as upholder of the rule of law and of the citizen's rights; and they fully justified their appointment to the Supreme Court if one has regard "solely to their efficiency and capacity," in the words of the Law Commission.

The Law Commission's recommendation is:

"For the performance of the duties of Chief Justice of India, there is needed, not only a judge of ability and experience, but also of competent administrator capable of handling complex matters that may arise from time to time, a shrewd judge of men and personalities and, above all, a person of sturdy independence and towering personality who would, on the occasion arising, be a watch-dog of the independence of judiciary. In our view, therefore, the filling of a vacancy in the office of Chief Justice of India should be approached with paramount regard to the considerations we have mentioned above. It may be that the senior most puisne judge fulfils these requirements. If so, there could be no objection to his being appointed to fill the vacancy."

If the qualities needed, according to the Law Commission, in the Chief Justice were to be the sole criteria, there was the strongest possible case for not superseding the three judges.

Further, until 1973, there had been an unbroken convention of appointing the senior most judge of the Supreme Court as the Chief Justice. The Law Commission's Report makes it clear that the convention of appointing the Chief Justice of India regardless of seniority should first be laid down before any such appointment is made, whereas in the present case the appointment was made without any such new convention being first established. The exact words of the Law Commission are:

"It is, therefore, necessary to set a healthy convention that appointment to the office of the Chief Justice rests on special considerations and does not as a matter of course go to the senior most puisne judge. If such a convention were established, it would be no reflection on the senior most puisne judge if he be not appointed to the office of the Chief Justice."

Judges Suitable from Government's Point of View

At first, government led the people to believe that it had merely implemented the recommendation of the Law Commission. Later, on 2nd May, 1973, a Cabinet Minister very frankly admitted in Parliament, without mincing words, that the government was motivated by the consideration that the Chief Justice would be one who would "help" the government and whose political philosophy would be "the most suitable" from the executive's point of view.

First, let us consider the plea that the Chief Justice must be one whose philosophy or outlook is "the most suitable" from the government's viewpoint. This means that the Chief Justice should be selected on the basis of his suitability, not from the viewpoint of the Constitution and the Constitutional duties and functions he has to discharge, but from the angle of the executive. The Government of India is the single largest litigant in the whole country. It has more cases pending against it than any other party or authority. If this litigant can select judges suitable to itself, that would be the end of the judicial system which has still now served so admirably as the citizen's palladium against unconstitutional laws and arbitrary executive action.

Secondly, the Minister suggested that the government is entitled to select judges having regard to their philosophy. Every government naturally thinks that it is forward-looking and its opponents are backward-looking; and the Minister said that in appointing the Chief Justice, "we are entitled to come to the conclusion that the philosophy of this judge is forward-looking and of that judge backward-looking and to decide that we will take the forward-looking judge and not the backward-looking judge." In other words, what the government really wants is that the Chief Justice should subscribe, not to the philosophy of the Constitution but to the philosophy of the ruling party. This attitude towards the judiciary is typical of communist countries where the judiciary has to be committed to the philosophy of one and only party permitted to function and where the judiciary exists to "help" the government in implementing its programmes. It is also the philosophy of dictators and absolute monarchs like the old English Kings who established the Star Chamber Court which was expected to "help" the king, be "suitable" to his needs and share his "philosophy" and "outlook" as regards the unfettered powers of the monarch. Charles I removed three judges, Charles II got rid of ten, and James II dismissed thirteen during his three years on the throne. In the words of Lord Denning, "Those were the evil days when the judges took their orders from the executive. But, the people of England overthrew the government which assailed their liberties, and passed statutes which gave the writ its present power. Never, therefore, have the judges taken their orders from anyone."

Experience should teach us that while it is desirable to inject justice into politics, it is disastrous to inject politics into justice. Consider how untenable is the government's claim that it is entitled to have Supreme Court judges who subscribe to the ruling party's philosophy. Suppose a party is in power whose philosophy differs from that of the Constitution, is the judge to uphold the philosophy of the Constitution or that of the ruling party? The Constitution requires the Supreme Court judge to take an oath that "he will bear true faith and allegiance to the Constitution…and…will uphold the Constitution and the laws." One of the hallmarks of our Constitution is the great importance attached to human freedoms. Some powerful political parties in India have no regard for the citizen's rights and civil liberties; and if the judge has to share philosophy of such a ruling party, he would necessarily be false to his oath. The President of India would be equally false to his oath in appointing such a judge, since the President has to take an oath that he will to the best of his ability, "preserve, protect and defend the Constitution".

Again, our Constitution believes in religious freedom. Assume the party in power at a future date does not believe in religion or in religious freedom, should the judgments of the Supreme Court be in conformity with such "forward-looking" view?

After a Supreme Court judge is appointed, a new political party may come into power at the centre whose philosophy and outlook may be quite different from those of the outgoing government. Should the judge change his colours like a chameleon? Further, different political parties may be in power in different States. Chaotic conditions would prevail if the judges of different High Courts are equally expected to be "suitable" to the different parties in power in the States.

A committed judge is a contradiction in terms. You cannot have a committed judge any more than you can have boiling ice-cream. Either a man is committed or he is a judge in the true sense; he cannot be both. A man is wholly unfit to be a judge and is necessarily false to his oath unless his exclusive commitment is to the Constitution regardless of the outlook and changing fortunes of political parties.

Thirdly, the Minister refers to the "prerogative" of the government to appoint that judge to be the Chief Justice whom he regards as the most suitable. "Prerogative" is an archaic concept which belonged to the feudal age. Kings and dictators, fascists and totalitarian rulers, have prerogatives, but not ministers who are merely the democratically elected servants of the people. Our Constitution recognizes no prerogative whatsoever; it recognizes merely rights, duties and discretions. The difference between "prerogative" and "discretion" is clear. A person who has a prerogative can act arbitrarily or irrationally and yet his decision must be treated as legal and valid. On the other hand, if a person has the discretion, and not the prerogative, to make a decision, the discretion can only be exercised fairly and reasonably; otherwise, his act is void on the ground that there is no valid exercise of discretion in the eye of the law. The President of India has only a discretion in appointing the Chief Justice and other judges; and neither the President nor the Cabinet has any prerogative in the matter.

Fourthly, the Minister argued that the government wants a Chief Justice who "is able to recognize that Parliament is sovereign; that Parliament's powers in relation to the future are sovereign powers." This ability required of the Chief Justice makes a mockery of the Constitution. Parliament has no unfettered sovereignty. The Constitution is supreme over Parliament; and not Parliament over the Constitution. The fundamental rights which are the basic human freedoms are fetters on Parliament's powers. The Supreme Court had held by majority in the Fundamental Rights case (*Kesavananda Bharati* vs. *State of Kerala*, A.I.R. 1973, S.C. 1461) that Parliament has no power to amend the Constitution in such a way as to alter the basic structure or framework of the Constitution; and the government's arguments to the contrary were expressly rejected. The Minister's statement amounted to a refusal to accept the law as laid down by the Supreme Court.

It would be a work of supererogation to spell out the frightening consequences for the entire country if the executive is permitted to appoint judges who share the philosophy of the ruling party. Every judge of the Supreme Court could then be selected on such reprehensible considerations.

If the Salt Lost Savour

So long as there is a judiciary marked by rugged independence, the citizen's civil liberties are safe even in the absence of any cast-iron guarantees in the Constitution. But, once the judiciary becomes subservient to the executive and to the ruling party's philosophy, no enumeration of fundamental rights in the Constitution can be of any avail to the citizen, because the Courts of Justice would then be replaced by the government's courts. "If the salt has lost its savour, wherewith shall it be salted?" In the last analysis, the final guarantee of the citizen's rights is the personality and intellectual integrity of our Supreme Court (*Our Constitution Defaced and Defiled,* N.A. Palkhivala, Macmillan, pp. 93-106).

Looking to the statements of Law Minister Kiren Rijiju and the maiden speech of Vice-President Dhankhar in the Rajya Sabha, it seems to be as clear as day light that the Modi government is set to replace the Collegium system. A layman like me thinks that the government should take no decision in haste. It should think dispassionately and find solution which will be acceptable to both judiciary and the government in the interest of justice to people at large. This could be done by removing flaws in the Collegium system or by removing the defects in the National Judicial Appointments Commission as pointed out by legal luminaries. In any way it should be borne in mind that the Supreme Court is not required to find faults and strike the Bill again.

9
ED and CBI Raids

Prime Minister Narendra Modi, in his address on 15th August, 2022, from the rampart of Red Fort reiterated his vow to weed out corruption from India, in spite of the history and rampant corruption as given in Chapter 6. His actions in this direction by launching ED raids speak for his pious intentions.

ED Team's Search

The Enforcement Directorate (ED) searched 40 locations in four States in connection with the alleged irregularities in the Delhi excise policy case. The premises linked to the beneficiaries, distributors and their associates in and around Delhi and Andhra Pradesh, Karnataka and Tamil Nadu were covered. The officials searched some places purportedly related to YSR Congress Party MP M. Srinivasulu Reddy, including one at Nellore in Andhra Pradesh. The agency also recorded the statement of Delhi Government Minister Satyendra Jain.

On 6th September, 2022, the ED searched over two dozen locations in Delhi, Gurgaon, Faridabad, Uttar Pradesh, Punjab and Mumbai. The money laundering probe is based on an FIR registered by the CBI on 17th August, 2022, against Manish Sisodia and others.

Amongst the accused, public servants named in the FIR are then Excise Commissioner, Arva Gopi Krishna, Deputy Commissioner, Arvind Tiwari and Assistant Commissioner, Pankaj Bhatnagar. The others are Vijay Nair, former Chief Executive Officer of Mumbai-based entertainment and event management company named Only Much Louder; Manoj Rai, former employee of Pernod Ricard; Amandeep Dhal, Director of Indospirit Group; Buddy Retail and its Directors Amit Arora and

Dinesh Arora; and Mahadev Liquors, its authorized signatory Sunny Marwah, Arun Ramchandra Pillai and Arjun Paney.

The agency has alleged that undue favors were extended to the license holders—license fee was waved or reduced, and L-1 license was extended without the competent authority's approval. The illegal gains were diverted to the accused public servants and false entries were made by the private parties concerned in their books of accounts to hide the money trail (*The Hindu*, 17th September, 2022).

Supplementary Chargesheet against Raut

The ED filed supplementary chargesheet against Shiv Sena MP Sanjay Raut in a money laundering case linked to a redevelopment project in sub-urban Mumbai. The ED also opposed bail to Raut stating that he had played a major role in the offence through his 'proxy and confidant' co-accused Pravin Raut and had been 'operating behind the curtain' to avoid the trail.

The ED claims that Raut utilized proceeds of crime to the tune of ₹ 3.27 crore received from Pravin from the sale of the Floor Space Index (FSI) of the land where the project was to be developed in Patra Chawl in Goregaon. The ED claimed that the amount was utilized in creating assets apart from spending the proceeds of crime in pleasure trips and other expenses.

Among the transactions flagged by the ED was the amount of ₹ 37.50 lakh received by Raut and his wife Varsha, from Prathamesh Developer, a business entity of Pravin. The ED also claimed that while Raut had invested ₹ 29.50 lakh, he received ₹ 37.50 in return within a month of the investment.

"The subject money was also utilized for the purchase of flat. The manner of receipt of money clearly indicated that the claim of the applicant is false. Nowhere such huge money gets returned on cancellation of booking of land. In fact, as per practice, normally the land seller cuts a certain percentage of the booking money and returns the amount whereas in the present case, the land owner gave ₹ 37.50 lakh over and above the invested amount of ₹ 29.50 lakh," the ED said.

The case relates to a cheating case filed in connection with the redevelopment of Patra Chawl. While 672 tenants were to be rehabilitated through the project, they were, instead, allegedly cheated by directors of infrastructure company HDIL and a company named Guru Ashish Constructions of which Pravin was the director. While the proceeds of crime from this sale is alleged to be ₹ 1,039.79 crore, part of this was received in the bank account of HDIL and Pravin received ₹ 112 crore, the agency said. The ED has alleged that the transfer of money from Pravin to Raut was from the proceeds of crime. It said that as developers, the accused did not have the right to sell the FSI of the land but it was done and never utilized for completion of the project. The ED had previously filed a chargesheet against Pravin and others.

Chinese Loan Apps Case

Continuing its investigation into loan and betting apps run by Chinese companies, the ED carried out search operations at six business and residential premises in Delhi, Ghaziabad, Mumbai, Lucknow and Gaya. It also froze ₹ 46 crore in accounts of Paytm, Razorpay, Cashfree and Pune-based Easebuzz Private Limited in connection with its money laundering probe into the App-based token named HPZ.

The ED said that searches were also conducted at 16 other locations of banks, payment gateway branches and offices in Delhi, Gurgaon, Mumbai, Pune, Chennai, Hyderabad, Jaipur, Jodhpur and Bangaluru.

The ED case is based on an FIR registered on 8th November, 2021, by the cyber-crime police station at Kohima, Nagaland. "Various incriminating documents had been recovered and seized. Huge balance was found to be maintained in the virtual accounts of the involved entries with payment aggregators. ₹ 33.36 crore was found with Easebuzz Private Limited, Pune; ₹ 8.21 crore with Razorpay Software Private Limited, Bangaluru; and ₹ 1.28 crore with Cashfree Payments India Limited, New Delhi. Total amount of around ₹ 46.67 crore was detected and frozen in various bank accounts and virtual accounts," as ED statement said.

According to ED, the HPZ Token was an app-based token that promised users of large gains against investments in mining machines for crypto currencies. The modus-operandi was to first lure the victims to invest in the company on the pretext of doubling their investment (*The Indian Express*, 18th September, 2022).

There have been ED raids at other places including a place like Jalna in Maharashtra where crores of rupees and kilos of gold have been seized.

On the spade of ED raids, the opposition parties are making hue and cry that raids are to crush the opposition. But, to me the cry has no meaning when the tons of money and kilos of gold are being unearthed. According to me this is the first round of ED raids and Modi will commence second round in 2023 as the elections draw near against his own party men, which will turn the wind in his favour to win 2024 general elections.

Opposition Leaders in CBI Net

In the past 18 years, spanning the governments of rival Congress and BJP, of the close to 200 key politicians whom the CBI has booked, arrested, raided or questioned, over 80% have been from the ranks of the Opposition. A trend that has got sharply more pronounced since the NDA took charge in 2014—reveals an investigation by *The Indian Express* of court records, official documents, agency statements and reports.

Under the Congress-UPA's 10 years at the helm (2004-14), at least 72 political leaders came under the CBI scanner and 43 of them (60%) were from the Opposition. Under the BJP-led NDA-II's eight years in power so far, even the Opposition's political footprints has shrunk, at least 124 prominent leaders have faced CBI probes and as many as 118 of them are from the Opposition that is 95%.

And just as in the UPA, when a leader switches sides, the CBI case against him/her is relegated to the back-burner. The entire list of 72 from the UPA and 124 leaders from the NDA in the CBI net has been compiled and published on Indianexpress.com. Leaders have been listed under the political parties to which they belonged, along with the posts they held, when the CBI initiated action against them.

The CBI did not respond to a question from *The Indian Express* on this trend but an agency official called it merely coincidence and denied that Opposition leaders are targeted. However, key patterns in the list are telling.

- With a number of scams clouding the UPA rule, from the 2-G spectrum case to the Commonwealth Games and coal block allotment cases, of the 72 key leaders the CBI probed from 2004 to 2014, 29 were either from the Congress or its allies such as DMK.
- Under the NDA-II, the tilt is overwhelmingly against non-NDA parties with just six leaders of note from the BJP facing the CBI probe.
- Of the 43 Opposition leaders under probe by the CBI during the UPA, the BJP had the largest share with 12 of its leaders being questioned, raided or arrested, including Union Home Minister Amit Shah, then a Gujarat Minister, who was arrested by the agency in connection with the alleged encounter killing of Sohrabuddin Sheikh. Other key NDA leaders under probe included former Karnataka Chief Minister B.S. Yediyurappa, Bellary mining baron G. Janardhan Reddy and former Defence Minister George Fernandes. The CBI continued its probe against Pramod Mahajan even after his death, when it named him in a chargesheet related to the 2-G spectrum allocation probe in 2012.
- Under the NDA-II beginning 2014, CBI probe against political leaders gained momentum. Of the 118 key Opposition politicians under probe, on the top of the list is TMC (30) and Congress (26). Besides, the CBI probed close relatives of key Congress politicians such as party President, Sonia Gandhi; Rajasthan Chief Minister, Ashok Gehlot; former Madhya Pradesh Chief Minister, Kamal Nath and former Punjab Chief Minister, Captain Amarinder Singh.

- For the TMC, the Saradha Chit Fund case and the Narada sting operation case have made it the party having the largest number of key political leaders under the CBI scanner. For over two months, TMC Minister Partha Chatterjee was under CBI arrest for his alleged involvement in the "school jobs for cash" case. And party leader Anubrata Mondal was held for his alleged role in a cross-border cattle-smuggling racket.
- After these two parties, the highest number of non-NDA politicians under probe are from the RJD and BJD, 10 each. Incidentally, these two Opposition parties are in power in Bihar and Odisha, respectively.
- The Opposition's party wise break-up of prominent leaders is: TMC (30), Congress (26), RJD (10), BJD (10), YSRCP (6), BSP (5), TDP (5), AAP (4), SP (4), AIADMK (4), CPM (4), NCP (2), DMK (2), PDP (1), TRS (1), and independent (1).

Beyond these numbers, the timing of the CBI raids under the UPA and the NDA-II have been repeatedly raised by Opposition leaders, both inside Parliament and in protests outside.

In 2013, two days after DMK walked out of the UPA, the CBI raided party leader and current Tamil Nadu Chief Minister, M.K. Stalin's house in Chennai in a case related to the import of luxury cars. According to the officials at that time, the Department of Revenue Intelligence (DRI) had provided information about the case involving 33 cars to CBI a month before the raid, but the agency registered a case only after the DMK broke its alliance with the Congress. Similarly, the CBI raided multiple premises associated with RJD leaders, including one allegedly linked to Bihar's current Deputy Chief Minister Tejashwi Yadav, on the day the new JD (U)-RJD government was facing the trust vote in the Assembly. Days earlier, the JD(U) had snapped ties with the NDA.

Then again, during the UPA regime, the ruling coalition was accused of "misusing" the CBI to bully potential allies. In 2007, a Preliminary Enquiry (PE) was raised against SP leader and former Uttar Pradesh Chief Minister, Mulayam Singh Yadav and his family in a case of alleged disproportionate assets. A year later, the SP helped the coalition survive after the Left pulled out of the government on the US nuclear deal. The disproportionate assets case was closed in 2013. Similarly, the CBI began an investigation into alleged corruption cases against Y.S. Rajasekhara Reddy's government in Andhra Pradesh after his son Y.S. Jagan Reddy rebelled against the Congress following his father's death in 2009.

Under NDA-II, the CBI's action against the AAP, which came to power in Delhi in 2015, has drawn criticism. In 2015, the agency raided the offices of Chief Minister Arvind Kejriwal's principal secretary Rajendra Kumar in a case of corruption. Ahead of the Punjab polls in 2017, the agency initiated multiple probes against AAP leaders, including Deputy Chief Minister Manish Sisodia and Health Minister Satyendar Jain. During the Gujarat elections, the CBI booked Sisodia and raided his residence in connection with a case of alleged corruption related to Delhi's liquor policy.

Under NDA-II, the agency has also been accused of going soft on past cases against senior leaders of the ruling dispensation. The CBI did not file an appeal against the discharge of Amit Shah by a special court in Sohrabuddin Sheikh case. While the agency raided premises associated with the then Congress leader from Assam, Himanta Biswa Sarma, in the Saradha chit fund scam and questioned him, there was no action against Sarma after he joined the BJP. Sarma is now Chief Minister of Assam and a key leader for BJP in the North East. Similarly, the then TMC leaders Suvendu Adhikari and Mukul Roy had been put under scanner by the CBI and ED in the Narada Sting Operation case; Adhikari and Roy joined the BJP before the West Bengal polls and the cases against them have not seen any significant development.

The ED was also the first agency to conduct searches on the premises of the then TDP MP Y.S. Chowdhary and attach his assets in early 2019. Months later Chowdhary joined the BJP. The ED, however, chargesheeted him later.

The ED had also been at the forefront in building cases against the Gandhi family. With Rahul Gandhi and former

Congress president Sonia Gandhi facing a probe in the National Herald case after a Delhi court took cognizance of a private complaint by BJP's Subramanian Swamy. The agency was the first to raid a company associated with Sonia Gandhi's son-in-law Robert Vadra questioning him multiple times in a money laundering case.

Besides, the agency had pursued former Finance Minister P. Chidambaram and his son Karti in connection with the Aircel Maxis case. Its probe had resulted into two more cases—the INX Media case and the bribes for visa case—against Chidambarams.

Kerala CPI (M) leader Kodiyeri Balakrishnan's son is also facing an ED probe. In July 2020, as the Ashok Gehlot government in Rajasthan faced a revolt by the deputy chief minister Sachin Pilot, the ED raided premises associated with Gehlot's brother, Agrasen, in connection with a probe into alleged diversion of fertilizers in 2007-09.

At the same time, records also show that the ED booked BJP leader Sudhanshu Mittal's brother-in-law Lalit Goyal of the IREO Group for allegedly defrauding investors and home buyers. The other senior Opposition politicians facing probe under NDA-II include D. Shivkumar from Karnataka, former Haryana CM Bhupender Singh Hooda, and the late Rajya Sabha MP Ahmed Patel, who was Sonia's aide.

The list also includes over a dozen prominent TMC politicians, including West Bengal Chief Minister, Mamata Banerjee's nephew Abhishek Banerjee. Also, among the notable political figures are NCP leaders Sharad Pawar, Ajit Pawar, Anil Deshmukh, Nawab Malik and Praful Patel; Shiv Sena's Anil Parab; as well as the former Bihar Chief Minister Lalu Prasad and his family.

The agency is also probing five BJP politicians, including Karnataka mining baron Gali Janardhana Reddy and former Rajasthan chief minister Vasundhara Raje Scindia's son Dushyant Singh.

During the UPA regime, prominent BJP politicians under the ED scanner included Laxmikant Sharma (Vyapam case) and former Karnataka Chief Minister B.S. Yediyurappa.

The list also includes TMC politicians Sudip Bandyopadhyay (Rose Valley Chit Fund case) and Kunal Ghose, Srinjoy Bose, Madan Mitra, Arpita Ghosh, Mukul Roy and Tapas Paul (Shardha case).

Under the UPA, the ED moved against Congress politicians such as former Maharashtra Chief Minister, Ashok Chavan (Adarsha Housing case), Suresh Kalmadi (Commonwealth Games case), and Naveen Jindal (coal blocks case). The agency also took action against UPA alley DMK's A. Raja and Kanimozhi (2G case), and Dayanidhi Maran (Aircel-Maxis case).

When asked by *The Indian Express* to explain the skew against the Opposition, the ED declined to comment. But, an agency official said: "The ED is the last agency you can accuse of political bias as it cannot register cases on its own. Only after a politician is booked by a state police or any central agency can the ED register a case of money laundering. We are also probing many BJP politicians. A fresh case against Gali Janardhan Reddy was initiated after the Modi Government came to power."

The official further said: "Also, we register cases after proper scrutiny. All our chargesheets are being taken cognizance of by the courts. The accused are unable to secure bail because courts are not convinced of their innocence."

The official added: "Of the 21 cases where trial has been completed, we have secured conviction in 18, 30 accused stand convicted and sentenced. Our conviction rate is higher than that of the CBI" (*The Indian Express*, 21st September, 2022).

However, *The Indian Express* in its editorial of 20th August, 2022, said: "Fighting corruption is key to cleaning up politics but the way agencies target mainly the Opposition, even Centre is in the dock. The Central Investigative agencies under the BJP-led government are paying excessive and excessively focused attention to the BJP's political rivals. Even a cursory look throws up a clear pattern that is worrying in a system in which the independence of these agencies is—or should be—a central tenet. There is a sharp jump in the number of political leaders against whom the ED has taken action in the NDA years compared to those in the tenure of the UPA, and within this, Opposition politicians have been targeted overwhelmingly disproportionately."

"The cases are piling up against non-BJP politicians and all the incriminating images of stashes of cash found in addresses linked to TMC minister Partha Chatterjee, now in custody, cannot counter the growing impression of a government aggressively (mis)using all it came to settle political scores. It is not as if other governments have not made central agencies dance to a political tune—the CBI was called the Congress Bureau of Investigation and it was also in the tenure of Congress-led UPA that the apex court famously described it as a 'caged parrot'. But, the gloves seem to have come off much more, the political calculation seems far more bare-knuckled now. Both, the frequency with which the agencies are wielded against political opponents, and the scale of these operations, have shown a quantum leap under the BJP-led NDA. And in some cases, when the politician has switched sides, the agencies have turned forgiving overnight."

10
Dynasty and Family Rule in Congress

Narendra Modi has been speaking of dynasty and family rule with contempt after his becoming prime minister. There are various versions about as to who after Jawaharlal Nehru.

Nehru himself was quite often asked to name his successor. His reply was: "This business of picking an individual successor is something I find quite alien to my way of thinking. I am not going to start a dynasty. I am not capable of ruling from the grave. How terrible it would be if, I after all I had said about the process of democratic government, were to attempt to handpick a successor. The best I can do for India is to help our people as a whole to generate new leadership as it may be needed."

Mark Tully and Zareer Masani's Version

Mark Tully and Zareer Masani, in their book, *From Raj to Rajiv: Forty Years of Indian Independence*, wrote: "Motilal Nehru had his differences with Mahatma Gandhi, but one thing they agreed upon was that the future of Congress lay with Motilal's radical young son, Jawaharlal. It was as a result of the joint canvassing that Jawaharlal succeeded his father as President of Congress in 1930. From then onwards, Jawaharlal Nehru, remained loyal to Mahatma and Gandhi in turn, ensured that Nehru became India's first prime minister."

"Even so, the two men did have a serious disagreement over the future of Congress. The Mahatma saw it as an independence movement which should be disbanded after it had achieved its aim. But Nehru insisted that Congress was the only institution with the deep roots in the villages which were essential if democracy was to survive and flower. It is those very roots which have dried up; and they have dried up because the Nehru dynasty has become like a great banyan tree, in the shade of which nothing grows."

"Nehru's later years were dominated by the question, 'After Nehru who'? One of the candidates on everyone's short-list was his daughter Indira Gandhi. But was it really the intention of Nehru to found dynasty? Morarji Desai believed it was. Shortly before Nehru died, he introduced Kamraj Plan. It required Morarji and some other senior ministers to leave their government posts and dedicate themselves to party work. Morarji Desai maintained that the real aim of Kamraj Plan was to get rid of him and clear the road to power for Indira Gandhi."

Durga Das's Version

Durga Das, in his book, *India from Curzon to Nehru and After*, gives his version as follows: "Nehru had his own plans for his daughter. That was the time when people at home and abroad had started asking: 'After Nehru, who?' All manner of guesses were being made. However, few realized then that Nehru was, building up Indu, as he affectionately called her, to carry forward the Nehru legend for the third successive generation."

Durga Das says: "In fact, I disclosed Nehru's succession plan in my weekly Diary in the *Hindustan Times* as early as 18th July, 1957. I wrote: 'It is wrong to suggest that Mr. Nehru is trying to build Mr. Menon, or anyone else, as his successor. If Mr. Nehru is consciously building up anyone, he is building up his daughter'.

Before writing my column, I checked my impression with Abul Kalam Azad the previous Sunday. To my surprise, he had independently reached the same conclusion."

Durga Das further says: "Nehru did not relish my comment and sent for me. He said that Tandon as Congress President had made Patel's daughter, Maniben, a member of the Working Committee but I had nothing to say about it. I replied that Maniben had been an active Congress worker since 1920, when she commanded the women's corps at Ahmedabad session of the

Congress. She had gone through the mill, whereas Indira had been given place in the High Command without any experience of the organization. Nehru said Indira had refused a ticket for Parliament. We, however, parted smiling as I said that the publicity, she has received through my column would stand her in good stead for a public career."

Durga Das says: "Nehru was upset by the publication about the paragraph on succession. He again sent for me and enquired my basis for writing it. I recalled the previous talk I had with him and said this impression was shared by those who were in very close contact with him. Nehru said my comment might hurt his daughter. But I again replied that this might, on the contrary, prove useful as a seed sown in the popular mind. I also pointed out that Nehru might find one day that I had unconsciously done his daughter a good turn. This made him relax. I did not tell him that the paragraph was based on the impression given me by Azad and Pant, his closest associates."

A year later U.N. Dhebar resigned from Congress Presidentship after the Nagpur Session and Indira succeeded him, to the great astonishment of all after the intense drama behind the scenes.

In this connection, Durga Das writes: "But, thereby, hangs another story, told to me by those present and confirmed by Pant, Kamraj and others. All the leaders present had agreed that S. Nijalingappa be appointed as president. At various functions held in connection with the Session, Nijalingappa was thereafter the centre of attention, as the delegates vied with one another to felicitate him. A large crowd even collected at the station to give him a hearty send-off when he left for Bangalore. The same evening, Dhebar called an unscheduled meeting of the Working Committee. When it met, Kamraj asked what it was about. Dhebar replied that it was about the next president. Kamraj said: 'But the matter has been settled.' Thereupon Lal Bahadur Shastri quietly suggested that Indira might be asked to become president.

Pant, unaware of the background moves, was surprised by Shastri's proposal and said: 'But Indiraji is not keeping good health. She must first....' Before he could complete the sentence,

Nehru agitatedly interrupted to say: 'There is nothing wrong with Indu's health. She will feel better once she has work to herself busy.' That ended the argument."

Even before Indira became Congress President, Nehru started building her up as a public personality. Whenever he invited a distinguished Indian or visitor from abroad to lunch or dine with him, he would tell Indira to invite such guests to an entertainment of her own. Thus, Nehru had a formal luncheon for the Nelson Rockefeller and Eleanor Roosevelt, Indira played host to them at an informal coffee party. The aim of this policy was twofold: to give Indira the confidence she lacked in meeting outsiders and to establish her as a hostess in her own right.

When Indira became Congress President in 1959, Nehru meticulously planned her tours and ensured they were rewarding and successful. Later, under his patient and watchful guidance Indira grew into an important figure on the national scene, particularly after the Chinese attack, when he appointed her the Chairman of the Citizens' Central Council.

Nehru realized that the task of building up Indira politically could not be completed in his lifetime. Therefore, he wanted a successor whom he trusted and who would treat Indira well. Shastri fitted the role eminently by his general conduct and his attitude towards Indira. A person very close to Nehru at the time told Durga Das: 'that is why he brought in the Kamraj Plan and later built-up Shastri'.

When Shastri died, the struggle for succession, averted in 1964 by Kamraj's consensus formula, was not to be similarly warded off. Morarji Desai was determined to resist all attempts to get him to withdraw from a contest. The Congress president flew to Delhi from Madras with Indira Gandhi's name in his pocket; he preferred her to Desai. Indira's willingness to contest was hedged in by reservations in the early stages. But, as the other likely candidates faded into the background, she was not averse to a trial of strength. To have Kamraj on her side was a decisive advantage and when a majority of chief ministers entered the list in her favor everything was over except the counting of votes.

Morarji Desai's Version

Morarji Desai, in his autobiography, *The Story of My Life*, writes: "When Lal Bahadur Shastri passed away, it became necessary to elect a new leader of the Congress Parliamentary Party. Shri Gulzarilal Nanda, who was No. 2 in the cabinet of Shri Lal Bahadur Shastri, was again sworn in as temporary Prime Minister and a meeting of the Party was called for electing a new leader."

"Shri Kamraj had got prejudiced against me in 1964 and his prejudice continued. He did all that he could to see that not I but Smt. Indira Gandhi was elected leader of the Congress Parliamentary Party. Shri Jagjivan Ram initially supported me, but Shri Kamraj won him over by promising him a ministership in the new cabinet. Shri Jagjivan Ram met me and told me that I did not have the support of the majority, and that he would go with the majority. I did not try to persuade him to do otherwise; it would have been futile to do so. He had taken his decision. I told him that he was free to do what he considered proper."

"It is possible that if I had made bargains with some members, I could have won the election. Some colleagues even told me that it did not pay to be quite straight in politics and that one must resort to manoeuvres and intrigues. But I do not believe in such methods as I am convinced that if one wants to pursue truth one must observe it in every action of one's life. If one wants to pursue truth, one cannot resort to intrigues or manoeuvres. I had also no doubt that even if I had succeeded in winning the contest by such means and become the Prime Minister, I could not have served the country well and that if I could not serve the country properly it was better that I did not become the Prime Minister. It was not my ambition to be the Prime Minister, but I did not consider Indiraji to be suitable for this office and considered it my duty to oppose her in the election. Some of my colleagues also pressed me to contest. Indiraji won by very large majority. I got 169 votes; she got more than double that number. But most people felt that the number of votes I got constituted a moral success. I was not disappointed at being defeated as I knew from the very beginning that I would be."

Morarji Desai further writes: "Shri Kamraj and some of his friends were determined to prevent me from being elected to this office and they had put up Smt. Indira Gandhi only in order to defeat me. They probably thought that nobody except Smt. Indira Gandhi could contest against me successfully. They opposed me because they felt that I was a man with a very strong mind and would not allow myself to be controlled by anybody."

"Indiraji had publicly said that Shri Kamraj was her leader and was also the President of the Congress and that she would do whatever he asked. This is probably why Kamraj and his friends felt that Indiraji would act on their advice and their influence in the Congress would be maintained. Later events, however, have shown how they went wrong in their calculations. I had warned several colleagues about this in the very beginning."

Smt. Indira Gandhi succeeded Nehru as the third Prime Minister not immediately after him, but after Lal Bahadur Shastri.

The party's old guard who chose her as Shastri's successor did not think much of her qualities of leadership. They chose her because they believed that her lack of experience would make clay in their skill hands. At first, they seemed to be right, because the woman who later came to be described as the Empress of India made a very hesitant start. L.K. Jha, who continued as principal secretary under the new Prime Minister, remembers her early days in office as: "She was unsure of herself, because she had got elected with a very strong challenge from Morarji Desai, and a lot of party members would have preferred him. More important, her party itself was not in a tremendously strong position, and the Opposition was very, very strong. Then, she did not have enough self-confidence to be able to make an extempore speech; she had to prepare the text; and the Opposition knowing that she was speaking from a text, would try to interrupt her. But the speed with which she picked up was quite impressive. Once she began to gain in political strength, then all her other abilities blossomed forth."

Romesh Thapar, then a member of what became known as her kitchen-cabinet, says that the Congress split of 1970 brought out the best in her. Thapar says: "She was a transformed character, and I realized suddenly her basic strength; she knew every Congressman, his relationships, his compromises in the past. She knew exactly how to place them, how they would vote. She was human computer where the Congress party was concerned."

The two most controversial populist measures she took were to nationalize banks and to strip the Indian princes of the privileges and privy purses guaranteed to them by her father.

After introducing these measures and putting her opponents on the defensive, Smt. Indira Gandhi called on early general elections. Her main slogan was *Garibi Hatao,* and electorate responded to it by sending her opponents into the political wilderness and giving her a two-thirds majority in Parliament (*From Raj to Rajiv: Forty Years of Indian Independence,* Mark Tully and Zareer Masani, Universal Book Stall, New Delhi, pp. 107-09).

Smt. Indira Gandhi had a far greater reliance on image politics than any of her predecessors. The most alarming development was that the cult of personality began to take on an increasing dynastic flavor. A sure indication of this was the growing influence of her younger son, Sanjay, which led serious disagreements between Smt. Gandhi and her principal secretary, P.N. Haksar.

According to N.K. Seshan, who was the Prime Minister's private secretary, her indulgence of Sanjay eventually led to Haksar's resignation. "Sanjay was given a free hand," says Seshan, "and he was totally irresponsible. But she never used to curb him. In the beginning, she used to shout at him, but later she did not bother at all about it. Haksar did not approve of Sanjay's activities at all."

According to Seshan, Haksar tried hard to warn Smt. Gandhi about the damage her son was doing and even tried to persuade her with an analogy from the Hindu epic, the *Ramayana.* The hero, Lord Rama, he pointed out to her, had been sent into exile for fourteen years by his father, so that he could prove himself; and he had returned in triumph. He went on to suggest that she should send Sanjay for three years to Kashmir to stop him interfering. But, as it turned out, it was Haksar, not Sanjay, she chose to dispense with.

Allegations of corruption caused an almost continuous uproar in Parliament and spilled into the press. Romesh Thapar, till then a friend and supporter of Smt. Gandhi was one of those who tried to warn her of the damage this was doing to her reputation. Thapar says: "I began a series of collusions with Smt. Gandhi over all this corruption. She used to get very indignant and say: 'You know that I do not do anything like this, and it is absurd.' I said: 'Well, if you are not prepared to accept what people are feeling, then we will call it a day'. 'No, no,' she said, 'I'm not saying that. I'm just saying that you must discipline yourself and think of all the problems I have to face.' So, I said: 'Well, I'm just telling you that people think you're corrupt.' She said: 'I am not.' I said: 'They say you're the queen bee that sends them out to make the collection.' She was very upset, and so we started meeting less frequently. Frankly, she was getting adjusted to this new role of a kind of mafia queen."

Smt. Gandhi shut her ears to the advice of her more disinterested well-wishers and dismissed all allegations against her son as prejudice and exaggeration. Smt. Gandhi once publicly replied to Sanjay's critics by saying: "There is nothing wrong in a young man proving his capacity. His product will have to stand the test of the public."

The Opposition demanded her resignation after the Allahabad High Court judgment in her election. Fearing that even a temporary resignation was too risky in the prevailing political climate, a small group of her advisers, including Sanjay, persuaded Smt. Gandhi to proclaim a state of emergency instead and crack down hard on her opponents.

'The President proclaimed emergency,' Smt. Gandhi announced in her broadcast. 'This is nothing to panic about. I'm sure you are all conscious of the deep and widespread conspiracy which has been brewing ever since I began introducing certain progressive measures of benefit to the common man and woman of India.' But most Indians interpreted the Emergency as a bid to save the ruling dynasty. That was hardly surprising when the

President of the Congress Party endorsed the Emergency with the immortal words: "India is Indira, and Indira is India."

According to Inder Gujral, then Information Minister in Smt. Gandhi's government, it was clear from the very first Cabinet meeting after the declaration of the Emergency that Sanjay Gandhi was calling the shots.

Smt. Gandhi took the extraordinary step of calling a general election in February 1977, at a time when the Emergency, still in force, was at its most unpopular.

What did the most damage to Smt. Gandhi in the election campaign were the allegations of forcible mass sterilizations throughout northern India. There were instances of unmarried couple, young men, and also old men in their seventies, who claimed that they had been forced to undergo this operation by Sanjay's over-zealous followers. In many places, villagers said that they used to hide *en masse* in the fields whenever officials arrived, in case they had come to sterilize them. The Congress party was routed in its traditional stronghold of northern India, and the prime minister and her son were defeated by large margins.

The new government was formed by the Janata Party with Morarji Desai as Prime Minister. But, it survived for only 27 months because of their infighting. Elections were held in January 1980 and voters put their faith again in the Nehru-Gandhi dynasty. Sanjay Gandhi masterminded the campaign and selected candidates. Smt. Gandhi seemed totally under his influence. Khushwant Singh said: "Sanjay was a very powerful character, a bit of a bully. Smt. Gandhi could not say 'no' to the man. I was not quite able to understand why. She professed a lot of affection for him, but I think in fact she was a little scared of him. I have a feeling that he had some kind of access to family secrets which may have given him some kind of power of blackmail. I do not know. But, I felt that, although he was extremely courteous and polite to her—they kept up a lot of formality in this family—there was no stopping him. When he wanted something, he got it done, even if she did not seem to agree with him."

There was even a speculation that Sanjay might oust his mother; but that was not to be. Shortly after election he died, flying his own light aeroplane. There were many who heaved a sigh of relief at Sanjay's removal from the political scene, arguing that he would have turned India fascist, had he lived.

Despite the cruel blow that fate had dealt her, Smt. Gandhi did not forsake her dynastic plans. She asked her elder son, Rajiv, to join the family business and had little difficulty getting her party accept him as the new heir-apparent. Until his brother's death, Rajiv was out of politics, pursuing his career as a pilot with India's state-owned domestic airline. He lived with his Italian wife, Sonia, in the same house as his mother, brother and sister-in-law Maneka.

Khushwant Singh remembered Rajiv as an unwilling candidate for the greatness that was thrust upon him by his brother's death. When I mentioned the subject, he recalled, "Smt. Gandhi repeated many times: 'Rajiv has no interest in politics. Sonia threatens to divorce him if he enters politics.' And then he did enter politics" (*From Raj to Rajiv: Forty Years of Indian Independence,* Mark Tully and Zareer Masani, Universal Book Stall, New Delhi, pp. 128-31).

Rajiv was not only systematically introduced to government decision-making but also to the intricate and convoluted processes involved in decision-taking. He was familiar to the party top brass. His exposure to the organizational hassles of the ASIAD, the NAAM Summit, the CHOGAM, etc., further enabled him to add to his accumulated experience of public relations and organization. Even as a young man, he had been exposed to the visiting VIPs from foreign lands, who met Smt. Gandhi for informal talks at the residence. He was introduced to the world leaders in a manner befitting a potential Prime Minister. Whether it was President Brezhnev of the Soviet Union, or US President Ronald Reagan, or British Prime Minister Margaret Thatcher, it was made evident that he was the man they would have to deal with in the absence of Smt. Indira Gandhi. The Soviet leaders extended to him all the courtesies due to a head of the government (*Resurgence of Rajiv Gandhi: Assassination of Indira Gandhi and after,* Rai Singh, pp. 78-79).

In the early 1980s, Punjab was in deep turmoil as a section of the Sikhs had become very belligerent and day-to-day life in the State had become immensely disturbed. This section included militants who were demanding a separate nation to be called 'Khalistan'. They began killing innocent civilians on a large scale in Punjab and the neighboring states. Prime Minister Smt. Indira Gandhi tried her level best to control the situation, but the extremist elements nullified all her efforts. The leader of the extremists was Jarnail Singh Bhindranwale, a Sikh preacher, who along with his followers, managed to take control of Sikhism's holiest shrine—Sri Harmandir Sahib or the Golden Temple in Amritsar.

On 6th June, 1984, the Indian Army entered the premises of the Golden Temple in Amritsar to flush out the militants who had taken refuse there under the leadership of Bhindranwale. It took only a few days for the army to clear the Golden Temple of the militants. In the process, some of Sikhism's highly venerated structures were damaged. They were later restored to their original condition to the extent possible. The operation came to be known as 'Operation Blue Star'.

Four months later, India paid a tragic price for it when Smt. Indira Gandhi was shot by two of her bodyguards, both Sikhs, in the garden of her house in Delhi.

Smt. Indira Gandhi was critically injured and had been rushed to the All India Institute of Medical Sciences (AIIMS). On that day many important persons were out of Delhi such as the President Zail Singh was in Mauritius, Home Minister Narasimha Rao in Andhra Pradesh, Rajiv Gandhi and Pranab Mukherjee in Calcutta, Cabinet Secretary, Krishnaswamy Rao Sahib and Prime Minister's Secretary, Dr. P.C. Alexander in Mumbai.

The first to reach Delhi were Krishnaswamy Rao and P.C. Alexander. They were immediately driven to AIIMS. The news of Smt. Indira Gandhi's death had not yet been announced. Dr. K.P. Mathur, personal physician to the Prime Minister told

Krishnaswamy Rao and Alaxander, "all is over, the body is being stitched up".

Dr. P.C. Alexander swung in action to continue the legacy of Nehru-Gandhi dynasty by getting Rajiv Gandhi sworn in as Prime Minister. The details given by him, in this respect, in his book, *Through the Corridors of Power: An Insider's Story*, from pages 216 to 222 speak volumes. He writes: "It was my firm conviction as soon as I received the news of the tragedy that the most feasible arrangement would be to have Rajiv sworn in immediately as prime minister without going in for an interim prime minister. I held hurried consultations with Shivshankar and B. Shankaranand, senior ministers in Indira Gandhi's cabinet, who had rushed to AIIMS. They both expressed their strongly held view that Pranab Mukherjee should not be sworn in as interim prime minister, although he was high up in the hierarchy. By then chief ministers from the Congress-ruled states had arrived at the institute and were standing together on the eighth floor in one section of verandah. I thought it would be prudent to quickly ascertain the views of the chief ministers, the ministers and other senior members of the party present there on the question of succession. I sought the opinions of N.D. Tiwari, chief minister of Uttar Pradesh, Janaki Ballabh Patnaik, chief minister of Orissa, Bhajan Lal, chief minister of Haryana and Shiv Charan Mathur, chief minister of Rajasthan and discussed with them the idea of having Rajiv sworn in as prime minister, thereby discarding the option of having an interim prime minister. All of them enthusiastically agreed with the idea. I then went to another section of the verandah and highlighted the salient points to those present there, of my brief talk with the chief ministers. I found that everyone was in agreement with the suggestion that Rajiv should be administered the oath forthwith. Within a few minutes Narasimha Rao reached the eighth floor. I told him quickly that there was unanimity among all the chief ministers and the ministers present at the institute that Rajiv should be sworn in directly as prime minister and he fully endorsed the proposal.

Rajiv arrived at 3.15 p.m. along with Pranab Mukherjee and Arun Nehru (one of Rajiv's cousins). After greeting us with folded hands, Rajiv quickly went inside the room adjacent to the operation theatre, where his wife Sonia Gandhi had been standing near the wall and sobbing.

I quickly told Pranab Mukherjee that everyone had agreed that Rajiv should be administered the oath of office as PM without going in for an interim arrangement. Without any hesitation, Pranab Mukherjee gave his assent to this suggestion. A group of individuals, with malicious intent, later spread a canard that Pranab Mukherjee had staked his claim to be sworn in as interim PM and had to be persuaded with great difficulty to withdraw his claim. The obvious objective was to create discord between Rajiv Gandhi and Pranab Mukherjee. But I should record here the true fact that Pranab Mukherjee had readily endorsed the suggestion I made to him.

While Rajiv was inside the room with Sonia, a serious controversy was brewing among the persons standing on the verandah of the eighth floor. Arun Nehru took me aside and told me in a very serious tone that Rajiv should be sworn in immediately by the vice-president without waiting for the president's arrival, scheduled for 5 p.m. Arun Nehru confirmed that he had the approval of all the ministers present there as also that of the Lok Sabha Speaker, Balram Jakhar. Parthasarthi and many others also strongly supported the proposal.

I was quite surprised to find that Arun Nehru and almost all the dignitaries present on the eighth floor believed that a swearing in by the vice-president was necessary to ensure Rajiv's assumption of office without any complications. They were of the view that president Zail Singh could not be trusted to accept Rajiv's nomination without a formal election by the Congress Parliamentary Party. They were genuinely apprehensive that because of the recent deterioration in the relations between Zail Singh and Indira Gandhi, he might use his position to prevent Rajiv from becoming prime minister and may administer the oath to Pranab Mukherjee as interim prime minister. Such a development could lead to serious difficulties as far as Rajiv's election later was concerned. I was more aware than anyone else present on the eighth floor of AIIMS at that time about the gravity of the strained relations between Indira Gandhi and Zail Singh. However, I was quite convinced that it would be ethically very wrong and politically very unwise if the president were made to feel that he had been deliberately denied the exercise of his most important responsibility, namely, choosing the prime minister and administering the oath of office to him. I was seriously worried that if Rajiv were administered the oath by the vice-president, Zail Singh would view this step as a challenge to his authority and may even take the extreme step of not recognizing the oath administered by the vice-president. Anyway, the president was on his way back to Delhi as quickly as possible. Zail Singh had not authorized the vice-president to exercise his functions in his Absence.

I decided to take determined stand on the issue of administration of the oath of office, as I wanted to ensure that the correct procedures were followed in such a crucial matter. I turned to Shivshakar, the Union Law Minister, and asked whether or not he agreed with my views. He replied that he agreed that my stand was legally valid, but he was not prepared, at that point of time, to support it. Everyone knew very well that there was no time for holding a meeting of the Congress Parliamentary Party to formally elect Rajiv as leader. Recognizing this practical difficulty, I suggested that the Congress Party's Parliamentary Board could formally recommend Rajiv's name to the president, which could be ratified by the CPP later. However, Arun Nehru, supported by a few like-minded individuals, was quite firm in his stand that no risk could be taken in this matter. He asked me, in a very defiant tone, as to who would accept the responsibility for the consequences if Zail Singh refused to administer the oath to Rajiv. My immediate response was that the person who was the most concerned about, and who would be most affected by, this decision was Rajiv and, first of all, his own wishes in the matter ought to be ascertained. Arun Nehru declared that he would go into the room where Rajiv was standing with Sonia and talk to him, but I preempted him and I quickly went inside the room.

What I saw on entering the room was Rajiv clasping Sonia with both hands and earnestly conveying to her the message that he considered it his duty to take on the responsibility as prime minister. Sonia was holding him tightly and tears were rolling down her cheeks. She was pleading with him not to yield to the forceful request of his party colleagues to accept the top post. Rajiv was kissing her forehead repeatedly and trying to convince her that his duty was to abide by the decision of his party. Time was ticking away and I was very keen to talk to him. I went near the couple and gently touched Rajiv on the back of his shoulder to indicate that I had some very urgent work with him. He released himself from Sonia's arms and turned around to talk to me. He quickly led me to the bathroom attached to the room so that we could talk without being noticed by anyone else who may enter the room.

I briefly informed him that the proposal of Arun Nehru and most of his senior party men present there was to have him sworn in as prime minister by the vice-president without waiting for the arrival of the president, as they were concerned that Zail Singh might not agree to administer the oath to him without being first elected as leader of the CPP. Moreover, he may insist on appointing Pranab Mukherjee as interim prime minister, which could cause complications later. I then explained all the reasons why I personally felt that the correct and even prudent course would be to wait till the president arrived and asked him (Rajiv) for his own wishes on this matter. Rajiv listened to me patiently and, much to my relief, told me that he fully agreed with my views and that the risk, if any, was worth taking. He said he would talk to Arun Nehru later, but that I, for my part, should go ahead with making the necessary arrangements for the swearing in by the president, presuming that he would agree with the proposal. I came out of the bathroom and conveyed Rajiv's decision to everyone present on the eighth floor. Nobody raised any objection after that.

Time was racing by. At 4.10 p.m., Pranab Mukherjee and Narasimha Rao went to 1, Akbar Road to arrange for the meeting of the Congress Party's Parliamentary Board, which was to recommend to the president the nomination of Rajiv by the party for the post of prime minister. As swiftly as possible, the Congress Parliamentary Board passed a resolution nominating Rajiv Gandhi as the party's candidate for the post of prime minister and recommending his appointment for the consideration of the president.

Zail Singh reached Rashtrapati Bhavan along with Rajiv within a few minutes of these fast-paced events; Arun Nehru and R.K. Dhavan also arrived there close on their heels. I met the president in his office immediately on his arrival and informed him that Narasimha Rao and Pranab Mukherjee were waiting to meet him. They were immediately called in and they gave the letter to the president. I came to know later that the president, as soon as he arrived at AIIMS, had informed Rajiv that he wanted him to be sworn in as prime minister without going in for an interim arrangement. Thus, all apprehensions and misgivings on the part of the Congress leaders had proved unwarranted.

The entire ceremony of administering the oath to Rajiv and his four cabinet colleagues was completed in twenty minutes and the first meeting of the new cabinet was held in Rashtrapati Bhavan itself immediately thereafter. The cabinet then took a series of decisions. The cremation was fixed for 3 p.m. on 3rd November at Shanti Van, near Raj Ghat in Delhi."

Dr P.C. Alexander further writes: "During an exchange of views with Rajiv at Bangalore on 8th February, 1991, I got the distinct impression that he was quite confident of staging a big come back if general elections were to be held that year. In fact, he was sure that general elections would have to be held early because of the continued instability of the government at the centre. However, all calculations about Congress' return to power went awry as a result of Rajiv's assassination in a bomb blast at Sriperumbudur in Chengalpet district near Madras. He was blown to bits at 10.30 p.m. on 21st May, 1991, right in the middle of the elections."

"Rajiv had just arrived at Sriperumbudur to address an election meeting when the bomb strapped on the body of a female suicide bomber belonging to the LTTE killed him instantly."

The LTTE a terrorist outfit was demanding a separate Tamil State in northern Sri Lanka. The well-armed LTTE had been in a state of conflict with Sri Lankan Army since 1983. The killing was apparently in relation for Rajiv Gandhi sending Indian troops to fight the LTTE in 1987.

Rajiv's body was completely mutilated and could be identified mainly from the special brand of shoes that he used to wear. Sonia and daughter Priyanka went by the IAF plane to Sriperumbudur to bring the body to Delhi. After the plane returned, the body was taken to the AIIMS and from there to his residence at 10, Janpath. Later Rajiv's body was taken to Teen Murti House where the scenes from the tragic incident of 31st October, 1984, when Indira Gandhi was assassinated, were to have their somber return.

The cremation rites were performed on 24th May. In every detail they were a repetition of the ceremonies performed for Indira Gandhi, about seven years earlier; in the place of Rajiv in 1984, Rahul, his son was there in 1991 to light the funeral pyre.

Even when Rajiv's body was lying in state at Teen Murti House on 23 and 24 May, Congress leaders from various parts of the country, in small clusters, had been busy confabulating with each other about who should take over as the Congress president and lead the party in the remaining states where the election to the Lok Sabha were yet to be held. One group, consisting of Arjun Singh, Makhan Lal Fotedar, Satish Sharma and others close to Rajiv family, had decided among themselves that Sonia should succeed Rajiv as Congress president. The Congress Working Committee met and hurriedly approved her name even without consulting her. Sonia, who was in a state of indescribable grief and shock, was in no mood even to think about such matters. She used the earliest opportunity to issue a statement declining to serve as the president of the party and, thus, the question of finding a successor to Rajiv remained wide open.

Arjun Singh, in his autobiography, *A Grain of Sand in the Hourglass of Time*, on page 239 and 240, writes: "Towards the end of May 1991, the first Congressman whom we approached was Sitaram Kesri, the Treasurer of the All India Congress Committee, an old-timer from Bihar, was not surprised at our choice of candidate for party president and agreed to support Sonia Gandhi. Soon, Kesri and Fotedar and I went to see P.V. Narasimha Rao, a very senior Congressman. On hearing our suggestion, Rao kept quiet for a few minutes with a grave expression on his face. Suddenly, he burst out in anger and virtually yelled out words to the effect that whether it was essential that the Congress Party should be treated like a train where the compartments have to be attached to an engine belonging to the Nehru-Gandhi family or were there other alternatives? I was dumbfounded by Rao's outburst but kept quiet. Kesri, however, pursued the matter further and contended that it would be in the fitness of things if we were to offer the post of the Congress president to Sonia Gandhi first. Rao realized that he had perhaps spoken too much too soon and had exposed his anti-Nehru feelings very clearly. He, therefore, thoughtfully queried: 'There is no harm in making the suggestion, but will she accept it?' We had no immediate answer to his query except that we would have to approach Sonia Gandhi and seek her reaction."

Narasimha Rao launched a county-wide campaign from 3rd June onwards in those states where the elections were yet to be completed. Considerable sympathy for the Congress had been generated in most states because of the dastardly assassination of Rajiv Gandhi; still it was doubtful whether the sympathy could be converted into votes.

By the first week of June of 1991, rumours gained ground in political circles that Sharad Pawar, the powerful chief minister of Maharashtra, would emerge as a contender for the top slot of the CPP. The Congress was expected to win an overwhelming majority of seats in Maharashtra and Pawar knew very well that this factor would provide him a solid base if he decided to stake his claim for the leadership of the CPP.

Meanwhile Arjun Singh's name cropped up as a likely contestant for the leadership of the CPP along with that of Sharad Pawar. Narasimha Rao had to tread cautiously. He had to make sure that Arjun Singh and Sharad Pawar did not reach an agreement to share the two top posts between them, leaving him in the lurch. However, Rao did not want to take any risk and decided to reach an understanding with Arjun Singh and his supporters.

When the results of the elections to the Parliament were declared, the entire scenario underwent a major change, which could be attributed to the fact that the Maharashtra Congress had secured 37 of the total 48 seats in the Lok Sabha and had emerged as the largest chunk of votes for the Congress in the country. On the basis of this impressive tally, Pawar's chances of winning, if a contest for the CPP leader became necessary, suddenly looked much brighter. He arrived in Delhi on 17th June evening and straight away began consultations with various sections within the Congress. Very soon a powerful 'Pawar Group' emerged and immediately demanded that the elections of the CPP leader should be on the basis of secret ballot. This group seemed to believe that a secret ballot would boost the chances of Pawar's victory if a contest became necessary.

Dr. P.C. Alexaner, in his book, *Through the Corridors of Power: An Insider's Story*, writes: "Narasimha Rao had asked me to ascertain Pawar's views on the election of the CPP leader. He told me that I should convey to Pawar that he (Rao) would like him to occupy a senior position in the Central cabinet when it would be formed. I thought of conveying this message to Pawar through an intermediary than doing it directly. Consequently, on 19th June, I decided to rope in P.C. Chacko, a Congress leader of Kerala and a friend of Pawar, for the cause. I told Chacko that Narasimha Rao was expecting full cooperation from Pawar for his election as leader of the CPP and that it was Rao's intention, if elected as leader, to invite him (Pawar) to join the Central Government in a senior position. My own personal advice to Chacko was that Pawar should accept the assurances given by Narasimha Rao and not contest the post of leader of the CPP as, in my considered assessment, the chances of Pawar winning were not very high."

Alexander further writes: "Chacko called on me on 19th June at 1.30 p.m. after discussion with Pawar and told me that Pawar would not contest for the post of leader of the CPP but expected to be offered the post of deputy prime minister taking into account the fact that he had the support of a sizable block of MPs from all over the country, though not of a majority. I told Chacko that Narasimha Rao would definitely be against any arrangement that would look like a 'deal' and that Rao expected Pawar to assert and affirm the solidarity and unity within the Congress at a time when the party was trying hard to recover from the trauma it had suffered as a result of the assassination of Rajiv Gandhi. Nevertheless, I informed Chacko that I would convey his suggestion to Narasimha Rao and also let him know Rao's reaction immediately."

"On the same day, at 2.15 p.m., I took Chacko with me to Narasimha Rao's house. I met Rao alone while Chacko waited in one of the rooms. Rao was very firm in his stand that the number two slot could not be offered to Pawar or to any other leader in the Congress. Instead, he repeated his earlier assurance, which had been already conveyed by me to Chacko that Pawar would be inducted into the Central cabinet in a senior post. I conveyed Narasimha Rao's reply to Chacko and came to know later that Pawar was not particularly happy with Rao's reply. He sent a signal through his aides that he was serious about contesting the election to the post of the CPP leader. A veteran Congress leader, N.K.P. Salve, had by now become the focal point for organizing support for Pawar within the party. Almost 48 high-ranking Congress leaders, who were ardent supporters of Pawar, had prepared a statement asking for a secret ballot for the election of the CPP leader. The CPP Board met on 19th June and fixed 21st June as the date for the election. The board had also authorized K. Karunakaran and Sidhartha Shankar Ray (a former chief minister of West Bengal) to ascertain the views of individual MPs about their choice of the CPP leader. By this time, most of the MPs had arrived in Delhi and they had gathered at Rao's house to express their support for him. The 'Pawar Group' had by late 19th June night realized that if a contest took place, Narasimha Rao would gain a clear majority."

"In the afternoon of 20th June, Sharad Pawar held a press conference where he announced that he would not be a contestant for the post of CPP leader. Pawar, along with senior leaders supporting him, went to Rao's house at noon on the same day and informed him about this decision. Consequently, Rao emerged as unanimous choice. The CPP met at 4 p.m. and elected Rao as the leader. The swearing in ceremony was fixed for 12.50 p.m. on 21st June."

The version of Natwar Singh, who was Foreign Minister, is somewhat different. He, in his autobiography, *One Life is not Enough*, wrote: "After the funeral (Rajiv Gandhi), there was intense political activity. The aspirants to the post of Congress President included Arjun Singh, N.D. Tiwari, Sharad Pawar and Madhavrao Scindia. Sonia Gandhi herself refused to be the President when it was suggested to her. I told her that the time had come for her to indicate her preference for the role; whoever she chose would naturally become prime minister. For so momentous a decision, I suggested that she ask P.N. Haksar for advice. She said she would let me know. In the meanwhile, she consulted several people, including M.L. Fotedar.

The next day, she asked me to bring Haksar to 10 Janpath. Haksar's advice was to offer the post to Vice-President Shankar Dayal Sharma. He suggested that Aruna Asaf Ali and I should sound out the VP. Aruna Asaf Ali conveyed Sonia's message to the VP. He gave us a patient hearing. He said he was touched and honored by Soniaji's placing so much trust in him. What followed staggered Arunaji and me. The VP continued, 'The Prime ministership of India is a full-time job. My age and health would not let me do justice to the most important office in the country. Kindly convey to Soniaji the reasons for my inability to take on so awesome a responsibility'."

Natwar Singh further wrote: "After hearing of the VP's refusal, I asked Sonia to once again send for P.N. Haksar, who advised her to call P.V. Narsimha Rao. Thereafter, the Congress Working Committee met and unanimously elected P.V. as Congress President."

"The problem lay in pacifying Sharad Pawar and Arjun Singh. If my memory serves, a solution was found by which Sharad Pawar withdrew his candidature. Arjun Singh also withdrew from the prime ministerial election as he was led to expect that he would become Congress President. P.V. Narsimha Rao agreed to this, but once he became Prime Minister, he decided that he would hold on to the post of Congress President as well"

(*One Life is not Enough,* Natwar Singh, Rupa Publications, New Delhi, pp. 288-89).

Natwar Singh further wrote: "The Congress Party with Sitaram Kesri as President was not an effective or assertive outfit. Sonia asked me how she should proceed. 'Reinvent Party,' I advised, a counsel that was easier offered than implemented. Would she be up to the job? What would her priorities be? These questions were being asked in clandestine, disgruntled group meetings. It was abundantly clear that without Sonia at the helm, the future of the Congress looked bleak."

Natwar Singh continued: "Kesri did not last long. A coup did him in, even though he had the support of several senior members of the CWC. Sonia was unanimously elected to succeed him. Immediately after Sonia's election as Congress President, the Tiwari Congress dissolved itself and returned to the parent party. But it was not all smooth going. The well-entrenched old turkeys worked behind the scenes to block the Tiwari Congress's return. Sonia saw through their unseemly designs, though, and overruled them" (*Ibid.,* p. 296).

Natwar Singh further continued: "In 2004, the NDA, led by Atal Bihari Vajpayee, lost the Lok Sabha elections. They could not manage to sell the 'India Shining' mantra to the voting public. Sonia and the leaders of several non-NDA parties put together the United Progressive Alliance (UPA) with Sonia as chair-person. The expectation was that Sonia would occupy 7 Race Course Road as Prime Minister."

See what Natwar Singh wrote. He wrote: "The Gandhi family, however, was a house divided. Rahul was vehemently opposed to his mother becoming prime minister, fearing that she would lose her life, much like his grandmother and his father. Matters reached a climax after Rahul said that he was prepared to take any possible step to prevent his mother from taking up the prime ministership. Rahul is a strong-willed person; this was no ordinary threat. He gave Sonia 24 hours to decide. Manmohan Singh, Suman Dubey, Priyanka and I were present at that moment.

Sonia was visibly agonized and in tears. As a mother, it was impossible for her to ignore Rahul. He had his way. That was the reason for her not becoming Prime Minister. She called a meeting in which she announced that she was offering the post of PM to Manmohan Singh" *(Ibid.,* pp. 318-19).

On pages 329 to 331 of his book, Natwar Singh wrote: "Sonia choosing Manmohan Singh as Prime Minister did not go down well with senior Congress leaders. Most members of the Congress Working Committee were senior to him. This was a bitter pill to swallow. The members were also resentful of having been kept in the dark."

Natwar Singh further wrote: "Our next big problem was to get the UPA partners to accept Sonia's decision. Senior CWC members were deputed to meet the alliance leaders to plead with them to accept what Sonia had decided. M.L. Fotedar and I were asked to meet V.P. Singh, Lalu Prasad Yadav and Ram Vilas Paswan. Lalu and Paswan both were furious. Lalu gave us a tongue-lashing in chaste Bihari, demanding to know why he had not been consulted and why he had to hear the news on television. Ram Vilas Paswan delivered the same message in less colourful language. It was a colossal mess and I found my diplomatic skills being stretched to breaking point."

"Sonia Gandhi called a meeting of the alliance partners at 10 Janpath the same afternoon. The heavyweights arrived, fuming—Harkishan Sing Surjeet, M. Karunanidhi, A.B. Bardhan, Sharad Pawar, Lalu Prasad Yadav, Ram Vilas Paswan, Farooq Abdullah and E. Ahmad, among others. They had, in good faith, elected Sonia Gandhi as UPA Chairperson, not Manmohan Singh. Why had they been kept in dark? It took more than an hour to bring them around. Sonia was exhausted by the end of it but her inner strength pulled her through."

Manmohan Singh government was sworn in on 22nd May, 2004.

11
Sonia Gandhi, De Facto Prime Minister

Sanjaya Baru, who was media adviser to Prime Minister Dr. Manmohan Singh, in his book, *The Accidental Prime Minister*, published by Penguin Books, gives in detail as to how Dr. Manmohan Singh became Prime Minister and Sonia Gandhi was made President of the Congress and Chairperson of UPA, which eventually made her de facto Prime Minister during UPA I and UPA II.

Sanjaya Baru says: "It became clear, that Sonia had got enough seats to form a new coalition government led by Congress party. Shortly before I flew to Washington D.C. to speak at a conference organized by the historian Sunil Khilnani, I typed out an editorial comment that appeared on 15th May with the title 'Thoughts on a Government'. My advice to the victorious Congress President Sonia Gandhi was simple—Invite Dr. Manmohan Singh to take charge as Prime Minister and make herself the Chairperson of the Congress and allies coordination committee that would oversee the functioning of the government."

"My suggestion that Dr. Singh be made PM was not a new idea. I had floated it five years earlier, almost to the date, on 25th May, 1999, in a column in *Times of India*. This was shortly after Sonia Gandhi's failed attempt to form a Congress-led coalition government after the fall of a BJP-led government. She had famously and, as it turned out, erroneously announced, 'We have 272 (MPs), and we hope to get more.' Provocatively titled 'Perils of Sonia Gandhi as PM,' my column advised Sonia to resist the temptation of claiming the job and, instead, name Manmohan Singh as PM, were Congress to form government."

"On the day I arrived in DC, 15th May, news reports suggested that Sonia Gandhi was in two minds on whether or not to head the government that was now likely to be formed. Sycophantic as ever, the rank and file of the party demanded that she become prime minister. On the other hand, BJP leader Sushma Swaraj, who had campaigned vociferously against an Italian-origin prime minister, was dramatically threatening to shave her head if Sonia did so."

"Rohit Bansal, resident editor of the Delhi edition of the *Financial Express* announced, 'Sonia says she will not be PM'. I thought to myself: Step one, she will not be PM. Step two, she will make Dr. Singh PM. Sonia announced that Dr. Singh would head a coalition government."

Sanjaya Baru further writes: "The Congress allies in UPA-I nominated their own ministers and bargained for their portfolios with Sonia, not with Dr. Singh... Thus, Sharad Pawar, who had been defence minister in Narsimha Rao's cabinet, could not climb Raisina Hill, since his party, the NCP had only nine seats in the new Parliament, he had to be content with agriculture. On the other hand, DMK that won all the 16 seats it had contested in Tamil Nadu, made sure it got key economic ministries with, to use a popular phrase, 'rent-seeking' opportunities."

"As far senior Congress leaders, they owed their cabinet posts almost entirely to Sonia Gandhi, who did, however, consult Dr. Singh and close aides before finalizing the names. Prithvraj Chavan was Dr. Singh's protégé but he knew that his political career depended on demonstrating loyalty to Sonia and Rahul."

"Dr. Manmohan Singh saw himself as an 'accidental prime minister,' by which he meant that he was not the natural choice for the job. After all, had Sonia not been born an Italian she would have kept the job for herself. The fact of her alien status had made it necessary for her to choose another leader and Dr. Singh was the man she chose."

"Dr. Manmohan Singh emerged as Sonia's right-hand man in the years between 1999 and 2004. It was Manmohan Singh, not Arjun Singh or Pranab Mukherjee, who was by her side when she met foreign heads of government. Therefore, while he neither planned nor schemed to become prime minister, Dr. Singh was not taken by complete surprise when he got the job."

Managing Coalition

A couple of years before Sonia Gandhi took charge of the Congress, the communist ideologue Mohit Sen wrote a persuasive column in the *Times of India* underlying the historical role Sonia would be called upon to play and urging her to do so. The first woman president of the Indian National Congress, he argued, was also a European woman Annie Basant. The party, he stressed, should once again be led by another.

Sanjaya Baru, in this connection, in his book, writes: "When Mohit's column landed on my table—I was then the editorial page editor of the *Times of India*—I called Mohit and told him that his suggestion that Sonia should take charge of the Congress was an outlandish idea. As the political party of India's freedom struggle, surely it had to have a future independent of Nehru-Gandhi family. How could he suggest that Sonia becomes the party's president merely because she was Rajiv's widow? I told him people would laugh at him for his political naivete and suggested the column be junked. He was most offended and threatened to go elsewhere if I refused to publish his piece. Finally, I agreed to use it because of my affection and regard for him. Mohit's column was the first credible public call for Sonia's induction into public life."

Sanjaya Baru on pages 63 to 65 writes: "I assumed that Mohit, as an Indira loyalist, had a special regard for her heirs. But his opinion that Sonia should enter politics was also based on his conviction that without a Nehru-Gandhi family member at the top, the Congress party would splinter and wither away. This view was also encouraged by members of the Delhi Darbar—a power elite, to use sociologist C. Wright Mill's term, comprising civil servants, diplomats, editors, intellectuals and business leaders who had worked with or been close to the regimes of Nehru, Indira and Rajiv. Some of them inhabited the many trusts and institutions that the Nehru-Gandhi family controlled. They had all profited in one way or another, over the years, from their loyalty to the Congress's first family."

"In opposition to this view was the one held by a Congressman like Narasimha Rao who, while ironically titling his semi-autobiographical book *The Insider,* believed he was an 'outsider' among Delhi's Nehru-Gandhi power elite. Rao believed that a political organization that was more than a century old, the party of India's freedom movement, inspired and led by a Gandhi, a Mahatma who was no relative of these Gandhis, ought to imagine for itself a life beyond the Nehru-Gandhi family. Many small regional parties might have become feudal, even despotic, family-led parties, but how could a grand old political organization like the Indian National Congress link its future only to the fortunes of one political family? This view had few takers among family loyalists, who took charge of the party after the unceremonious ouster of Sitaram Kesari, the man Narasimha Rao chose as his successor and who in turn placed the party's crown in Sonia's hands."

Further writes Baru: "When Sonia Gandhi decided to join active politics and take charge of the Congress party, becoming its president in 1998, few thought through how her elevation would affect the relationship between the party and a future Congress government. While her loyalists argued there is nothing to resolve here, since she would become prime minister, her detractors in the party said they were willing to accept her party president but not as future PM because of her Italian origin. It was this issue that led Sharad Pawar and others to exit the party in 1999 and form the NCP."

When Sonia turned sixty, Dr. Manmohan Singh sent her a personal letter praising her courage and fortitude. She had been widowed at a young age, and had to bring up her children in the very difficult social and security context of Delhi. And she had allowed herself to be persuaded to take on the mantle of party presidency by Congressmen who feared the party would disintegrate without her at the helm. Recounting these facts, Dr. Singh praised her for her courage and her poise in the face of such adversity and for the energy and wisdom with which she had led the Congress party back to power.

For Congress MPs, the leader to please was always Sonia. They did not show loyalty to the PM as a political necessity, nor did Dr. Singh seek loyalty in the way in which Sonia and her aides sought it.

With Sharad Pawar, the boss of the NCP and Lalu Prasad Yadav, the feisty politician who headed the Rashtriya Janata Dal (RJD), both of which were constituents of the UPA, Dr. Manmohan Singh had a good equation even if he did not approve of their conduct. With Sharad Pawar, there was a special relationship. Dr. Singh often recalled how Pawar always lent support to him whenever his policies came under attack from within the Congress party. He regarded Pawar as an 'ally' against his critics in the cabinet, like Arjun Singh, A.K. Antony and Vayalar Ravi. And it is true.

Sharad Pawar: The Great Enigma written by me was released by Dr. Manmohan Singh on 23rd December, 2017 at Aurangabad. In his speech on the occasion Dr. Manmohan Singh said: "I am happy to be in this ancient and graceful city of Aurangabad and that too for a function which seeks to honour Shri Sharad Pawar through release of his biography."

"I have been benefitted enormously from Sharadji's sustained and long friendship and for me he is supreme embodiment of the word in shastras which describes a *Karmayogi*. Sharadji is truly *Karmayogi*."

"Shri Sheshrao Chavan has produced a magnificent book, which highlights the life and work of Sharadji. This book clearly brings out that Sharad Pawar is ideally suited to handle any situation of crisis."

Dr. Manmohan Singh further said: "In 1991, I had privilege to be associated with Sharadji as a minister in Narasimha Rao's cabinet. Sharadji was the Defence Minister. I was Finance Minister at a time when the treasury was nearly empty. I had no other option but to go each of my colleagues asking them to cut their budget. No other minister saw my predicament, but Sharadji most gracefully agreed to cut the defence budget by ₹ 500 crores and set an example for the rest of the cabinet colleagues to follow."

"I have been associated as Finance Minister with liberalization move for economic reforms, which was launched by Narasimha

Rao government in 1991-96, but the credit for those reforms also goes to Sharadji, because even before he became minister in Narasimha Rao Government, in his lecture, he delivered in Pune to Maratha Chamber of Commerce, he set out what was needed to reform and rebalance the Indian Economy and for that, therefore, if any credit has to be given, it is to Sharad Pawar as equal partner in carrying out those reforms."

Dr. Manmohan Singh further said: "I also recall that when our government was to be formed in 2004, the choice of ministers was being discussed, my prayer was agriculture portfolio should be given to Sharad Pawar, because I knew that no other politician has paid so much attention to agriculture as Sharad Pawar has done as chief minister of Maharashtra. My prayer was accepted and Sharadji became for ten years Agriculture Minister. He was the most successful, the most prominent and the most creative agriculture minister that India has produced."

Dr. Manmohan Singh continued: "In the cabinet I could always look up to him for guidance and support and even when I was in difficult times, Sharad Pawar always held my hand. Whatever remarkable work Narasimha Rao Government or United Front Government did, the large part of the credit goes to my esteemed friend Sharad Pawar."

Concluding his speech, Dr. Manmohan Sing said: "Blessed is the land, which gives birth to citizens like Sharad Pawar and therefore I pray to God to give him long life, many, many years of productive life so that India and Maharashtra can derive benefits of his learning, scholarship and statesmanship."

Thus, even as some in the Congress party targeted an ally like Sharad Pawar, Dr. Manmohan Singh sought to maintain good relations with him. Such relationships were Dr. Singh's real source of strength. Political analysts and reporters who skimmed the surface only saw Dr. Singh as 'Sonia's puppet.' Those who had a deeper knowledge of the power play within the wider coalition knew that Dr. Singh had the backing of the coalition partners some of whom were more loyal to him than to his own party leaders.

In other words, Dr. Singh became prime minister as Sonia's nominee, but he settled down and retained his office as the consensual and implicit choice of all the UPA allies, especially Karunanidhi, Sharad Pawar and Lalu Prasad Yadav, and indeed even the Bengal faction of the CPI (M).

Sanjaya Baru, in his book on pages 91 and 92, writes: "In the UPA, however, Congress party spokespersons let it be known to all concerned that Sonia Gandhi would remain the boss even though she was not the PM, despite her renunciation of power. Even a Left Front Leader like Sitaram Yechury, would remind political reporters that this was not the first time that the head of the party was seen as more important than the head of government, recalling Jyoti Basu's early days as CM. In the case of UPA-I, what the arrangement also implied was that the credit for all the good work done by the government would go to Sonia, and all the blame for any mistakes or failure would go to Dr. Singh."

"Dr. Singh never shied away from this political reality. When confronted with a difficult political demand from an ally, or from leaders of other political parties, he would confess to them that he did not have the last word on the matter, that he was an accidental Prime Minister and that the buck stopped with Sonia. Fully conscious of this political Achilles heel, he nevertheless tried bringing into line difficult colleagues."

On page 126 of the book, Baru says: "It was a relatively smooth ride with the media for Dr. Singh in UPA-I. His problem always was that he did not want to become more popular with the media and the general public than Sonia. Whenever a TV channel or newsmagazine conducted an opinion poll and showed that his popularity, while rising, was a few notches below that of Sonia, he would feel relieved. 'Good,' he would say with mischievous smile. That defined the limit to his projection and brand-building."

Looking to the above facts, it would not be exaggeration to say that during UPA-I and UPA-II, Sonia Gandhi as its chairperson was acting as de facto Prime Minister.

12
Dynastic Rule in Opposition Parties

It is true that Jawaharlal Nehru wanted in his heart of heart his daughter Indira to succeed him and she did succeed. Indira brought her son Rajiv in politics after the death of Sanjay with a sole object of grooming him to succeed her, and after her tragic assassination, Rajiv stepped in her shoes as Prime Minister. After Rajiv's murder at Sriperumbudur, it appeared that the Nehru-Gandhi family will cease to rule India. But, the conspiracy of circumstances in the Congress dragged Sonia in the Congress and made her Congress President. Had she not declined under the pressure of Rahul, as said by Natwar Singh, she would have certainly become Prime Minister. However, she got Dr. Manmohan Singh installed as Prime Minister and became chairperson of UPA-I and UPA-II and virtually functioned as de facto prime minister for ten years from 2004 to 2014.

The UPA was defeated in 2014, but Sonia Gandhi continued to be the saviour of the Congress as its President until Mallikarjun Kharge was elected as Congress President in 2022 to replace Sonia Gandhi.

In India, it is not only the Nehru-Gandhi family that ruled but the families of other political parties including BJP have also been ruling, which will be evident from the following facts.

The BJP currently has 303 members in the Lok Sabha and 85 in the Rajya Sabha. Of these 388, 45 MPs have dynastic linkages, around 11 per cent. This number stands in stark contrast to the way Prime Minister Narendra Modi and Union Home Minister Amit Shah have often mocked the Congress and its members for their family connections in politics, such as calling Rahul Gandhi '*shehzada*' (prince) and contrasting his '*naamdaar*' (known for their name) status with their own '*kaamdaar*' (known for their work).

The BJP national president, J.P. Nadda too attacked Rahul Gandhi, asking why the dynast wanted a weak India and a strong China.

The BJP has added several dynasts in the Rajya Sabha, including four out of 17 in the last round of polls held in June 2020. Previous Karnataka Chief Minister, Basavaraj Bommai, was an addition to a lengthening list of dynasts in the Bharatiya Janata Party (BJP), which believes that dynastic politics is the "biggest enemy" of democracy. Basavaraj's father, S.R. Bommai, was the chief minister of Karnataka during 1988-89, making them the second father-son duo, after H.D. Deve Gowda and H.D. Kumaraswamy, to occupy the CM's chair in Karnataka.

Prime Minister Narendra Modi has been attacking dynastic politics, saying that it gives rise to a new form of dictatorship in democracy and burdens the country with incompetence. But, his dislike for dynasties hasn't come in the way of inducting dynasts into the BJP or in his own team of ministers. Many prominent faces in his own Cabinet come from political families—Piyush Goyal, Dharmendra Pradhan, Anurag Thakur, Nirmala Sitharaman, Kiren Rijiju and Jyotiraditya Scindia.

The BJP possess a pragmatic approach when it comes to promoting dynasts within the party and importing them from the opposition camp. The BJP welcomed Jitin Prasada, son of prominent Congress leader Jitendra Prasada, into the party fold. In West Bengal assembly election, the BJP inducted CM Mamata Banerjee's former aide, Suvendu Adhikari, and also his father, former union minister Sisir Adhikari. Suvendu Adhikari went on to become the Leader of Opposition in the state assembly.

In the run-up to the Lok Sabha elections in 2014, Modi, then the BJP's PM candidate, taunted the Gandhi family, referring to Rahul Gandhi as "*shehzada*" and the then UPA government as "Delhi sultanate".

"While the country has been destroyed by the governments of mother and son, Uttar Pradesh has been destroyed by a father-son government," Modi had said during his campaign in Uttar Pradesh, referring to the Samajwadi Party duo of Mulayam Singh Yadav and Akhilesh Yadav. Modi and his party colleagues have continued to train guns at the opposition parties for promoting dynastic culture even as members from prominent political families continue to join and thrive in the BJP.

The *Print* had reported in 2019 that around 11 per cent of the BJP MPs had a dynastic background. In the 2019 Maharashtra and Haryana assembly elections, the BJP and the Congress seemed to be in competition when it came to fielding dynasts. Seventeen of the 29 dynasts the BJP fielded across Maharashtra and Haryana won. The figure for the Congress stood at 21 out of 36.

"As if they didn't have their own dynasts in Dushyant, Pankaj Singh, Anurag Thakur, Punam Mahajan, Jayant Sinha, Pravesh Verma and so on, the BJP is also importing dynasts from other parties. Now they have another dynast as CM of Karnataka in Bommai," said senior Congress leader Pawan Khera. He further added: "Between in-house dynasts and imported dynasts, BJP has more dynasts than the Congress. They should stop using this stale bogey of dynastic politics against Congress. It sounds hypocritical and boring."

Is there a Difference?

Rahul Verma, fellow at the Delhi-based Centre for Policy Research, pointed out that around 30 per cent of the MPs are from political families if the last three Lok Sabhas are considered.

"The cadre-based parties like the BJP and CPM have slightly lower representation of dynasts, but even these parties have a significant number of politicians belonging to such families," said Verma.

"As far as the induction of dynasts like Jyotiraditya Scindia or promotion of B. Bommai as the chief minister in Karnataka is concerned, its impact on the BJP and Modi's politics of attacking political dynasties will be zero. The BJP will keep inducting dynasts as long as it can take advantage by having such leaders on board. At the same time, they will keep attacking Rahul Gandhi and the regional parties for dynastic culture," he added.

Verma, however, pointed out a difference between the BJP and the opposition parties in terms of the importance of dynasts.

"The Congress and other regional parties are dynastic in nature, i.e., the party organization is controlled by a single family. For example, in the case of a Samajwadi party, Trinamool Congress, or the DMK, the president (or the main leader) of the party as well as the chief minister-designate come from the same family," he said.

"As far as the impact of political dynasties on Indian democracy is concerned, if more political family members continue to be wooed by political parties across the spectrum, then it will create more barriers for commoners to enter the electoral arena as political families have more access to all kinds of resources that puts them in an advantageous position," he added.

This trend reflects at the state level too—just three weeks ago, when Shivraj Singh Chouhan expanded his Madhya Pradesh cabinet, he included Om Prakash Saklecha, son of former CM Virendra Saklecha, as a minister. Chouhan's cabinet also includes Vishvas Sarang, son of senior BJP leader Kailash Sarang.

Jyotiraditya Scindia: Scindia is the son of the late Madhavrao Scindia, the former Congress leader and union minister, and grandson of the late Vijayaraje Scindia, the Jana Sangh/Janata Party/BJP stalwart, and scion of the erstwhile royal family of Gwalior. Jyotiraditya Scindia became MP in 2002, soon after his father's death, and also served as a union minister under Manmohan Singh's Congress-led UPA-2 government.

Udayanraje Bhosale: Hailing from the erstwhile royal family of Satara in Maharashtra, Bhosale was a three-time Nationalist Congress Party MP before joining the BJP ahead of last year's Maharashtra assembly elections. He is now a Rajya Sabha MP, having lost the Satara bypoll necessitated when he resigned from the NCP and joined the BJP. He has also served as a minister in the Shiv Sena-BJP Maharashtra government in the 1990s. His cousin, MLA Shivendra Raje, also quitted the NCP and joined the BJP.

Vivek Thakur: Vivek is the son of five-time MP and renowned physician C.P. Thakur, who served as the union health minister under Atal Bihari Vajpayee. Thakur senior is regarded as an influential leader of the Bhumihar caste in Bihar, and Vivek's Rajya Sabha ticket earlier this year is being seen in that context, with an eye on the assembly polls.

Leishemba Sanajaoba: The titular king of Manipur was elected on the lone Rajya Sabha seat in the state amid high drama, defeating the Congress candidate by four votes despite the BJP-led coalition government being in jeopardy at the time. Upon his election, he said that he would like to be addressed by his fellow MPs as 'Maharaja', because that is his "birthright".

Neeraj Shekhar: The son of former prime minister Chandra Shekhar was a sitting Rajya Sabha MP from the Samajwadi Party but switched to the BJP last year and became a member of the Upper House again.

Neeraj Shekhar fought three Lok Sabha elections on SP tickets, but didn't get one in 2019, and, therefore, joined the BJP.

Sambhaji Chhatrapati: A descendent of Chhatrapati Shivaji, Sambhaji got nominated to the Rajya Sabha by the President on the BJP's recommendation. He was the face of the Maratha reservation stir in 2016-17, and the BJP sent him to the Rajya Sabha to bring the agitating community into its fold.

Nabam Rebia: Former speaker in the Arunachal Pradesh assembly from the Congress, whose brother Nabam Tuki served as CM, Rebia was elected to the Rajya Sabha on a BJP ticket in June 2020.

Continuing Trend: Even as Modi carried out his election campaign on the '*naamdaar*' versus '*kaamdaar*' plank, a number of dynasts were elected to the Lok Sabha on BJP tickets. The list included Anurag Thakur, son of former Himachal Pradesh CM Prem Kumar Dhumal; Dushyant Singh, son of former Rajasthan CM Vasundhara Raje; B.Y. Raghavendra, son of four-time Karnataka CM B.S. Yediyurappa; Rajbir Singh, son of former UP CM Kalyan Singh; Pravesh Verma, son of former Delhi CM

Sahib Singh Verma; Sanghamitra Maurya, daughter of UP cabinet minister Swami Prasad Maurya; Poonam Mahajan, daughter of late union minister Pramod Mahajan; Pritam Munde, daughter of late union minister Gopinath Munde; Jayant Sinha, son of former Union minister Yashwant Sinha; and Varun Gandhi, son of BJP MP Maneka Gandhi.

The trend is very noticeable in UP and Maharashtra in particular. In the western state, Pankaja Munde, another daughter of Gopinath Munde, served as a minister in the Devendra Fadnavis government, while Raksha Khadse (daughter-in-law of former state revenue minister Eknath Khadse), Sujay Vikhe Patil (son of prominent former Congress leader Radhakrishna Vikhe Patil) and Shrikant Shinde (son of Eknath Shinde, Chief Minister of Maharashtra) are Lok Sabha MPs.

In UP, Union Defence Minister Rajnath Singh's son Pankaj Singh is an MLA, while Rita Bahuguna Joshi, daughter of former state Congress chief and former CM Hemwati Nandan Bahuguna, was a minister in Yogi Adityanath's government. Sharad Tripathi, the son of state BJP president Ramapati Ram Tripathi, was also an MP, but was denied a ticket after a video surfaced showing him assaulting a party MLA with a shoe.

What's the Harm?

An IndiaSpend study published by BloombergQuint (now, BQ Prime) in March 2019 stated: "Since 1999, the Congress has had 36 dynastic members of Parliament elected to the Lok Sabha, with the BJP not far behind with 31. In 1999, the beginning of the 13th Lok Sabha, 8 per cent of Congress MPs were either descended from or married to former MPs, only slightly ahead of the 6 per cent among the BJP. The most similar density of dynastic politicians was in 2009 when the Congress and BJP had 11 per cent and 12 per cent dynasts elected, respectively."

Sanjay Kumar, director of the Centre for the Study of Developing Societies, said every party believes in dynastic politics. He said: "It helps them to win elections easily with less effort, but in recent times, it doesn't matter whether you are dynast or non-dynast—if the candidate has the potential to swing the arithmetic, the BJP has awarded them."

But, Rajbir Singh, the Lok Sabha MP and son of Kalyan Singh, asked what was the harm in following one's father's profession? "What is the harm in getting into politics if one's father is also politician? We never question if a doctor's son becomes a doctor or IAS officer's son becomes an IAS officer. We never call them dynasts," he told *The Print*.

BJP's Narrative for 2024 to be 'Dynasty-free Bharat'

The theme would be that while the BJP is devoted to the nation, dynasty-run parties are 'devoted to families'.

Dynastic politics is perhaps the antithesis of democracy. Critics say it is amongst many political evils in the Indian democratic setup where most parties, are being run like family enterprises. The paradox lies in the emergence and coexistence of numerous regional satraps within a democratic framework over the past 75 years. More are emerging.

National parties are at the forefront of the phenomenon across all states. Except for a handful like the communist parties, only seven or eight of the fifty relevant parties in India are free from dynastic rule.

During the 42nd Foundation Day of Bharatiya Janata Party, Prime Minister Narendra Modi observed, "There are still two kinds of politics going on in this country. One is the politics of family devotion (dynasts), and the other (like BJP) is committed to patriotism." While 'Congress-free' Bharat and 'corruption-free' India were prominent slogans of the BJP in the last two Lok Sabha elections, the narrative for the 2024 campaign would be 'dynasty-free Bharat'. The theme would be that while the BJP is devoted to the nation, the other parties are "devoted to families". The narrative covers regional parties also, most of which are family-oriented.

The BJP has now realised that the real threat comes from the family-ruled regional parties in several states. After sidelining the Congress dynasty, the BJP has identified eight prominent families that dominate state politics nationwide; the BJP intends to decimate them politically, failing which it will join them as an ally. Telangana, Meghalaya, Nagaland, Tripura, Karnataka,

Chhattisgarh, Madhya Pradesh, Mizoram, and Rajasthan will hold Assembly elections in 2023. Therefore, eliminating the provincial czars would be Modi's next big project.

The question is whether it is possible to eliminate the dynasts as visualised by the BJP? It is indeed ambitious. From Kashmir to Kanyakumari, there are many dynastic families like the Abdullahs. Tall leaders among them mesmerised their electorate. The Muftis in Kashmir, the Badals and Captain Amarinder Singh in Punjab, the Rajes and Pilots in Rajasthan and Madhya Pradesh, and the Yadavs in Uttar Pradesh and Bihar are such dynasts. On the other hand, the Patnaiks in Odisha, the Gowdas and Bommais in Karnataka, the Gogois in Assam, the Karunanidhis in Tamil Nadu, the Raos and the Reddys in Telangana and Andhra Pradesh, the Sorens in Jharkhand, and the Chautalas and Hoodas in Haryana are notable.

The southern states are currently under the sway of regional satraps—Telangana Rashtra Samithi's K. Chandrashekar Rao, Y.S. Jagan Mohan Reddy in Andhra Pradesh, M.K. Stalin in Tamil Nadu, and Pinarayi Vijayan in Kerala. The BJP aims to weaken all of them in their next project.

The party currently has just four MLAs in Tamil Nadu (riding piggyback on the AIADMK) and none in Andhra Pradesh or Kerala. In Telangana it has three MLAs, which it has won on its own steam. Therefore, the first step would be to weaken them. There are 120 Lok Sabha seats in the five states in the South. Despite all its efforts, the BJP could not find a hold in southern states except in Karnataka.

Now comes the question as to why do these dynastic leaders sway people? Firstly, family-oriented parties choose their kith and kin to succeed because they feel they are more an asset than a liability. They find it easy to install and train them to take over when they die. Secondly, candidates from family are more likely to get elected than new candidates. Thirdly, some regional czars have realised that establishing family rule gives them loyalty and confidence. A party like the DMK is also reconciled to dealing with the Karunanidhi dynasty.

On the other hand, the BJP and many others think that dynastic politics is not good in a democracy as it enables only those leaders who have strong connections with the family. New fiefdoms boasting of family rule have emerged all over India.

Dynastic politics discourages new talents from coming forward. But, the BJP is not alien to it. Critics point out that this does not seem to apply to dynasts such as Jyotiraditya Scindia, Piyush Goyal, Dharmendra Pradhan, Anurag Thakur, and Kiren Rijiju—all Cabinet ministers in the Modi government. Nor does it apply to the BJP's chief ministers such as Basavaraj Bommai of Karnataka or Pema Khandu of Arunachal Pradesh.

It is premature to expect the end of political dynasties as it may take a while because people are stuck with the dynasts for now. The present-day leaders are not ashamed of projecting their family members as political heirs. Dynastic families have three advantages—name capital, cultural capital and financial capital. Though the BJP wants a dynasty-*mukt* Bharat, as long as dynasts can attract voters with a coherent narrative and possess the ability to convince them, they will hold on to their fiefdoms. The only consolation is that even the dynasts have to come through the electoral process.

There is no doubt that Jawaharlal Nehru, in his heart of heart wanted his daughter to succeed him one day and she did succeed him. But, it is not only Nehru-Gandhi dynasty which continued to rule India. There are instances to show that certain dynasties or families ruled India, such as Mulayam Singh Yadav in Utter Pradesh; Lalu Prasad Yadav in Bihar; Scindias in Madhya Pradesh; and Sharad Pawar in Maharashtra. The BJP is also no exception. The difference is only that before independence it was hereditary rule—monarchy, after independence it has become democratic monarchy. If one looks around, he will find that the elected representatives, be they ministers or Members of Parliament or Members of Legislatures, be they of any political party, their lifestyle is no less than kings and queens.

At the first meeting of the BJP Parliamentary Party after the Assembly elections in five States, Prime Minister Narendra Modi cautioned partymen about the ills of dynastic politics, which he said, led to casteism. Addressing the gathering Modi said many partymen sought ticket for their children but it was his decision that it should be denied, and that the onus of this refusal was on him.

"Several Members of Parliament and party leaders were seeking ticket in the recently concluded elections for their children and many of them were denied. For those who are not given tickets for the children, the responsibility entirely lies with him," the prime minister said.

"There would be no place for dynastic politics in the BJP and the family-led political parties would continue to be challenged," he stated. He was clear that a message needs to go to people that family and dynastic politics are not leading the country anywhere.

At an event in Paraunkh, ancestral village of former President Ramnath Kovind in Kanpur, prime minister said: "When he targets *parivarvad* or dynasticism in politics, he does not hold any personal resentment against any political party or particular individual and asserted that he wants a strong Opposition in the country."

"I want a strong Opposition liberated from the clutches of dynasty which he termed as a disease that is hollowing out Indian democracy. I want parties in the grip of *parivarvad* free (*mukta*) themselves from this disease and get themselves treated," Modi said.

"I do not have personal *narazgi* (resentment) against any political party or particular individual," prime minister said.

Modi said that while we discuss the strength of democracy in the context of a person from a rural background going on to become President of the country, "we must also beware of challenges such as *parivarvad*."

"It is *parivarvad* that strangulates talent not just in politics but in all fields and prevents them from moving forward," said prime minister.

Modi said that when he talks of *parivarvad*, some people feel it is a political statement and that he is speaking against a political party. This is how it is publicized. I see that those who fit my definition of *parivarvad* are furious at me. These *parivarvadis* in different corners of the country are uniting against me.

He further said that *parivarvadis* are also unhappy that the youths are taking his stance against *parivarvad* seriously. He advised his political opponents, the *parivarvadis*, to get themselves treated and that this would strengthen democracy in the country. This would also provide the youth of the country more opportunities to enter politics (*The Hindu*, 4th June, 2022).

Narendra Modi will be true to his thinking, if he frees his own party from dynastic rule, until then it would be a mere wishful thinking.

Anil Baluni, who is an MP and BJP's National Media Head, in his write up in *The Indian Express* of 16th June, 2022, says: "In the past four-five decades, family-based parties have choked talent and created road-blocks to the development of States. Dynasty-based political parties have neither ideology nor vision. Their only goal has been to grab power and cling to it. This resulted in these parties playing the politics of vote-banks and appeasement. The Congress adopted the same strategy at the Centre. Today, the Congress is no longer a national party, it has been reduced to the party of a brother-sister duo."

"So, engrossed were these parties in serving the interests of their kith and kin that they completely ignored overall development and holistic growth... Under dynastic rule, the dangerous and negative politics of appeasement flourished which led to the poor getting poorer while the oppressed were reduced to second-class citizens."

"The common man had deep anger and mistrust over the politics of dynasty, vote-bank and appeasement. His anger started coming out in 2014 when he saw in Narendra Modi a hope for the nation and himself. He has seen the nation and its politics changing fast."

In conclusion of his write up Baluni says: "It is heartening that the electorate has rejected parties dominated by dynasts. The recent election results in five States are the latest indicator of this trend. The BJP has been persistently fighting family-based political outfits. Under the dynamic leadership of PM Modi, we have been able to fight the politics of casteism, dynasty, nepotism and appeasement. The struggle to rid the nation of dynasty politics is long and hard. Its effect must be felt in all parts of the country—from Maharashtra to Telangana, from Bihar, Uttar Pradesh, Jharkhand to Jammu and Kashmir and Tamil Nadu."

Baluni needs to go for introspection to see whether the statements he made about Congress are not equally applicable to the BJP. The Indian politics has reached such a stage that no political party can survive without encouraging dynasty or family.

13

Constitution of India: Document of Collective Wisdom

Those entrusted with the task of framing the Constitution of India were fully alive to their historic role and the supreme importance of their assignment. Most of them were politicians but that was the age when politics attracted the best in society. Those were also the times when politics signified an attachment to certain values, and adherence to certain convictions and willingness to suffer, if need be, for those values and convictions. The top leaders also saw to it that in the election of members of the Constituent Assembly partisan considerations should not stand in the way of selecting others from outside the Congress party who had made a mark in various fields. The Constituent Assembly as such represented the very cream of those in the public life of the country. Apart from the fact that its members were inspired by a high sense of idealism and were sincerely attached to the great values of life, it was a body of persons who for sheer brilliance and talent, for breadth of vision and comprehension of basic problems for deep learning and erudition was unrivalled on our history. And in the drafting of the Constitution, the members of the Assembly were assisted by a band of civil servants and jurists who combined within themselves great ability and a high sense of devotion and dedication. Apart from sheer talent, the membership of the Constituent Assembly wielded tremendous influence and enjoyed immense popular confidence.

Dr. Rajendra Prasad who was Chairman of the Constituent Assembly, in his address on 26th November, 1949, described the method, which the Constituent Assembly adopted in connection with the making of the Constitution. The first step was to lay down its norms of reference as it were in the form of Objectives Resolution. It then proceeded to appoint a number of committees to deal with different aspects of the Constitutional problems. Several of these had as their chairman either Jawaharlal Nehru or Sardar Patel to whom thus goes the credit for fundamentals of our Constitution. They all worked in a business-like manner and produced reports, which were considered by the Constituent Assembly, and their recommendations were adopted as the basis on which the draft Constitution had to be prepared. This was done by Sir B.N. Rau who brought to bear on his task a detailed knowledge of conditions of other countries and an extensive knowledge of the conditions of his own country along with his own administrative experience. The Constituent Assembly then appointed the Drafting Committee which worked on the original draft prepared by Sir B.N. Rau and produced the draft Constitution, which was considered by the Constituent Assembly at great length. It was not only the members of the Drafting Committee who were giving their close attention to the Constitution, but other members were vigilant and scrutinizing the draft in all its details.

Dr. Rajendra Prasad said: "There were not less than 7,635 amendments of which 2,473 amendments were moved. I am mentioning this only to show that it was not only the members of the Drafting Committee who were giving their close attention to the Constitution, but other members were vigilant and scrutinizing the Draft in all its details. No wonder, that we had to consider not only each article in the Draft, but practically every sentence and sometimes every word in every article. It may interest honourable members to know that the public were taking great interest in its proceedings and I have discovered that not less than 53,000 visitors were admitted to the Visitor's gallery during the period when the Constitution has been under consideration. In the result, the Draft Constitution has increased in size, and by the time it has been passed, it has come to have 395 articles and 8 schedules, instead of the 243 articles and 13 schedules of the original Draft of Mr. B.N. Rau."

Syed Muhammad Sa'adulla, who was a member of the Drafting Committee, said: "We were only asked to dress the baby and the baby was nothing but the Objectives Resolution, which the Constituent Assembly passed. We were told that the Constitution must conform and remain within the Four Corners of the Objectives Resolution. Moreover, whatever we did had to be considered and accepted by this House. How dare any member of the Drafting Committee be so arrogant as to thrust the opinion of seven members against a total member of 308 in this House."

Sa'adulla further said: "Many sections of our Draft Constitution had to be recast as many as seven times. A draft section is prepared according to the beat in each of the members of the Drafting Committee. It is scrutinized by the particular ministerial department of government. They criticized it and a fresh draft is made to meet their criticism or requirements. Then it is considered by the biggest block, the majority party in the House—Congress Parliamentary Party—which alone can give the *imprimatur* of adoption in this House; and sometimes we found that they made their own recommendations which had to be put into the proper legal and Constitutional shape by the members of the Drafting Committee."

Dr. B.R. Ambedkar himself said: "The Drafting Committee was charged with the duty of preparing a constitution in accordance with the decisions of the Constituent Assembly on the reports made by the various committees such as the Union Powers Committee, Constitution Committee, the Provincial Constitution Committee, and the Advisory Committee on Fundamental Rights, Tribal Areas, etc. I hope the Drafting Committee will be found to have faithfully carried out the directions given to it."

Dr. Ambedkar further said: "The credit that is given to me does not really belong to me. It belongs partly to Sir B.N. Rau, the Constitutional Advisor to the Constituent Assembly who prepared a rough Draft of the Constitution for the consideration of the Drafting Committee. A part of the credit must go to the members of the Drafting Committee who, I have said, have sat for 141 days and without whose ingenuity to devise new formulae and capacity to tolerate and to accommodate different points of view, the task of framing the Constitution could not have come to a successful conclusion. Much great share of the credit must go to Mr. S.N. Mukherjee, the Chief Draftsman of the Constitution. His ability to put the most intricate proposal in the simplest and the clearest legal form can rarely be equaled, nor his capacity to hard work. He has been an acquisition to the Assembly. Without his help, this Assembly would have taken many more years to finalize the Constitution."

Dr. Ambedkar continued: "The task of Drafting Committee would have been a very difficult one if this Constituent Assembly had been merely a motley crowed, a tessellated pavement without cement, a black stone here and a white stone there in which each member or each group was a law unto itself. There would have been nothing but chaos. This possibility of chaos was reduced to nil by the existence of the Congress Party inside the Assembly, which brought into its proceedings a sense of order and discipline. It is because of the discipline of the Congress Party that the Drafting Committee was able to pilot the Constitution in the Assembly with the sure knowledge as to the fate of each article and each amendment. The Congress Party is, therefore, entitled to all the credit for the smooth sailing of the Draft Constitution in the Assembly."

Dr. Ambedkar continued: "The proceedings of the Constituent Assembly would have been very dull if all members had yielded to the rule of party discipline. Party discipline, in all its rigidity, would have converted this Assembly into the gathering of 'yes men'. Fortunately, there were rebels. They were Mr. Kamath, Dr. P.S. Deshmukh, Mr. Sidhva, Prof. Saxena and Pandit Thakur Das Bhargava. Along with them, I must mention Prof. K.T. Shah and Pandit Hridya Nath Kunzru. The points they raised were mostly ideological. That I was not prepared to accept their suggestion does not diminish the value of their suggestion nor lesson the service they have rendered to the Assembly in enlivening its proceedings. I am grateful to them. But for them, I would not have had the opportunity, which I got for expounding the principles underlying the Constitution, which are more important than the mere mechanical work of passing the Constitution."

Granville Austin said: "Nehru and Patel were the focus of power in the Assembly. When they were divided on the issue, as in the case of property clause, factions could line up behind them and the debate would be lengthy. But, when they settled their difference, the factions among the rank and file could do little else but shake hands and make the decision unanimous. Nehru and Patel were not, however, the only powerful figures in the Assembly. Their colleagues in the oligarchy, Azad and particularly Prasad, exercised much influence. Prasad could not do this openly; his position as the presiding officer of the Assembly prevented that. But, his suggestions made behind the scene carried considerable weight. As a basically conservative individual, his sympathies often lay with Patel and the key provincial figures like Purushottam Das Tandon, who often used Prasad as a channel to communicate his ideas to the inner circle of Assembly leaders" (*Ambedkar and Social Justice,* Publication Division, Government of India, Vol. 1, p. 241).

M.V. Pylee, in his book, *Constitutional Government in India*, wrote: "It may, however, be pointed out that Ambedkar and other members of the Drafting Committee were not free agents. They had to work under the guidance of other agencies. In the most fundamental fields, the ideas and decisions of Nehru, Patel and Congress Party had to be accommodated. Nehru and Patel, the combination of the idealist and the realist respectively, had the final word in any matter."

In the editorial written to *Indian Constitutional Documents—Munshi Papers*, Dr. A.K. Majumdar wrote: "The Constituent Assembly was a sovereign body and took the ultimate decisions formally. Though the debates of the Constituent Assembly and the Committee reports are very instructive and informative, it should be remembered that many of the vital decisions were taken informally either by Pandit Nehru or by Sardar Patel" (*Ibid.,* pp. 32-33).

Shri Krishnaswami Bharati, a member of the Constituent Assembly, said: "No congratulations are due to Ambedkar for the provisions in the Draft for the simple reason they are not his. Most of the clauses in the Draft Constitution were discussed, debated and left over for incorporation by the Drafting Committee."

Sir Alladi Krishnaswamy Iyer, a member of the Constituent Assembly, said: "The Constitution has been settled by the Constituent Assembly in the light of the recommendations of the various committees appointed by this House and the Draft as originally submitted by the Drafting Committee and as revised later. The Constitution as it has finally emerged, truly reflects the spirit of the Objectives Resolution with which this Assembly started its work and the Preamble of the Constitution, which mainly founded on the Objectives Resolution."

Sardar Suchet Singh, a member of the Constituent Assembly, said: "Our Constitution carries in it the impress of the high-souled nobility of the President, Dr. Rajendra Prasad, the universal vision of Pandit Jawaharlal Nehru, the unfailing judgment and strength of Sardar Vallabhbhai Patel, the scintillating and penetrating intellectuality of Dr. Pattabhi Sitaramyya, the erudition and labors of Dr. Ambedkar and above all, the patriarchal blessings and divine inspiration of the Father of the Nation, our revered Mahatma Gandhi."

Dr. K.M. Munshi, who was also a member of the Drafting Committee, said: "We had several stages in which the constitutional provisions were discussed. First, we had the committees, which submitted their reports, followed by discussion there on in the Assembly. Then we had detailed discussions in the party meetings, followed by second readings of the draft, clause by clause. Later, the Drafting Committee discussed and revised each clause; then the Congress Party went over each clause; sometimes every word. Lastly there was the open discussion of the final Draft in the Constituent Assembly."

Dr. Munshi further said: "The Chief Ministers of the States who were the members of the Constituent Assembly contributed their experiences. On occasions, the departments of the central government and the states submitted the elaborate notes. There was always the encyclopedic knowledge of Sir B.N. Rau at the service of the Assembly. Above all, were Pandit Jawaharlal Nehru's vision of sovereign Democratic India and Sardar Patel's intuitive perception of the sources from which power and stability sprang."

Composition of the Constituent Assembly

The total membership of the Constituent Assembly was envisaged as 389, of which 93 were to be representatives of the Indian States and 296 were to represent British India (292 from the Governors' Provinces and four from the Chief Commissioners' Provinces). Elections were held in July and August 1946 for 292 seats allotted to the Governors' Provinces and the two seats allotted to Coorg and British Baluchistan. The members, representing Delhi and Ajmer-Merwara in the Central Legislative Assembly, automatically became the representatives of these provinces in the Constituent Assembly. The total number of seats allotted from the Governors' Provinces to Muslims was 78, to Sikhs four, and to the candidates in the general category 210. Of the 210 general seats, the Congress was able to capture 199. The Congress also won three of the four Sikh seats from Punjab and three Muslim seats from—one in the United Provinces and two in the North-West Frontier Provinces. In addition, the Congress was to secure three seats allotted to Coorg, Ajmer-Merwara and Delhi. It won the Coorg seat in an election; and the members of the Central Legislative Assembly from Ajmer-Merwara and Delhi (a Muslim), who became members of the Constituent Assembly, were both from the Congress. The Muslim League captured 73 Muslim seats out of total of 78 Muslim seats.

The party-wise break-up of the Assembly's British Indian membership was as follows:

Congress 208, Muslim League 73, Unionist 1, Unionist Muslims 1, Unionist Schedules Castes 1, Krishak Praja 1, Scheduled Castes Federation 1, Sikhs (non-Congress) 1, Communist 1, Independents 8—Total 296.

The composition of the Constituent Assembly was representative of almost all schools of political thought in the country. Its members, elected by the method of single transferable vote by the Legislatures of the Provinces, fell into four groups:

1. Congressmen
2. Independent members, occupying important positions in public life, drawn from all communities, elected, under the direction of the Congress High Command, by Congress members of the Provincial Legislatures.
3. Independent members elected by non-Congress, non-Muslim members of the Provincial Legislatures.
4. Members elected by the representatives of the Muslim League in Provincial Legislatures. On partition, most of such members migrated to Pakistan; the few who were left, continued in the Constituent Assembly.

The Congress was anxious that the Assembly should be as truly representative as possible of all elements in India's national life. It had gone out of its way to facilitate the election of distinguished men in all spheres, irrespective of the party to which they belonged. Of the 205 members elected to the Assembly from Governors' Provinces on the Congress vote, as many as 30 were from outside the party. The concern of the Congress in regard to minorities was evident from the liberal representation given to them. From the minorities, the Scheduled Castes accounted for 29, the Indian Christians six, Anglo Indian three, Parsis three and Tribals four.

The Congress leaders had recognized the need to bring together a body of experts, regardless of party affiliation, in formulating principles and working out details. Mahatma Gandhi gave the lead in commanding to the Congress executive 16 eminent persons to be elected on the Congress ticket so that they could participate in the work of Constitution-making. The presence of such persons as Alladi Krishnaswamy Iyer (an eminent advocate), Gopalaswami Ayyangar (a former civil servant), H.C. Mookherjee (an educationist), S. Radhakrishnan (a philosopher and educationist), H.N. Kunzru (President of the Servants of India Society), and others, enhanced the prestige and authority of the Constituent Assembly.

Ultimately, the Constituent Assembly produced the world's longest Constitution, laying about the law and structure of government and the rights and duties of citizens. Granville

Austin's classic account presents the framing of the Indian Constitution as the stirring drama of a nation coming into its own as Constitutional Republic. He writes of the guiding of an "oligarchy"—Nehru, Patel, Rajendra Prasad and Maulana Abul Kalam Azad—steering the discussions and debates in the Constituent Assembly in Delhi. There were differences and misgivings, but in the end the adopted Constitution was presented to the nation as the realization of Nehru's aim: "It had been drafted with the welfare of four hundred million Indians in mind."

Dr. Ambedkar submitted the Draft Constitution as prepared by the Drafting Committee to the Constituent Assembly on 4th November, 1948, with his speech, which he concluded thus: "...The Constitution as settled by the Drafting Committee is good enough to make in this country a start with. I feel that it is workable, it is flexible and it is strong enough to hold the country together in peacetime and in wartime. Indeed, if I may say so, if things go wrong under the new Constitution, the reason will not be that we had a bad Constitution. What we will have to say is that man was vile."

The Constitution as drafted by the Drafting Committee was adopted by the Constituent Assembly on 26th November, 1949. Before the Constitution was adopted by the Constituent Assembly, Dr. Ambedkar delivered his address on 25th November, 1949, highlighting the salient features of the Constitution, the extracts of which are given below:

"On 26th January, 1950, India will be an independent country. What would happen to her independence? Will she maintain her independence or will she lose it again? This is the first thought that comes to my mind. It is not that India was never an independent country. The point is that she once lost the independence she had. Will she lose it second time? It is this thought which makes me most anxious for the future. What perturbs me greatly is the fact that not only India has once before lost her independence, but she lost it by the infidelity and treachery of some of her own people. In the invasion of Sind by Muhammad ibn al-Qasim, the military commanders of

King Dahir accepted bribes from the agents of Muhammad ibn al-Qasim and refused to fight on the side of their King. It was Jaichand who invited Mahommed Ghori to invade India and fight against Prithvi Raj and promised him the help of himself and the Solanki Kings. When Shivaji was fighting for the liberation of Hindus, the other Maratha noblemen and the Rajput Kings were fighting the battle on the side of Moghul Emperors. When British were trying to destroy the Sikh Rulers, Gulab Singh, their principal commander, sat silent and did not help to save the Sikh Kingdom. In 1857, when a large part of India had declared a war of independence against the British, the Sikhs stood and watched the event as silent spectators."

"Will history repeat itself? It is this thought that fills me with anxiety. This anxiety is deepened by the realization of the fact that in addition to our old enemies in the form of castes and creeds we are going to have many political parties with diverse and opposing political creeds. Will Indian place the country above their creed or will they place creed above country? I do not know. But, this much is certain that if the parties place creed above country, our independence will be put in jeopardy a second time and probably be lost forever. This eventuality we must all resolutely guard against. We must be determined to defend our independence with the last drop of our blood."

"On the 26th of January 1950, India would be a democratic country in the sense that India from that day would have a government of the people, by the people and for the people. The same thought comes to my mind. What would happen to her democratic Constitution? Will she be able to maintain it or will she lose it again? This is the second thought that comes to my mind and makes me as anxious as the first."

"It is not that India did not know what is democracy. There was a time when India was studded with republics, and even where there were monarchies, they were either elected or were limited. They were never absolute. It is not that India did not know Parliament's Parliamentary Procedure. A study of the Buddhist Bhikkhu Sanghas discloses that not only there were Parliaments—for the Sanghas were nothing but Parliaments—but the Sanghas knew and observed all the rules of Parliamentary procedure known to modern times. They had rules regarding seating arrangements, rules regarding motions, resolutions, quorum, whip, counting of votes, voting by ballot, censure motion, regularization *re judicata,* etc. Although, these rules of Parliamentary procedure were applied by Buddha to the meetings of the Sanghas, he must have borrowed them from the rules of the political assemblies functioning in the country in his time."

"This democratic system India lost. Will she lose it second time? I do not know. But, it is quite possible in a country like India—where democracy from its long disuse must be regarded, as something quite new—there is danger of democracy giving place to dictatorship. It is quite possible for this newborn democracy to retain its form but give place to dictatorship infect. If there is a landslide, the danger of the second possibility becoming actuality is much greater."

"If we wish to maintain democracy not merely in form, but also in fact, what must we do? The first thing in my judgment we must do is to hold fast to Constitutional methods of achieving our social and economic objectives. It means we must abandon the bloody methods of revolution. It means that we must abandon the method of civil disobedience, non-cooperation and satyagraha. When there was no way left for Constitutional methods for achieving economic and social objectives, there was a great deal of justification for unconstitutional methods. These methods are nothing but the Grammer of Anarchy and the sooner they are abandoned, the better for us."

"The second thing we must do is to observe the caution which John Stuart Mill has given to all who are interested in the maintenance of democracy, namely, not to lay their liberties at the feet of even a great man, or to trust him with powers which enable him to subvert their institutions. There is nothing wrong in being grateful to great men who have rendered life-long services to the country. But, there are limits to gratefulness. As has been well said by Irish patriot Daniel O'Connell, no man can be grateful at the cost of his honour, no woman can be grateful at the cost of her chastity and no nation can be grateful at the cost of its liberty. This caution is far more necessary in the case of India than in the case of any other country. For India, *Bhakti* or what may be called the path of devotion or hero-worship, plays a part in its politics unequalled in magnitude by the part it plays in the politics of any other country in the world. *Bhakti* in religion may be a road to the salvation of the soul. But, in politics, *Bhakti* or hero-worship is a sure road to degradation and to eventual dictatorship."

"The third thing we must do is not to be content with mere political democracy. We must make our political democracy a social democracy as well. Political democracy cannot last unless there lies at the base of it social democracy. What does social democracy mean? It means a way of life, which recognizes liberty, equality and fraternity as the principles of life. These principles of liberty, equality and fraternity are not to be treated as separate items in trinity. They form a union of trinity in the sense that to divorce one from the other is to defeat the very purpose of democracy. Liberty cannot be divorced from equality; equality cannot be divorced from liberty. Nor can liberty and equality be divorced from fraternity. Without equality, liberty would produce the supremacy of the few over the many. Equality without liberty would kill individual initiative. Without fraternity, liberty and equality could not become a natural course of things. It would require a constable to enforce them. We must begin by acknowledging the fact that there is complete absence of two things in Indian society based on the principle of graded inequality, which means elevation for some and degradation for others. On the economic plane, we have a society, in which there are some who have immense wealth as against many who live in abject poverty. On 26th January, 1950, we are going to enter into a life of contradictions. In politics, we will be recognizing the principle of one-man one-vote and one vote, one value. In our social and economic life, we shall, by reason of our social and economic structure, continue to deny the principle of one-man, one-value. How long shall we continue to live this life of contradiction? How long shall we continue to deny equality in our social and economic life? If we continue to deny it for long, we will do so only by putting our political democracy in peril. We must remove this contradiction at the earliest possible moment or else those who suffer from inequality will blow up the structure of political democracy which this Assembly has so laboriously built up."

"The next thing we are wanting in is recognition of the principle of fraternity. What does fraternity mean? Fraternity means a sense of common brotherhood of all Indians—of Indians being one people. It is the principle which gives unity and solidarity to social life. It is a difficult thing to achieve. How difficult it is, can be realized from the story related by James Bryce in his volume on *The American Commonwealth* about the United States of America."

"The story is: I propose to recount in the words of Bryce himself that some years ago the American Protestant Episcopal Church was occupied at its triennial Convention in revising its liturgy. It was thought desirable to introduce among the short sentence a prayer for the whole people, and an eminent New England divine proposed the words of O' Lord, bless our nation. Accepted one afternoon, on the spur of the moment, the sentence was brought up next day for reconsideration, when so many objections were raised by the laity to the word 'nation' as importing too definite a recognition of national unity, that it was dropped and instead there were adopted the words O' Lord, bless these United States."

"There was so little a solidarity in the U.S.A. at the time when this incident occurred that the people of America did not think that they were a nation. If the people of the United States could not feel that they were a nation, how difficult it is for Indians to think that they are a nation. I remember the days when political minded Indians resented the expression 'the People of India.' They preferred the expression 'the Indian nation.' I am of opinion that in believing that we are a nation, we are cherishing a great delusion. How can people divided into several thousands of castes be a nation? The sooner we realize that we are not as yet a nation in the social and psychological sense of the word, the better for us. For then only we shall realize the necessity of becoming a nation and seriously think of ways and means of realizing the goal. The realization of this goal is going to be very difficult—far more difficult than it has been in the United States. The United States has no caste problem. In India there are castes. These castes are anti-national: in the first place because they bring about separation in social life. They are anti-national also because they generate jealousy and antipathy between caste and caste. But, we must overcome all these difficulties if we wish to become a nation in reality. For fraternity can be fact only when there is a nation. Without fraternity, equality and liberty will be no deeper than coats of paint."

"These are my reflections about the task that lie ahead of us. They may not be very pleasant to some. But, there can be no gain saying that political power in this country has too long been the monopoly of a few and the many are not only beasts of burden, but also beasts of prey. This monopoly has not merely deprived them of their chance of betterment; it has snapped them of what may be called the significance of life. These downtrodden classes are tired of being governed. They are impatient to govern themselves. This urge for self-realization in the downtrodden classes must not be allowed to devolve into a class struggle or class war. It would lead to the division of the House. That would indeed be a day of disaster for as, has been well said by Abraham Lincoln, a House divided against itself cannot stand very long. Therefore, the sooner room is made for the realization, of their aspiration, the better for the few, the better for the country, the better for the maintenance of its independence and the better for the continuance of its democratic structure. This can only be done by the establishment of equality and fraternity in all spheres of life."

Concluding his speech, Dr. Ambedkar said: "Let us not forget that this independence has thrown on us great responsibilities. By independence, we have lost the excuse of blaming the British for anything going wrong. If hereafter things go wrong, we will have nobody to blame except ourselves. There is great danger of things going wrong. Times are fast changing. People including our own are being moved by new ideologies. They are getting tired of Government by the people. They are prepared to have Government for the people and are indifferent whether it is

Government of the people and by the people. If we wish to preserve the Constitution in which we have sought to enshrine the principle of Government of the people, for the people and by the people, let us resolve not to be tardy in the recognition of the evils that lie across our path and which induce people to prefer Government for the people to Government by the people, nor to be weak, in our initiative to remove them. That is the only way to serve the country."

Dr. Rajendra Prasad's Concluding Observations

It also seems apposite to refer to the words of Dr. Rajendra Prasad, who was the presiding officer and the last speaker in the Constituent Assembly:

"We have prepared a democratic Constitution. But successful working of the democratic institutions requires in those who have to work them willingness to respect the viewpoints of others, capacity for compromise and accommodation. Many things, which cannot be written in a constitution, are done by conventions. The way in which we have been able to draw the Constitution without taking recourse to voting and to divisions in Lobbies strengthens that hope."

"Whatever the Constitution may or may not provide, the welfare of the country will depend upon the way in which the country is administered. That will depend upon the men who administer it. It is a trite saying that a country can have the Government it deserves. Our Constitution has provisions in it, which appear to some to be objectionable from one point or another. We must admit that the defects inherent in the situation in the country and the people at large. If the people who are elected are capable and men of character and integrity, they would be able to make the best even of a defective Constitution. If they are lacking in these, the Constitution cannot help the country. After all, a constitution like a machine is a lifeless thing. It acquires life because of the men who control it and operate it, and India today needs nothing more than a set of honest men who will have interest of the country before them. There is a fissiparous tendency arising out of various elements in our life. We have communal differences, caste differences, language differences, provincial differences and so forth. It requires men of strong character, men of vision, men who will not sacrifice the interests of the country at large for the sake of smaller groups and areas and who will rise over the prejudices which are born of these differences. We can only hope that the country will throw up such men in abundance."

He then said: "I have no doubts that when the country needs men of character, they will be coming up and the masses will throw them up. Let not those who have served in the past, therefore, rest on their oars, saying that they have done their part and has now come the time for them to enjoy the fruits of their labours. No such time comes to anyone who is really earnest about his work. In India today, I feel that the work that confronts us is even more difficult than the work, which we had when we were engaged in the struggle. We did not have then any conflicting claims to reconcile, no loaves and fishes to distribute, no powers to share. We have all these now, and the temptations are really great. Would do God that we shall have the wisdom and strength to rise above them, and to serve the country which we have succeeded in liberating."

The vision and foresight shown by Dr. Ambedkar and the fears expressed by Dr. Rajendra Prasad in their speeches have almost come true during seventy-five years of independence.

14
Sharana Philosophy and Indian Constitution

A national seminar was organized in Delhi in October 2004 on the twelfth-century Sharana Revolution and the Constitution of India by the Akhil Bharat Sharana Sahity Parishad, Mysore, in collaboration with JSS Academy of Technical Education, Noida, Uttar Pradesh. The seminar was conducted with the purpose of highlighting the shared elements present in the thought processes of the Sharana philosophers and the framers of the Indian Constitution. Additionally, the significance of the Sharana Philosophy was explored, as it has nurtured a sense of divinity within the secular framework. The seminar aimed to demonstrate how these principles are reflected in the Indian Constitution.

Sharana Philosophy and *Stambhas* of Constitution

The seminar was inaugurated by Dr Karan Singh. In his inaugural address, Dr. Karan Singh said: "The Sharana concept can in a way be said to represent the basic spiritual foundation of the Indian Constitution. The Constitution reflected the deep commitment of our National Movement headed by Gandhiji and other great thinkers towards the pluralistic society."

Ekam Sat Vipra Bahudha Vadanti.

The truth is one, but we call it by many names. India is a pluralistic country. But, we have always accepted multiple paths to the Divine.

Yathā Nadyaḥ Syandamānāḥ Samudre'staṃ Gacchanti Nāmarūpe Vihāya;
Tathā Vidvānnāmarūpādvimuktaḥ Parātparaṃ Puruṣamupaiti Divyam.

—*Mundaka Upanishad*

As rivers and rivulets arrive from the different parts of the world but finally flow into the same ocean, so do all the different religions and sects arise in different parts but ultimately the goal cannot be different. These basic concepts of the Constitution are pre-figured in the twelfth-century Sharana Revolution. Our Constitution is based upon *Satyameva Jayate*, which has been taken from the *Mundaka Upanishad*.

Satyameva Jayate Nānṛtaṃ
Satyena Panthā Vitato Devayānaḥ
Yenākramantyṛṣayo Hyāptakāmā
Yatra Tat Satyasyaa Paramaṃ Nidhānamm

—*Mundaka Upanishad*

Truth can only be based upon acceptance of the Divinity inherent in all human beings—equality between men and women, a democratic pluralistic and open style of functioning, and rule of law which applies to everybody regardless of caste or creed or economic or social conditions. The foundational features of the Indian Constitution are greatly indebted to Basava and the Sharana revolution that emerged 900 years ago during the twelfth-century. These visionary concepts were boldly advocated by them and continue to shape the core principles of our Constitution today.

Indian Constitution Reflecting Spirit of Vachana Literature

His Holiness Dr. Shivamurthy Shivacharya Swamiji in his address said: "The central theme of the seminar is the comparative study between the Constitution of India and the Vachana literature. If you read the third part of the Constitution which speaks about the Fundamental Rights of the citizens in this country, every sentence appearing under this category for every word, for every sentence, with my knowledge of Vachana literature, I can quote you for every word the corresponding Vachana. For example, there are seven rights declared in the Fundamental Rights:

1. The right to equality;
2. The right to freedom;
3. The right against exploitation;

4. The right to freedom of religion;
5. The cultural and educational rights;
6. The right to property; and
7. The right to Constitutional remedies.

Under these headings if you read each and every line of it, you will find the parallel thoughts in Vachana literature. Take for example, under the category of the 'Right to Equality', it is said that the State shall not discriminate against any citizen on grounds of religion, race, caste, sex, place of birth or any of them. Again, under clause 2, it is declared that no citizen shall on grounds of religion, race, caste, sex, place of birth or any of them be subjected to any disability, liability, restriction or condition with regard to the use of wells, tanks, bathing ghats, roads, etc."

We already had a Spiritual Parliament, in the twelfth-century under the dynamic leadership of Basavanna just like we have our democratic Parliament.

Justice Shivraj Patil, a judge of the Supreme Court of India, as Chairperson of the seminar, said: "When one reads Vachana of Sharana and the Indian Constitution, one would find similarities between the several Vachanas and many Articles of the Indian Constitution."

"Whenever we look into any of the Universal religions or into the thoughts of the great personalities, the seers and the saints, we find that the Truth, the Non-violence, Dharma, Peace and Love are advocated. There is no superiority or inferiority among the human beings; there is no difference between the male and the female; and all the human beings have equal rights. All these ideas are found in the Vachanas, and in the Indian Constitution. We will also find them upheld in the U.N. Charter and the Universal Declaration of the Human Rights."

"When the Indian Constitution is read, one can find the quintessence of the Vachanas in the various Articles of the Constitution. Since the human values are intrinsically found in the Vachanas and the Articles of the Constitution, they must be read by laying emphasis on the human values and implementing them in practice with the same vigour and enthusiasm. Then it would do good to all the people in the society, and to all the living creatures."

"Spiritualism and Constitution, what does it mean? There is an answer to this question in the Sharana's Vachanas. There is a lot of similarity between the Vachanas and Sharanas and the Articles of the Constitution. If the message found in the Vachanas is honestly and meticulously followed, the Constitution would be spiritualized. The Sharanas contemplated socially, politically and culturally in the twelfth-century itself. The Sharanas said: 'see Divinity in the entire humanity'. They did not say that Kailasa is attained by Kakaya, emphatically argued that Kakaya itself is Kailasa."

Constitution Reflecting Vachana and Vedic Literature

Shri Shivraj Patil Chakurkar, who was then Home Minister of India delivered valedictory address in which he said: "The Preamble of the Constitution gives an essence of the Constitution. It emphasizes on freedom, on equality, on brotherhood, fraternity and such important aspects of life."

"If you study books on Constitution of India or for that matter any Constitution, freedom in a real sense cannot be understood. Is there a key in the Vachanas or in the Vedas or in the Upanishads or in the Constitution? What is given in the Constitution it is there in the Vachanas and in the Upanishads, but what is not given in the Constitution is also there in the Vachanas and the Upanishads. If we understand the meaning of freedom from that angle probably, we understand and enjoy the meaning of freedom better."

"The Constitution of India will speak in the name of fraternity and unity and equality. It is not possible to treat others with equality if we treat their religion as something inferior to ours."

Influence of Sharana Thought in Framing Indian Constitution

The Presidential address of the seminar was delivered by M.V. Rajasekharan in which he said: "The ideas of social justice, equality, fraternity found in the Preamble are based on Basava's Vachanas. Basavanna visualized a possibility of what would happen after 900 years when we got our independence, and what kind of Constitution we should have to groom."

"The preaching of the Shiva Sharanas of the twelfth-century could easily be compared to many of the provisions contained in the Indian Constitution. The revolutionary thought which our Constitution has incorporated, was preached and practiced by the Sharanas during the twelfth-century. The thought was kept in mind of the architects of the Constitution, and used it while discussions were held in the various sub-committees. The main motto of the twelfth-century movement was to achieve freedom, equality, fraternity, right to work and removal of untouchability."

"It is evident that the definition of the twelfth-century movement and the definitions of the modern-day Constitution of India appear to be one and the same. Many of the Articles and Clauses of our Constitution, when discussed along with the Sharana movement, such as equality, freedom of speech, non-exploitation, right to practice one's own religion and follow one's own faith, cultural and educational rights, Directive Principles of State Policy, fundamental duties, etc., we can easily find that how they are surprisingly similar to each other. We are fortunate in inheriting such a legacy which should be cherished not only by us but also by the generations to come" (*Sharana Revolution and the Indian Constitution* edited by K.M. Marula Siddhaih, published by Akhata Bharat Sharana Sahitya Parishad).

Dr. L.M. Singhvi, in his book, *Freedom on Trial*, at page 17, said: "Jawaharlal Nehru, who led the enterprise of making our Constitution magna carta between 1946 and 1949 in the Constituent Assembly of India conjured up in those four goals of fighting faiths of five major revolutions in the last 200 years of human history which had become catalyst and exemplars. These five revolutions, namely, the American Revolution, the French Revolution, the Soviet Revolution, the Gandhian and anti-Colonial Revolution and finally the Human Rights Revolution, were of crucial relevance to Constitution-making throughout the world. Human Rights Declarations became the battle cry of the allies in the Second World War. Its revolutionary credo was enshrined in the United Nations Charter and Universal

Declaration of Human Rights. It should be added that our Constitution represents not only the eclectic essence of all the five revolutions but is also the repository of our own heritage, both ancient and modern, and of our approach to national reconstruction and socio-economic transformation evolved during our freedom struggle."

15
Experts' Opinion on Constitution

I have given below the opinions of some of the Constitutional experts, which go to prove that Indian Constitution is a good one—nay as good as any other Constitution of the world.

Justice H.R. Khanna

Justice H.R. Khanna, in his book, *Law, Men of Law and Education*, published by N.M. Tripathy Pvt Ltd., Mumbai in 1981, says: "A constitution is a basic law relating to the Government of the country. It defines various organs of the State, enumerates their functions and demarcates their fields of operation. But, a constitution is more than that. It is the vehicle of nation's progress. It has to reflect the best in the past traditions of the nation; it has also to provide a considered response to the needs of the present and to possess enough resilience to cope with the demands of the future. A Constitution at the same time has to be a living thing, living not for one or two generations but for succeeding generations of men and women. It is for that reason that the provisions of the Constitution are couched in general terms, for the great generalities of the Constitution have a content and significance that vary from age to age and have, at the same time, transcendental continuity about them."

"The labour and experience of many generations of men, mould the work of those entrusted with the task of framing the Constitution. The framing of Constitution calls for highest statecraft. Those entrusted with it have to realize the practical needs of the Government and have, at the same time, to keep in view the ideals which have inspired the nation. Not anointed priests but men with proven grasp of affairs, who have developed resilience and spaciousness of mind through seasoned and diversified experience, through study of history not only of their country but also of other countries, through calm contemplation of the present, through deep thinking and sensitive awareness of the inarticulate feelings of their fellowmen, have to be the persons whom destiny and historical forces entrust with the task of drafting the Constitution. It is indeed a unique occasion in the history of a nation that a generation of men is called upon to frame the Constitution of a country. Such occasions do not recur and it becomes essential that those entrusted with the task should be conscious of their great role and the supreme importance of their assignment. On their wisdom and sagacity, their vision and foresight, their perspicacity and discernment depend on the mode of life and happiness of succeeding generations of men, women and children."

"Fortunately, for us those who were entrusted with the task of framing the Constitution of India were aware of their historic role and the supreme importance of the assignment. At a time when politics signified an attachment to certain values, an adherence to certain convictions, the Constituent Assembly represented the best talent and the cream of those in politics in the country. And in the drafting of the Constitution, they were assisted by a band of distinguished civil servants and jurists who combined within themselves great ability with a high sense of devotion and dedication."

"A Constitution is different from the ordinary statutes which are designed to meet the fugitive exigencies of the hour. The statutes can be amended when the exigencies change. A Constitution states, or ought to state, not the rules for the passing hour but principles for an expanding future. This does not, however, mean that there is something absolute about the Constitution. A Constitution is a human product and like all mortal contrivances it cannot claim absolute perfection. The framers of Constitution are always aware that in their actual working the Constitution may run into difficulties in some fields. It is for that reason that there is provision for amendment of the Constitution and it is an integral part of it. There are two distinctive features of our Constitution. It is one of the lengthiest Constitutions in the world and it has been subjected to, perhaps, the largest number of amendments."

"Stability at the centre is another matter of vital importance. This question was not important in the past as the party in power normally had an absolute majority of the members. Recent events have shown that this position may not hold true in future. The danger which we are facing is of political instability and uncertainty. One major consequence of that would be weakening of the Central Government and one cannot but shudder at this prospect. No serious peril can arise and nor great harm can be done to the nation by the bungling, failures and weakening of the administration of some states. As against that, weakening of the Central Government can imperil our very existence as an independent nation. It can indeed pose a threat to our liberty and integrity and undermine the very foundation of the nation."

"In the history of nations occasions can arise when it is not provisions of the Constitution which fail, it is the people or their representatives who fail the Constitution. I wonder if that is not true of us in India today. The success of the Constitution, it also needs to be mentioned, depends not so much on having well drafted and nobly worked provisions of the Constitution; it depends in the final analysis on the way those provisions are worked. There are few Constitutions in the world when drafted were hailed as more liberal in character and as enshrining within themselves more cherished values than the Weimar Constitution of Germany drafted soon after the First World War. Yet the manner in which the said Constitution was worked created tremendous disillusionment amongst the people. Those who were called to work that Constitution failed to live up to its ideals. The political bickering and internecine strife made its normal working more difficult. Way was, thus, paved for the emergence and rise of power of Hitler and we all know what happened thereafter."

"All this would show that whatever may be provisions of the Constitution, its ultimate success and effectiveness for public will depend upon the persons who work them and the way those provisions are worked. This necessarily postulates that the persons who are to work the system should be men of caliber, endowed with vision and possessed of catholicity of approach. They must also be attached to basic values which underlie the various provisions of the Constitution. They must be imbued, if not fully at least in substantial measure, with the spirit of idealism which inspired the founding fathers to enshrine them in the Constitution. The underlying assumption of our Constitution, as of every Constitution, is that each succeeding generation must share the faith and allegiance to values which inspired the drafting of the various provisions of the Constitution. Once this basic condition is lacking the working of the provisions of the Constitution is bound to run into rough weather."

"Petty minds ill go with the governance of great countries. The edifice of nations and national institutions, we should remember, take long to build. Behind them is the story of sweat, blood and tears of untold suffering and sacrifice; yet they can be destroyed overnight by the banishment of principles or by selfishness, petty-mindedness or folly of men. Eternal vigilance is the price of liberty and in the final analysis its only keepers are THE PEOPLE. Imbecility of men, history teaches us, always invites the impudence of power."

Justice Chandrashekhar Dharmadhikari

Justice Dharmadhikari, in his book, *Reflections on the Indian Constitution*, published by Sadhana Prakashan, Pune, said: "The Indian Constitution is the product of a long and arduous penance of political freedom and its moorings are embedded in our oceanic freedom struggle; that our national leaders and social reformers launched movements to secure for the people the rights which they never enjoyed; that these movements created hopes and aspirations in the minds of the common people and the Constitution reflects these hopes and aspirations. It is unexceptionable that the Constitution was framed not by the Constituent Assembly alone functioning between 1946 and 1950 but was shaped and moulded into the cast by the hundreds and the thousands of popular assemblies of the Indian masses which met from 1870 to 1947 throughout the length and breadth of the country. This historical assessment, though correct, is not comprehensive. There were four distinct eras of our national freedom struggle, represented by various political and social leaders; Dadabhai Naoroji and Ranade belonged to the first. Tilak and Gokhale to the second, C.R. Das, Motilal Nehru and Gandhiji to the third, and Jawaharlal Nehru, Maulana Abul Kalam Azad and Subhash Chandra Bose to the fourth. The history of the Indian freedom struggle cannot be said to be complete without reference to the part played by the generations of revolutionaries beginning with Nanasaheb Peshwa, Tatya Tope, Bahadur Shah, Vasudev Balwant, Chandrashekhar Azad, Savarkar and a host of others; their means may be questionable but their aim or goal of winning freedom for the country was not; their contribution to the national struggle far from being insignificant, gave inspiration to many and hence the agitation for political freedom and justice could be said to commence from 1857 rather than from 1870. It can legitimately be claimed that our Constitution is the product of the hopes and aspirations of the Indian people as moulded and became manifest during the period of 90 years of our freedom struggle. In a sense it was continuous process of Constitution making that crystallized into the final document in 1950."

"The objective of the Indian Constitution differs from the objective of the Constitution of the U.S.A. or that of the U.S.S.R. The American Constitution incorporates the ideas and ideals cherished by American leaders like Jefferson, Washington and Hamilton; the founding-fathers had recognized pursuit of happiness as an inalienable right of an American citizen. The Russian basic document has been framed to grant legal recognition to the new Social Order created by the Revolution of 1917. On the other hand, our Constitution reflects the hopes and aspirations of the people engendered during the freedom struggle. Hence, its objective is not merely to preserve law and order or to nurse the establishment but it is a dynamic instrument to forge and fashion the future of the Indian people so as to secure for all social and economic justice."

"Our Constitution is something much more than the idiom which defines the basic framework for legislation. It has provided guidelines for arming a political community with necessary sanctions to achieve essential social changes which were delayed by heavy handed stagnation of alien domination. Unlike, for instance, the Russian Revolution, where major changes of property ownership were achieved by force and later legalized by their new Constitution, the Indian situation created a sovereign authority by consent, and the tasks of translating freedom in terms of all-round development and social justice remained to be achieved afterwards. The direction and dynamism of such changes were to be provided by the Constitution. We can ill-afford to lose sight of this socio-political context in a community where all kinds of progress are retarded by pressures of economic interest-groups, the sway of superstition and caste arrogance. A situation of prolonged paralysis and entrenched inequalities of caste provides deep roots to feudal patterns of social relationships. The forces of change-resistance derive their strength from such a situation. It is to blast these reactionary trends that Directive Principles were enunciated as an integral part of the Constitution. They blazon the direction in which Indian polity had to advance in order to achieve its objective of social order through radical social and economic changes."

"The study of the Indian Constitution is not a simple straight forward matter. There are different ways of looking at the Constitution and, therefore, its nature as revealed to different outlook is also different. To the law courts, the study of the Indian Constitution is the integrated and consistent understanding of its various articles as interpreted by the Supreme Court. It is no doubt true that the Constitution is not to be construed in any narrow pedantic sense. The court of law has to gather the spirit of the Constitution from the language used. The established rules of interpretation require that the meaning and intention of the framers of the Constitution must be ascertained from the language used and the court is not concerned with the motives of those who framed it."

"A second way of looking at the Constitution is from the standpoint of the political scientist. He makes a comparative study of different Constitutions of the world. Important to his study is the extent to which the Indian Constitution has borrowed from other Constitutions in the world as also from the existing constitutional laws of the country. It is a very favourite thesis of Indian political scientists that our Constitution has borrowed profusely from the Constitutions of England, America, Russia, Australia, Canada, Ireland and other countries and also from the Government of India Act 1935."

"It is true that many Articles of our Constitution bear a close resemblance to various Articles of the Constitutions of these countries. But, it would be ridiculous to suggest that our Constitution is a quilt stitched out of borrowed pieces of cloth. Would it not be silly and stupid to say that all literature attributed to Shakespeare is made up of words stolen from the English Dictionary? Surely mere words taken out of a dictionary cannot produce a good literary piece. It is only when a writer imports contents to the words that creative literature is born. The various Articles of our Constitution have a significant socio-economic content—a product of our freedom struggle as well as various social and economic reform movements."

"Who are the real makers of the Constitution? In a democracy, the people are sovereign. It is the people who give themselves a constitution that is how we formally look at it. Even in the Preamble to the Indian Constitution there is a clear declaration that 'We the People of India give ourselves the Constitution.' A study of the Constitution which regards the people irrelevant must be considered to be a crude and insignificant study. Therefore, the Constitution ought to be studied in the context of the people, the common people who gave it to themselves."

Justice J.M. Shelat

Justice Shelat, in his book, *The Spirit of the Constitution*, published by Bharatiya Vidya Bhavan in 1967, expressed his views on Constitution of India as given below:

"The demand for equality involves three aspects, all of them are accepted in our Constitution—political equality in the sense of equal universal suffrage, social equality and equality of opportunity."

"The makers of the Constitution have shown considerable anxiety in ensuring that unnecessary encroachments are not made on the guaranteed freedoms in the name of common weal. Confines of rights, therefore, are as elaborately and precisely laid down as the rights themselves. As a further safeguard, the question whether a particular restriction is reasonable or not is not left to the decision of the legislature or the executive. It is the judiciary which has been entrusted with the task of ascertaining the reasonableness or otherwise of the restriction and its necessity in the interest of the society."

"None of the three organs can claim either to be supreme or superior to anyone of them. All legislators, ministers and judges take oath of allegiance to the Constitution. It is from its different provisions that they derive their respective authority and jurisdiction."

"By underwriting the classical freedoms of the individual which constitute the fundamental values of a civilized community, such as the freedom of speech, of life and liberty, of faith and conscience, of association and property, the Constitution ensures the liberty of the individual in its comprehensive meaning, giving him full opportunity for self-realization as a human being."

"The Constitution makers laid down a positive direction that the State should endeavour to secure a living wage and make exploitation of the weaker sections of the society impossible. They were not oblivious of the fact that a true democracy can thrive only in a regulated society, that there can, therefore, be no absolute freedoms without there being corresponding obligations, that insistence on absolute rights would thwart growth and advancement, social and economic, and that consequently those rights must give way where genuine interests of society in general reasonably require."

"The makers of the Constitution not only struck a reconciliation between the rights and obligations of the individual to the society but made the Constitution a living and dynamic organism, making it possible to expand so as to be able to cater to the demands of a growing society and the hopes and ambitions of large sections of it generated by the advent of independence and the large-scale industrialization following in its wake."

"Having effected a reconciliation between the conflicting interests of the citizens and the needs of society, the Constitution makers next proceeded to make a similar adjustment between the three great organs of government, the legislature, the executive and the judiciary. These three organs of the democratic fabric are expected to function not in a spirit of hostility, but rationally, harmoniously and in a spirit of concord, each operating within its allotted sphere and exercising the powers and functions respectively entrusted to them. For, it is only such regulated working by them which would conduce to the peaceful development, growth and stabilization of the democratic way of life chartered by the Constitution for the nation."

"It is manifest that the supreme concern of the makers of Constitution was the individual and his liberty, of securing to him dignity, welfare and happiness and an opportunity for development and self-realization. It is the individual who is the centre of new society which the Constitution envisages wherein the State is for him and not he for the State."

Dr. L.M. Singhvi

The following are the views expressed by Dr. L.M. Singhvi on the Constitution in his books, *Democracy and Rule of Law* and *Freedom on Trial*.

"The antecedent experience of the evolution of constitutional concepts during India's freedom struggle and the experience of Indian leaders with Parliamentary institutions during the colonial period provided certain basic inputs in the making of our Constitution. It is fair to say that the experience of India's previous constitutional history was not lost on the founding fathers. A Constitution drafted in 1895 under the inspiration of Lokmanya Bal Gangadhar Tilak, Swaraj Bill of 1895 and numerous constitutional; or semi-constitutional instruments drafted during the British regime were on the historical canvas of the Constituent Assembly. The Morley-Minto Reforms, the Montague-Chelmsford Reforms, and the 1935 Act were etched on the canvas. Those evolutionary stages were synthesized with the vision of *Poorna Swaraj* and the eclectic wisdom of different Constitutions of the world into the final constitutional document that emerged on 26th November, 1949, which embodied and constitutionally internalized the country's history, its outlook, its ethos and concerns. It was a living document, prepared by an elite which had the capacity to make it work. The Constitution was made in the name of 'We the People of India,' who had the wisdom and the maturity to understand and develop the cultural dynamics and dialectics of the discourse of democracy and rule of law. The Constitution of Burma was short-lived mainly because it did not belong to the Burmese society and no segment of Burmese society was prepared to own it or stand up for it. India had the inheritance of its own successive movements of renaissance from the early 19th century onwards. It was a continuous process of renaissance. We had the whole history of the freedom struggle and the values of the freedom struggle as a bulwark of the Constitution. We also had, a number of our own constitutional documents, not only the Swaraj Bill of 1895, but documents such as Commonwealth of India Bill which was prepared in 1920s under the inspiration of Annie Besant and Tej Bahadur Sapru, and the draft prepared by Motilal Nehru in 1920-30. These documents also provided the foundation and helped the organic assimilation of the constitutional aspirations of the Indian people."

"The Constitution of India epitomizes the new socio-political norms which were enthroned in the wake of our Independence. In the context of Indian life, these norms were doubtless radical and forward-looking. It is in this sense that the Constitution of India is a progressive, even a revolutionary document even though it accepted and perpetuated many colonial legacies. By and large, it was and continues to be ahead of the existing realities of Indian society."

"The Constitution of India is above all a democratic document. It proclaims the objective of social, economic and political justice as the mainspring of its inspiration. It is wedded to the ideals of equality in social and economic spheres. It guarantees fundamental freedoms for all individual citizens. It legalizes the Revolution. The Constitution of India is above all a democratic, liberal document, it does not contain the seeds of revolution so much as it represents flowering of certain revolutionary ideas and the possibility of the efflorescence of freedom. Achievement of or approximation to these ideas in the fabric of Indian life would be the material fulfillment of the spiritual raison d'etre of the Indian Revolution."

"The message of Indian revolution is enshrined in the soul stirring resolve which finds utterance in the Preamble of the Constitution which proclaims the resolve of the people of India to secure: Justice, social, economic and political; liberty of thought, expression, belief, faith and worship; and equality of status and of opportunity; and to promote among them all fraternity, assuring the dignity of the individual and unity and integrity of the Nation."

"In a country where injustice had been rampant for centuries in all walks of life, where liberty of thought and expression had been suppressed under colonial and monarchical rule for several generations and when Equality and Fraternity among all classes of its inhabitants had been more often than not denied, the declarations of the Indian Constitution are obviously exceedingly bold."

"In a sense, the Indian Constitution is such a courageous act of faith, in that it laid the foundation of a radical and constructive transformation of Indian society."

"After partition, the founding fathers found themselves face to face with the two-nation theory and its trauma and tragedy. But in the making of the Constitution of India they firmly resisted subscribing to obscurantist and divisive premise of a theocratic state or a state based on the dominance of any religious or subservience of others. It was a courageous decision consistent with India's liberal ethos, demographic diversities and cultural pluralism. It was a considered ideological position taken by the founding fathers that the Constitution had to be for all the people, not merely for the majority community and to the elite of India in the Constituent Assembly that while establishing a democracy based on the majority principle and despite the ideological communal onslaught of partition, the founding fathers established an organic social fabric of freedom, equality, justice, secularism, rule of law, judicial review and enforceability of fundamental rights as the foundation of our republic Constitution."

"It was an act of courage and an act of faith that the draft Constitution opted unhesitatingly for a liberal secular Constitution and kept the vision of the freedom struggle intact. The word secular was not used in the Constitution, except in one place, in respect of the management of certain aspects of religious institutions, but secularism, pluralism and liberalism were the pulsating ideologies and inspiration of our Constitution. It is a constitution of equal respect for different faiths, of respect for the minorities, of fundamental rights as basic human rights, and rule of law. At the time when our Constitution was being made, the issue of human rights was very much in the air. The Universal Declaration was proclaimed on 10th December, 1948, and is reflected fully in the Indian Constitution."

V.B. Kulkarni

Kulkarni, in his book, *The Indian Triumvirate: A Political Biography of Gandhi-Patel-Nehru*, said: "The Constitution has attempted to give practical effect to the Periclean prescription of political liberty and of social and economic justice by devoting two whole chapters to Fundamental Rights and Directive Principles of State Policy. The enunciation of Fundamental Rights in the manner it has been done has been proved to be wise since it has helped the law courts to check legislative and executive inroads into them."

"The Directive Principles of State Policy, no less detailed in their exposition of the social and economic rights of the people, promise a fair and generous deal to every citizen of the Republic, irrespective of his caste, creed or colour. Social justice, opportunities for employment and education, and preferential treatment for certain backward sections of the community are promised. The Directive Principles are, however, not justiciable. Nor can they override other constitutional provisions or any other law. Even so, they form an essential part of the Constitution and are similar to the provisions in the Irish Constitution."

"Besides providing for political liberty and freedom from want, the framers of the Constitution were anxious to ensure that the territorial integrity of India was fully safeguarded. Towards this end, they have clothed the Union Government with a plenitude of effective powers. At the same time, they have realized the need for allowing a large measure of internal autonomy to the constituent units since some 90% of the interests of the ordinary man are dealt with in the provincial sphere. We have, thus, in this country, a system of government, the form of which is both federal and unitary. In normal times, it can transform itself into a unitary state under the emergency provisions enumerated in Part XVIII of the Constitution. For this reason, the Indian statute is described as *sui generis.*"

"Even in normal times, the paramountcy of the Centre, represented by Parliament, the Union Government and the Supreme Court, over the rest of the country is well-established. Apart from the fact that Parliament has exclusive legislative jurisdiction over the Union List, consisting of a large number of subjects, it shares with the State Governments the right of legislating for the States on subjects included in the concurrent list. Besides, the law of the Union prevails in the event of a state law being repugnant to it. Again, Articles 256 and 257(1) are crucial in establishing the ascendency of the principal Government over the States. Not only are the States required to exercise their executive power in such a manner as to ensure compliance with the Union laws, but they are prohibited from doing anything calculated to impede or prejudice the exercise of its executive power by the Centre."

"In addition, all matters of national and international importance, such as defence, foreign affairs and communications, are reserved to the exclusive jurisdiction of the Centre. In financial matters also, its primacy is undoubted. The financial provisions in the Constitution have in fact been so devised as to strengthen further the country's administrative unity. The States cannot expect to prosper without generous financial assistance from the Union Government. Nor can they claim any permanence for their boundaries."

I have given the details as above to show that the Constitution is the document of collective wisdom and it has long history and background. So, the credit of preparing the Constitution cannot be given to one individual as being rampantly done in the recent past.

Since Narendra Modi has taken over as Prime Minister, there is a race to praise Dr. Ambedkar and the Constitution forgetting what RSS supremos have said about the Constitution and Dr. Ambedkar.

The Prime Minister, in his speech, thanked the framers of the Constitution of India for giving us the federal structure. He said our dreams are bound to be realized if we walk shoulder to shoulder by maintaining this spirit and respecting its sentiments in the *Amrit Kaal*.

The above statement of Narendra Modi on the Constitution amounts to his disagreement on the views of his patriarchs in RSS and its allied organizations on the Constitution. I reproduce below the views of RSS and its Supremos on the Constitution to refresh memory.

RSS published its White Paper denouncing the Constitution as anti-Hindu on 1st January, 1993. Its front cover page posed two questions—(i) Who is the destroyer of India's integrity, brotherhood and communal amity? (ii) Who has spread starvation, unemployment, corruption and irreligion? The answer provided in the White Paper was '*Vartman Samvidhan*'.

In the 'Foreword' of the White Paper, Swami Hiranand wrote: "The present Constitution is contrary to the country's culture, character and circumstances. It is foreign oriented. We will have to think afresh about our economic policy, judicial and administrative structure and our national institutions only after nullifying the present Constitution. It has to be discarded completely as a matter of high priority."

On 25th December, 1992, after the demolition of Babri Masjid, Swami Muktanand held a press conference in New Delhi jointly with Swami Vamdeo Maharaj. They gave a call to the nation to reject the anti-Hindu Constitution.

In January 1993, the RSS Sarsanghchalak Rajendra Singh said: "A Constitution more suited to the ethos and genius of this country should be adopted in future."

On 24th January, 1993, at Anantapur in Andhra Pradesh, Murli Manohar Joshi who was then President of BJP reiterated his demand for a fresh look at the Constitution.

Within a fortnight of Atal Bihari Vajpayee's thirteen months Government, a Constitution Review Commission was constituted. L.K. Advani, who was then Home Minister, said: "My party has felt the need for a comprehensive review of the Constitution, principally for three reasons. Firstly, with the passage of nearly 50 years since its adoption in 1950, it was evident that the schism had developed between the original ideals and goals of the Constitution and actual performance of the republic. This gap needed to be bridged. Secondly, the working and coordination between the institutional tripod of Parliamentary democracy, legislature, executive and judiciary left a lot to be desired. Also, growing demands for the devolution of powers from the Centre to the States, and from the State Governments to the Panchayat Raj institutions and municipal bodies had not been addressed. The third and the most pressing reason was the problem of political stability."

On 25th November, 1949, after the final draft of the Constitution was presented by Dr. B.R. Ambedkar in the Constituent Assembly, the RSS mouthpiece, the *Organizer* wrote that the worst thing about the new Constitution of Bharat is that there is nothing Bhartiya about it. There is no trace of ancient Bhartiya Constitutional Laws, institutions, nomenclature and phraseology in it.

A letter published in the *Organizer* expressed outrage at a writer who had praised Dr. Ambedkar as the 'Modern Manu' of Modern India. This said, the ideologue is an instance of depicting a Lilliput as Brobdingnag. It borders on ridicule to put Dr. Ambedkar on par with God-like Manu.

U-Turn of Mohan Bhagwat

Putting to rest the controversy, Dr. Mohan Bhagwat, the present RSS Sarsanghchalak asserted that "the RSS accepts and respects the Indian Constitution since its very beginning, as it has been put together on the basis of consensus in the nation. The RSS respects all the symbols and sentiments attached to the Indian Constitution. He stresses that the Sangh works on the basis of a sense of brotherhood enshrined in the Constitution."

Dr. Bhagwat seems to have genius in creating confusion and diverting attention from main issues, which is evident from his recent statement that every person living in the country is Hindu and the DNA of all Indians is the same, and that there is no need for anyone to change his/her way of offering rituals.

Addressing RSS volunteers, Bhagwat repeatedly highlighted unity in diversity as India's long-held tradition and said Hindutva is the only idea in the world that believes in taking everyone along. "We have been saying since 1925 (when RSS was founded) that everyone living in India is a Hindu. Those who consider India as their *Matrabhoomi* (motherland) and want to live with a culture of unity in diversity, irrespective of whatever religion, culture, language and food habit and ideology they follow, are Hindus," he said.

Bhagwat further said: "Hindutva is the only idea in the entire world that believes in unifying diversities because it has carried such diversities together in this country for thousands of years. This is truth and you have to speak it firmly."

Presuming that Bhagwat is right, but the million-dollar question is whether the Muslims and the Christens will agree and follow him.

RSS on National Flag

On 14th July, 1946, Sarsanghchalak Golwalkar Guruji said: "It was the saffron flag which in totality represented Bhartiya culture. It was the embodiment of God. We firmly believe that in the end, the whole nation will bow before this saffron flag." Even after independence, the RSS refused to accept the tricolor as the National Flag. Golwalkar Guruji wrote in his *Bunch of Thoughts*:

"Our leaders have set up a new flag for our country. Why did they do so? It is just a case of drifting and imitating. Ours is an ancient and great nation with glorious past. Then, had we no flag of our own? Had we no national emblem at all these thousand years? Undoubtedly, we had. Then why this utter void, this utter vacuum in our minds?"

Prime Minister Narendra Modi announced '*Har Ghar Tiranga*' campaign to hoist tricolour on every house from 13 to 15 August 2022. And people enthusiastically followed him including RSS headquarters in Nagpur.

Better than late, the wisdom seems to have dawned on Narendra Modi and RSS supremos to acknowledge the Constitution and Dr. Ambedkar.

Annexure

AZADI KA AMRIT MAHOTSAV

The Speech of Narendra Modi on 15th August, 2022

The Prime Minister Narendra Modi delivered his 76th Independence Day speech on 15th August, 2022 from the ramparts of the Red Fort as reproduced below.

Best wishes to my dear countrymen on the momentous occasion of completion of 75 years of Independence. Many congratulations to all! It is heartening to see our tricolor being unfurled with pride, honor and glory, not only in all the corners of India, but also worldwide by Indians who love their country immensely. I extend my heartiest congratulations to all the people spread across the globe who love India. My heartfelt greetings to all my dear Indians on this Amrit Mahotsav festival of celebrating our freedom. This is a day of historic importance. This is an auspicious occasion to step forward on a new path, with a new resolution and a new strength.

In the pursuit of Independence, the entire period of slavery was spent in struggle. No part of India or any time period remained untouched by the freedom struggle against several centuries of slavery and marked by people sacrificing themselves facing torture and making supreme sacrifice. Today is an opportunity for all of us countrymen to bow down and salute all such brave hearts, the legends of every sacrifice made by every great soul. This is an opportunity to also solemnly acknowledge their debt and pledge to fulfil their dreams at the earliest with deep resolve. All the countrymen are deeply indebted to Pujya

Bapu, Netaji Subhash Chandra Bose, Babasaheb Ambedkar, Veer Savarkar, who devoted all their life on the path of duty towards the nation. The path of obligation has been their sole life path. This country is grateful to Mangal Pandey, Tatya Tope, Bhagat Singh, Sukhdev, Rajguru, Chandrashekhar Azad, Ashfaq Ulla Khan, Ram Prasad Bismil and countless such revolutionaries of ours who shook the foundations of British rule. This nation is grateful to those brave women, be it Rani Lakshmibai, Jhalkari Bai, Durga Bhabhi, Rani Gaidinliu, Rani Chennamma, Begum Hazrat Mahal, Velu Nachiyar, who showed the mettle of women power of India. What is the resolve of India's 'Nari Shakti'? Every Indian is filled with pride while remembering the countless brave women who achieved the pinnacle of sacrifice.

Today is an opportunity to pay homage to countless such great men like Dr. Rajendra Prasad ji, Nehru ji, Sardar Vallabhbhai Patel, Shyama Prasad Mookerjee, Lal Bahadur Shastri, Deendayal Upadhyay, Jai Prakash Narayan, Ram Manohar Lohia, Acharya Vinoba Bhave, Nanaji Deshmukh, Subramania Bharati who fought the war of independence and built the country after independence.

When we talk about the freedom struggle, we cannot forget to acknowledge our tribal society living in forests. There are countless names like Bhagwan Birsa Munda, Sidhu-Kanhu, Alluri Sitarama Raju, Govind Guru, who became the voice of freedom movement and inspired tribal brothers and sisters, mothers and youth in the remotest jungles to live and die for the motherland. It has been the good fortune of the country that there have been many aspects of the freedom struggle. And one such aspect was when many such great men like Narayana Guru, Swami Vivekananda, Maharishi Aurobindo, Gurudev Rabindranath Tagore kept awakening the consciousness of India in every corner and every village of India, and kept this consciousness alive.

For the last year, we are witnessing how the country is celebrating the '*Amrit Mahotsav*'. It all began with Dandi Yatra in 2021. The people held programs in every district, every corner, of India to enlarge the scope of goals of the '*Amrit Mahotsav*' of Independence. This was perhaps for the first time in history that such a huge and comprehensive festival for a single purpose was celebrated. An attempt was made in every corner of India to remember all those great men who did not find mention in history for some reasons or who were forgotten. Today, the nation sought out all such heroes and great men, selfless, brave men from every corner of the country and paid tributes to them. It was an opportunity to pay tributes to all these great men during the '*Amrit Mahotsav*'.

Yesterday on 14th August, India also remembered the deep wounds of Partition on 'Partition *Vibhishika* Memorial Day' with a heavy heart. Crores of such people had endured a lot for the glory of the tricolour. They had endured so much due to their love for the motherland and they did not lose patience. Their determination to start a new life with their love for India is inspirational and worth saluting.

Today, as we are celebrating the '*Azadi Ka Amrit Mahotsav*', it is an opportunity to recall the contributions made by those who lived and died for the country, dedicated their lives for the country during the last 75 years, those who protected the country and fulfilled the country's resolutions; be it the army personnel, police personnel, bureaucrats, public representatives, administrators of the local self-government, state administration or central administration. Today we must also recall the contributions made by the crores of citizens of the country who have done everything possible to take the country forward despite various challenges in 75 years.

This journey of 75 years has been full of ups and downs. Amidst the shadow of good and bad times our countrymen have accomplished various achievements; they have made efforts and have not given up. They didn't let the resolutions fade away. It is true that the hundreds of years of colonial rule had inflicted deep wounds on India and the sentiments of the Indians, but the people were resilient and passionate. And that's why, Indians managed to revive the nation despite scarcity and denigration. When the freedom struggle was in its final stages, all measures were taken to frighten, disappoint and frustrate the country. There were apprehensions that after independence when the

British would leave, the country would be scattered and in shambles; people would die fighting internal wars; India would plunge into a dark age.

But they were not aware that this is the soil of India. This country has the unlimited potential to survive across centuries and influence even beyond the powerful rulers. It is as a result of such immense capabilities and resilience that our nation has emerged strong despite facing innumerable adversities be it food crisis or war. We have aborted challenges hurled at us by terrorist activities which killed our innocent countrymen. We endured proxy war, natural calamities, successes and failures, hopes and despair yet remained undaunted at all such junctures. But even in the midst of these abysmal stages, India has been relentlessly progressing. India's diversity, which others once thought was a burden to India, is proven to be the priceless power of India. A strong testimony of its power.

The world was not cognizant that India has an inherent potential of strong culture and values, a bond of thoughts deeply embedded in mind and soul; and that is India is Mother of democracy. And when those who have democracy pulsating in their minds walk with determination and resolve, it augurs doom for the most powerful sultanates of the world. This Mother of Democracy, our India has proven to all that we have this invaluable strength.

In the journey of 75 years, in the midst of hopes, aspirations, ups and downs, it is with everyone's effort that we could reach this far. And when in 2014, my countrymen gave me this responsibility, I was the first Indian born in free India, who got the privilege to sing praises of glory to my dear countrymen from the ramparts of the Red Fort. But whatever I have learned today is from all of you. I have been able to understand your happiness and sorrows. I could sense your soul calling about the hopes and aspirations you have for your country. With whatever I could embrace of your dreams, I immersed myself fully in empowering those countrymen during my tenure who were left behind and deprived from being a part of the mainstream. Be they the marginalized, outcast, exploited, victimized, deprived, tribals, women, youth, farmers, or the *divyang* people. From the farthest of India's east or west, north or south, ocean beds or Himalayan peaks, I have dedicated myself to fulfil Mahatma Gandhi's vision of inclusion. I have committed myself to his vision of empowering and uplifting the person sitting at the last mile. I can see the fruition of this mission in the past eight years because of the experience gained over several decades of independence. We are embarking on the glorious years of 75 years today on *Amrit Mahotsav*. On the first morning of this *Amrit Kaal*, I am filled with pride to see such an immensely endowed nation.

I am witnessing the biggest fortune today that Indians have emerged as an Aspirational Society. Being an aspirational society is the biggest asset for any nation. And we are proud that today every corner of India, every section and strata of our society is brimming with aspirations.

Every citizen of the country wants to change things, wants to see things change, but is not ready to wait. He wants these things to happen in front of his eyes and wants to do it as part of his duty. He wants speed, he wants progress. He is eager and excited to fulfill all the dreams cherished in 75 years before his eyes. It may cause problems to some people. Because when there is an aspirational society, then even the governments have to walk on the edge of the sword and also have to charge with the times. And I believe whether it is the central government, state governments, institutions of local self-government, no matter what kind of governance system, everyone has to address this aspirational society and we cannot wait longer for their aspirations. Our aspirational society has waited for a long time. But, now they are not ready to force their future generations to live in wait and hence the first dawn of this '*Amrit Kaal*' has brought a huge golden opportunity for us to fulfill the aspirations of that aspirational society.

Recently, we have seen and experienced one such force and that is the renaissance of the collective consciousness in India. The renaissance of such collective consciousness, a nectar of so many struggles for freedom, is now being preserved and compiled. It is turning into a resolution; the culmination of effort is reckoned and the path of accomplishment is visible. I think that this awakening of consciousness, this renaissance, is our greatest asset.

Look at this renaissance. Until 10th August, people would not even be aware of the power within the country. But, for the last three days, the way the country has set about celebrating the journey of the Tricolour, even the leading experts of social science can't imagine the power within my country which has been shown by the Tricolor. This is the moment of re-consciousness and renaissance. People are still to understand this. One can experience this consciousness when every corner of India comes out to observe '*Janata Curfew*'. There is a feeling of consciousness when the country stands shoulder to shoulder with the corona warriors by clapping and clanging utensils. This consciousness is felt when the country goes out to greet the corona warriors by lighting a lamp. During Corona, the world was grappling with the confusion whether to take vaccines or not or whether the vaccines are useful or not. At that time, even the poor people of my country's villages surprised the world with the administration of 200 crore vaccine doses. This is consciousness; this is potential, which has given new strength to the country today.

I can see an important potential. Like an aspirational society, like renaissance the attitude of the whole world towards India has changed in the same way after so many decades of independence. The world is looking at India with pride and with anticipation. The world has started looking for solutions to the problems on the soil of India, friends. This change in the world, this change in the thinking of the world is the result of our experience and journey of the last 75 years.

The world is observing the way we have started moving ahead with the resolution, and ultimately the world too is living with a new hope. The world has started realising where the power to fulfil the expectations actually lies. I see it as triple power or '*tri-shakti*' i.e., aspiration, re-awakening and the world's expectations. We are fully cognizant of this, today, my countrymen have a major role in awakening. 130 crore countrymen after several decades of experience have shown the world the importance of a stable government, the power of political stability, policies and how trust develops in the policies. The world too is now realising it. And now when there is political stability, dynamism in policies, speed in decision making, ubiquity and universal trust, then everyone becomes a partner in development.

We started our journey with the mantra of '*Sabka Saath, Sabka Vikas*', but gradually the countrymen have added more colours to it with '*Sabka Vishwas and Sabka Prayas*'. So, we have seen our collective power and collective potential. '*Azadi Ka Amrit Mahotsav*' is being celebrated with the campaign to build 75 *Amrit Sarovars* in every district today. People from every village are joining the campaign and offering their services. With their own efforts, the people are running a massive campaign for water conservation in their respective villages. Therefore, brothers and sisters, whether it is a campaign for cleanliness or the work for the welfare of the poor, the country is moving ahead with full force today.

But, brothers and sisters, if we continue to glorify our 75 years of journey in the '*Azadi Ka Amrit Kaal*' and keep patting our own backs, then our dreams might be pushed far away. So, even if the past 75 years have been wonderful, full of various challenges and certain unfulfilled dreams, yet today when we are entering the '*Azadi Ka Amrit Kaal*', the next 25 years are very significant for our country. And that's why today as I am talking about the strength of 130 crore countrymen, witnessing their dreams and feeling their resolutions from the ramparts of Red Fort, I believe we must focus our attention on the '*Panch Pran*' for the coming 25 years. You have to concentrate on your resolve and strength. And we must take up the responsibility of fulfilling all the dreams of the freedom fighters by embracing those '*Panch Pran*' by 2047 when the country celebrates 100 years of independence.

Speaking of '*Panch Pran*', the first vow is for the country to move ahead with a big resolve. And that big resolution is of a developed India; and now we should not settle for anything less than that. Big resolution! The second *Pran* is that in no part of our existence, not even in the deepest corners of our mind or habits should there be any ounce of slavery. It should be nipped there itself. Now, 100 per cent this slavery of hundreds of years has kept us bound, has forced us to keep our emotions tied up, have developed distorted thinking in us. We have to liberate ourselves from the slavery mind set which is visible in innumerable things within and around us. This is our second *Pran Shakti*.

The third *Pran* is that we should feel proud of our heritage and legacy. Since it is this same legacy which had given India its golden period in the past. And it is this legacy that has an innate capability of transforming itself with time. It is this rich heritage that transcends tests of tide and times. It embraces the new. And hence we should be proud of this heritage.

Fourth *Pran* which is equally important is unity and solidarity. Amongst 130 million countrymen when there is harmony and bonhomie, unity becomes its strongest virtue. '*Ek Bharat Shreshtha Bharat*'—is one of the unifying initiatives to actuate the dream of the fourth *Pran*.

Fifth *Pran* is the duty of the citizens, in which even the Prime Minister, Chief Minister cannot be an exclusion as they are also responsible citizens and have a duty towards the nation. This virtue is going to be the vital life force if we want to achieve the dreams, we have for the next 25 years.

When your dreams are big, your resolve is big, and therefore endeavours should also be bigger. Strength also adds up to a great extent. Recall the period of 40-42, it is difficult to imagine now how the country emerged from the shackles of the treacherous British rule. Some hands picked up brooms, while some chose spindles, while several chose the path towards satyagraha, some chose to struggle while many treaded the path of bravery of revolution. But, the resolve of each was big, that of Freedom. Just see the power of their big goal—they achieved freedom for us. We became independent. Had their resolution would have been small and limited, we would have prolonged our days of struggle and slavery, but kudos to their indomitable spirit and big dreams, we could finally attain our freedom.

As we wake up to this auspicious morning of 76th Independence, we must resolve to make India a developed nation in the next 25 years. The youth of today, all of 20-22-25 years, who I can see here shall be a witness to the glorious centennial celebrations of Independence. You will be 50-55 years old then, that means this golden period of your life, these 25-30 years of your age is the time to fulfill the dreams of India. Take a pledge and walk with me, friends, take the oath of the Tricolor and let us all join with full strength. This should be our great resolve that my country will be a developed country, we will develop a people-centric system in every parameter of development and we will have every human being and his hopes and aspirations at our center. We know that when India makes great resolutions, it also implements them.

When I first spoke about cleanliness during my first speech, the entire country embraced it. Everyone moved towards cleanliness as per his capacity and there is now antipathy towards filthiness. This is the country which has done it, is doing it and will continue to do so in future also. When the world was in a dilemma, this is the country which crossed the target of 200 crore vaccinations in a time-bound manner and broke all the previous records. We are dependent on the fuel from the Gulf. We had decided how to move towards bio-oil. The 10 percent ethanol blending seemed like a very big dream. Old experiences showed that it was not possible, but the country has realized this dream of 10 percent ethanol blending before time.

Providing electricity connection to 2.5 crore people in such a short time was not a small task, but the country has done it. Today the country is rapidly providing 'water from tap' to the homes of lakhs of families. Freedom from open defecation has become possible in India today.

Experience tells us that we can achieve our goals once we are determined. Be it the goal of renewable energy, the intention of building new medical colleges in the country or creating a workforce of doctors, the pace has increased a lot in every field. And that's why I say that the coming 25 years should be of huge resolutions, this should be our life and this should be our pledge.

The second thing that I have mentioned is the mentality of slavery and the attitude of the country. Brothers, how long will the world continue to give certificates to us? How long will we live on the certificates of the world? Shall we not set our own standards? Can a country of 130 crores not make an effort to exceed its standards? Under no circumstances should we try to look like others. It should be our temperament to grow with our own potential. We want freedom from slavery. The element of slavery should not remain in our mind even under the distant seven seas, friends. And I look with hope the way the new National Education Policy has been formulated with a lot of brainstorming, with the exchange of ideas from various people and is at the root of the country's education policy. The skill that we have emphasized is such a power, which will give us the strength to be free from slavery.

We have seen that sometimes our talent gets tied in the shackles of language. This is the result of slave mentality. We should be proud of every language of our country. We may or may not know the language, but we should be proud that it is the language of my country and it is the language given to the world by our ancestors.

Today we are witnessing the structure of Digital India. We are looking at start-ups. Who are these people? This is that pool of talent who lives in Tier-2 and Tier-3 cities, or in villages and belongs to poor families. These are our youngsters who are coming before the world today with new discoveries. We have to give up the colonial-era mentality. Instead, we must rely on our capabilities.

Secondly, we must feel proud of our heritage. Only when we connect with our land, we will be able to fly high, and when we fly high, we will be able to provide solutions to the world too. We have seen the impact when we take pride in our heritage and culture. Today the world is talking about holistic health care. But when it talks about holistic health care, it looks towards India's yoga, India's Ayurveda and India's holistic lifestyle. This is our legacy that we are providing the world with. The world is being influenced by it today. Now, look at our strength. We are the people who know how to live with nature. We know how to love nature. Today the world is facing environment related problems.

We have that legacy and the solutions to the problems of global warming. Our ancestors have given us the same. When we talk about an environment-friendly lifestyle and LIFE mission, we attract the attention of the world. We have this power. Coarse paddy and millets are household items. This is our heritage. Due to the hard work of our small farmers paddy flourished on small pieces of land. Today the world is moving ahead to celebrate the millet year at the international level. That means our heritage is being appreciated around the world today. Let us learn to be proud of it. We have a lot to offer to the world.

When it comes to social stress, people talk of our family values; whenever it comes to personal stress, people talk of yoga. When it comes to collective tension, the people talk of the family system of India. The joint family system is an asset. Due to the sacrifices made by our mothers and sisters over the centuries, the 'joint family system' has evolved as a legacy. This is our legacy. How can we not be proud of this heritage? We are those people who see Shiva in every living being. We are those people who see Lord Narayana in every man. We are people who call women 'Narayani'. We are people who see the divine in the plants. We are the people who consider the rivers as mother. We are those people who see Shankar in every stone. This is our power. It is our potential to see every river as a form of mother. Such enormity of the environment is our pride! When we are proud of such heritage, the world too will feel proud of it.

We are the people who have given the world the mantra of '*Vasudhaiva Kutumbakam*'. We are the people who believe in '*Ekam Sad Vipra Bahudha Vadanti*'.

In the period of 'holier than thou' mentality, today the world is facing a severe crisis due to conflicts caused by the attitude of one upmanship—the reason for all tensions. We have the wisdom to resolve this. Our scholars have said '*Ekam Sat Vipra Bahudha Vadanti*' meaning that absolute Truth is one but it is manifested differently. This is our glory. We are the ones who say '*Yat Pinde Tat Brahmande*', such a wise thought that whatever is in the universe is in every living being. We were the proponents of such human values.

We are the people who have seen the welfare of the world; we have been on the path of collective good and individual good, not only for our people but the whole world by believing in '*Sarve Bhavantu Sukhinaḥ, Sarve Santu Nirāmayāḥ*'. It is ingrained in our values that we will pray that may all be prosperous and happy, may all be free from illness, may all see what is auspicious, and may no one suffer. It is our heritage to care for the happiness and good health of all. Hence, we should learn to honour and feel proud of our heritage and value system. It is the strength of our resolve that will be crucial in achieving the dreams in the next 25 years.

Another very important issue is unity and solidarity. We need to celebrate the diversity of our huge country. The peaceful co-existence of innumerable traditions and creeds are our pride. For us all are equal. No one is inferior or superior; all are our own. This feeling of oneness is important for unity. The foundations of unity can be laid in every home only if son and daughter enjoy equality. If the family seeds gender discrimination across its generations, then the spirit of unity can never be woven in society. Gender equality is our first stipulation. When we talk of unity, why not have only one parameter or standard—that of India First. All my endeavours, everything that I am thinking, saying, envisioning or visualising is in accordance with India First. This way the path to unity can be opened for all of us my friend. This is the mantra we need to embrace to bind all of us in oneness. I have full faith that we can, thus, diminish the discrimination prevalent in our society. We endorse the value of *Shramev Jayate* which means that it should be in our nature to respect the labourer.

From the ramparts of Red Fort, I also want to share one of my enduring pains. I cannot hold myself from expressing my pain. I am mindful that it may not befit the podium of the Red Fort. But I will still express my deepest feelings of agony to my countrymen. If I do not open up in front of the countrymen, then where will I say it after all? What I wish to share is that it hurts me to say that we have witnessed a perversion in our day-to-day speaking, behavior. We have been casually using language and words that are insulting to women. Can we not pledge to get rid of everything in our behavior, culture and everyday life that humiliates and demeans women? Women's pride is going to be a huge asset in fulfilling the dreams of the nation. I see this power and, therefore, I am insistent on it.

I will now talk about the fifth life force, *Pran*, which is the duties of citizens. While trying to understand all the countries in the world that have made progress; every country that has achieved something, even in personal life, few things emerged. One is disciplined life, and the other is devotion to duty. There should be success in the life of the individual, of the society, of the family, of the nation. This is the fundamental path and the fundamental vital force.

It is the job of the government to make efforts to provide 24 hours electricity but it is the duty of the citizen to save as many units as he can. It is the responsibility and efforts of the government to supply water to every field, but a voice should come from each of my fields that we will move forward by saving water by focusing on 'per drop more crop'. It is our duty to do chemical-free farming, organic farming and natural farming. Friends, whether it is police or people, ruler or administrator, no one can be untouched by this civic duty. If everyone performs the duties of a citizen, I am sure that we can achieve the desired goals ahead of time.

Today is also the birth anniversary of Maharishi Aurobindo. I bow at the feet of that great man. But, we need to remember the great man who gave a call for '*Swadeshi* to *Swaraj*' and '*Swaraj* to *Suraj*'. This is his *mantra*. We all need to think how long we will be dependent on other people of the world. Can we outsource when our country needs food grains? When the country decided that we will meet our food requirements, did the country demonstrate it or not? Once we take a resolution, it is possible. And, therefore, '*Aatma-Nirbhar Bharat*' becomes the responsibility of every citizen, every government and every unit of society. '*Aatma-Nirbhar Bharat*' is not a government agenda or a government programme. This is a mass movement of society, which we have to take forward.

My friends, today we heard this sound after 75 years of independence for which our ears were yearning to hear. For the first time after 75 years, the Made in India cannon has saluted the Tricolour from the Red Fort. Will there be any Indian who will not be inspired by this sound? My dear brothers and sisters, today I want to congratulate the soldiers of the army of my country from my heart. I salute the way the army jawans have shouldered this responsibility of self-reliance in an organized way and with courage. The soldier of the army carries death in his hands. He stands firmly in the middle when there is no gap between death and life. The resolution of our country is not small when the armed forces make a list and decide not to import 300 defence products.

In this resolution, I can see the seed of a bright future of '*Atmanirbhar Bharat*' that will convert this dream into a banyan tree. Salute! Salute! Salute to my army officers!

I also want to salute the little children between 5 and 7 years of age. The nation's consciousness has been awakened. I have heard from countless families that 5–7-year-old children tell their parents that they do not want to play with foreign toys. When a 5-year-old child makes such a resolution, it reflects the spirit of self-reliant India in him.

Speaking of the PLI scheme, one lakh crore rupees, people from around the world are coming to India to try their luck. They are bringing new technology along with them. They are generating new employment opportunities. India is becoming a manufacturing hub. It is building a foundation for a Self-reliant India. Be it manufacturing of electronic goods or mobile phones, today the country is progressing at a very fast pace. Which Indian wouldn't be proud when our Brahmos is exported to the world? Today the Vande Bharat train and our metro coaches are becoming objects of attraction for the world.

We have to become self-reliant in the energy sector. How long will we be dependent on others in the field of energy? We should be self-reliant in the fields of solar energy, wind energy, and various other renewable energy sources like Hydrogen and bio-fuel.

Today natural farming is also a way of becoming self-reliant. Today the factories of Nano Fertilizer have brought a new hope in the country. But, natural farming and chemical-free farming can give a boost to self-reliance. Today, new employment opportunities in the form of green jobs are opening up very fast in the country. India has opened up 'space' through its policies. India has come up with the most progressive policy regarding drones in the world. We have opened up new doors of opportunities for the youth of the country.

I also call upon the private sector to come forward. We have to dominate the world. One of the dreams of a self-reliant India is to ensure that India does not lag behind in fulfilling the needs of the world. Even if it is the MSMEs we have to take our products to the world with 'Zero Defect-Zero Effect'. We have to be proud of *Swadeshi*.

Till today we always remember our revered Lal Bahadur Shastri ji for his inspirational clarion call of *Jai Jawan Jai Kisan* meaning "Hail the Soldier, Hail the Farmer". Later Atal Bihari Vajpayee ji added a new link of *Jai Vigyan* which meant "hail science" and we gave it utmost importance. But, in this new phase of *Amrit Kaal* now, it is imperative to add *Jai Anusandhaan* that is "hail innovation".

Jai Jawan Jai Kisan Jai Vigyan Jai Anusandhaan.

I repose my utmost faith in our youth of the nation. Witness the power of indigenous innovations. Today we have many success stories to show to the world—UPI-BHIM, our digital payment, and our compelling position in the domain of Fintech. Today in the world, 40 percent of real time digital financial transactions are happening in my country. India has shown innovation prowess to the world.

Today we are all set to enter the 5G era. You don't have to wait too long before we match the global steps. We are ensuring that optical fiber reaches each and every village until the last mile. I am fully informed that the dream of Digital India will be attained through rural India. Today I am happy that four lakh Common Service Centers of India are being developed in villages which are being managed by the youth of that village. Nation can take pride in the fact that four lakh Digital Entrepreneurs are being nurtured in the villages, and the rural population is becoming accustomed to benefit from all the services. Such is the power of India to become a technology hub in itself.

This Digital India movement of developing semiconductors, entering the 5G era, spreading the network of optical fibers is not just to establish ourselves as modern and developed, but it is possible because of three intrinsic missions. The complete transformation of the education ecosystem, revolution in health infrastructure and improvement in the quality of agricultural life will be possible only through digitalization.

I can foresee that India will march ahead phenomenally in this decade which is hailed as the techade for humanity. It is a decade of technology. In the field of IT, India has become a force to reckon with globally. We have the competencies to contribute in this techade.

Our Atal Innovation Mission, our incubation centres, and our startups are developing a whole new sector, opening up new opportunities for the younger generation. Whether it is a matter of space mission, whether it is about our Deep Ocean Mission, whether we want to go deep into the ocean or we have to touch the sky, these are new areas, by which we are moving forward.

Let us not forget this and India has seen this for centuries, while some model works are needed in the country, some great heights must be achieved, but at the same time we should remain rooted and grounded while accomplishing heights as a nation.

Potential of the economic advancement of India is dependent on the strength of the grassroot. Hence, we must acknowledge and strengthen the potential of our small farmers, entrepreneurs, small and medium sized enterprises, cottage industries, micro industries, street vendors, domestic labourers, daily wagers, auto rickshaw drivers, bus service providers, etc. These form the largest population who need to be empowered. Being able to do so shall guarantee India's potential and, therefore, our efforts are going in the direction of giving maximum emphasis to this stratum which is the fundamental grass root force of our economic development.

We have 75 years of experience, and we have also achieved many accomplishments in these 75 years. We have cherished new dreams and taken new resolutions in 75 years of experience. But, what should be the optimum outcome of our human resources for the '*Amrit Kaal*'? How to get the optimum outcome of our natural wealth? We have to move forward with this goal. I want to say something from the experience of the last few years. You must have seen the power of '*Nari Shakti*' in courts who are working in the field of Law. Look at the public representatives in the rural area. Our '*Nari Shakti*' is devotedly engaged in solving the problems of our villages. Look at the field of knowledge or science, the '*Nari Shakti*' of our country is visible right at the top. Even in the police force, our '*Nari Shakti*' is taking the responsibility of protecting the people. In every walk of life, whether it is the playground or the battlefield, the '*Nari Shakti*' of India is coming forward with a new strength and a new belief. I can see the manifold contribution of '*Nari Shakti*', my mothers, sisters and daughters, in the next 25 years compared to the contribution in the last 75 years of India's journey. And hence, it is beyond assessment. Everything is beyond your parameters. The more we pay attention to this aspect, the more opportunities and facilities we provide to our daughters, they will return us much more than that. They will take the country to a new height. If the considerable efforts of our '*Nari Shakti*' are added to the hard work that is required to fulfill the dreams in this '*Amrit Kaal*', then it will take less hard work and our time limit will also be reduced. Our dreams will be more intense, vivacious and resplendent.

Therefore, friends, let's move ahead with our responsibilities. Today I also want to thank the framers of the Constitution of India for giving us the federal structure. Our dreams are bound to be realized if we walk shoulder to shoulder by maintaining this spirit and respecting its sentiments in this '*Amrit Kaal*'. Programs may differ, working styles may differ, but resolutions can't differ, dreams for a nation cannot be different.

Let us move towards such an era. I remember the government at the Centre did not belong to our ideology when I was the Chief Minister of Gujarat. But, I used to follow the same *mantra* that the progress of Gujarat is for the progress of India. India's progress should be at the core of our heart wherever we are. There are many states of our country, which have played a great role in taking the country forward, have led and worked as examples in many fields. This gives strength to our federalism. But, today the need of the hour is that we need cooperative federalism as well as cooperative competitive federalism. We need competition for development.

Every state should feel that it is moving ahead, that it will race ahead by toiling hard. If a particular state has done 10 good tasks, others shall do 15 good tasks. If a state has completed a job in three years, others should complete the same job in two years. There should be an atmosphere of competition between the states and all the units of the government which should strive to take us to new peaks of development.

When we talk of the 25 years of *Amrit Kaal*, I know that there would be many challenges, limitations and problems. We do not underestimate these. We keep on looking for ways and are constantly striving but I wish to discuss two things here. There may be many issues to discuss but considering the time constraint, I would like to talk about two things right now. And I believe that because of all these challenges and problems if we do not take corrective steps while there is still time during 25 years of '*Amrit Kaal*', then it could take a turn for the worse. So, I do not want to discuss everything but would definitely want to focus on two issues. One is corruption and the other is nepotism and the dynasty system. In a democracy like India where people are struggling with poverty and do not have a place to live, there are people who do not have a place to keep their ill-gotten money. This is not an ideal situation. So, we have to fight against corruption with all our might. In the last eight years, we have been successful in working for the betterment of the country by saving two lakh crore rupees which used to go into the wrong hands, using all the modern systems like Direct Benefit Transfer, Aadhaar and Mobile. Those who fled the country after looting banks during the tenure of the previous government, we have seized their property and are trying to get them back. Some have been forced to go behind the bars. We are trying to ensure that those who looted the country are compelled to return.

I can clearly see that we are entering a crucial period against corruption. Even the big ones will not be able to escape. With this spirit, India is now stepping into a decisive period against corruption. And I am saying this with a great responsibility from the ramparts of the Red Fort. Brothers and sisters, the corrupt are eating away the country like termites. I have to fight against it, intensify the fight and have to take it to a decisive point. So, my 130 crore countrymen, please bless me and support me! Today I have come to seek your support and cooperation so that I can fight this battle. I hope the country becomes victorious in this war. The lives of the ordinary citizens have been ruined by corruption. So, I want to make sure that the ordinary citizens are once again able to live with dignity. My dear countrymen, it is a matter of great concern that although abhorrence of corruption in the country is visible and expressed, sometimes the generosity towards the corrupt is shown which is not acceptable in any country.

And many people have gone so shameless that despite being convicted in court, having been proved corrupt, having been sentenced for imprisonment, while still serving in jail, they continue to glorify, take pride and continue to elevate their status. Unless there is hatred towards filth in the society, the consciousness for cleanliness does not arise, unless we develop hatred towards the corrupt and corruption, until we relegate these people to social shaming, such mentality will not change. And that's why we need to be very aware of corruption and corrupt people.

Another point to highlight is rampant nepotism. And whenever I talk about nepotism or dynasty, people think I am talking only in the context of politics. Not at all. Unfortunately, it is being nourished in other Indian institutions as well. Family bias, nepotism has gripped many of our institutions today. This is sadly harming the immense talent pool of our country. The future potential of my country is suffering. Those who are legitimate contenders of these opportunities and are genuinely eligible get sidelined due to nepotism. This is a good reason for corruption. Since they feel that they stand no chance to avail opportunities as per norms, these potential and deserving candidates resort to paying bribes to get a job. All of us have to work hard on fighting nepotism by becoming more aware and creating an antipathy for this. Only such efforts can save our institutions and ingrain ethical behaviour in our future generations. This is mandatory to ensure a bright future of our institutions. Similarly, in politics too, family bias or dynasty has done the most injustice to the country's strength. It becomes a way to benefit only the family and has no connection towards the national good.

And therefore, while remembering the Constitution of India, standing under the tricolour from the ramparts of the Red Fort, I want to say with an open heart to all the countrymen—let us all join hands for the purification and cleansing of Indian politics and for the cleansing of all the institutions of India, we have to liberate the country from this family mentality and move towards taking the country forward on the basis of merit. It is more imperative now than ever. Otherwise, everyone will carry heavy resentment that s/he was deserving but could not succeed as there was no family member vouching for them in the ecosystem. Such a mentality is not good for any country.

Dear youth of my country, for your bright future, for your dreams, I seek your support in the fight against nepotism. I want your support in the fight against dynastic politics. I consider this as my constitutional responsibility. The responsibility of a democracy. I believe in the power of words spoken from the ramparts of this Red Fort. And hence, I request you to support this opportunity. We have noticed this in the accolades we received at the sports world in the last few days. It's not that we did not have such great talent in the past. It is not that our sons and daughters, the youth of India, are not achieving anything in the world of sports. But, sadly they have been pushed out due to the nepotism channel. The ones that qualified to reach the competition in other countries were least bothered about winning medals for the country. But, when transparency was reinstated, selection was on the merit of the sportsperson and the talent was honoured on the playgrounds. It is a moment of pride today to see the tricolor flying high and the national anthem reverberating at the stadiums globally.

One feels proud when there is freedom from dynasty and nepotism, and such results come along. My dear countrymen, there are many challenges no doubt. But, if there are crores of problems before this country, then there are also crores of solutions and I have faith in 130 crore countrymen. When 130 crore countrymen take one step ahead with a set goal and the commitment to resolve, India moves 130 steps forward. We have to move forward with this capability. This is the first dawn of the '*Amrit Kaal*' and we should not forget a single moment for the next 25 years. To live for the motherland each day, every moment of time and every particle of life will be our true tribute to the freedom fighters. Only then, the virtuous remembrance of all those who contributed in taking the country to this point in the last 75 years will be of use.

I urge the countrymen to start the '*Amrit Kaal*' today by nurturing new possibilities, realizing new resolutions and moving ahead with confidence. The '*Amrit Mahotsav*' of freedom has turned in the direction of '*Amrit Kaal*' and, therefore, '*Sabka Prayas*' is necessary in this '*Amrit Kaal*'. '*Sabka Prayas*' is going to yield this result. The spirit of Team India is going to take the country forward. This Team India of 130 crore countrymen will realize all the dreams by moving forward as a team.

Prime Minister concluded his speech with *Jai Hind, Bharat Mata Ki Jai* and *Vande Mataram*. (This is an approximate translation as the original speech was delivered in Hindi)

It would be seen that after paying glowing tributes to the freedom fighters, Narendra Modi highlighted the achievements of his government during eight years in office. He also addressed the problems facing the country such as corruption, dynastic rule, nepotism, etc. He suggested *Panch Pran* to solve them.

Index